TITANIC
Names

A COMPLETE LIST OF THE PASSENGERS AND CREW

Second Edition

Lee William Merideth

Rocklin Press

To LINDSAY WEAVER

BEST WISHES!

JUNE 13, 2010

COLUMBUS, OK

Titanic Names: A Complete List of the Passengers and Crew
Second Edition
By Lee William Merideth

© 2002, First Edition
© 2007, Second Edition

Includes bibliographic references

Printing Number, First Edition
10 9 8 7 6 5 4
Printing Number, Second Edition
10 9 8 7 6 5 4 3 2 1
Second Edition, First Printing: November 2007

ISBN 978 0-9626237-7-6

Cover design: Jim Zach
Cover photography: Ross Mehan

Rocklin Press
An imprint of
Historical Indexes Publishing Co.
P O Box 64142
Sunnyvale, CA 94088
RocklinPress@earthlink.net
www.rocklinpress.com

Other Books by Lee William Merideth

Civil War Times and Civil War Times, Illustrated 30-Year Comprehensive Index
    (April 1959 to February 1989)
Guide To Civil War Periodicals, Volume I
Guide To Civil War Periodicals, Volume II

1912 Facts About Titanic
Grey Ghost: The Story of the Aircraft Carrier Hornet
Titanic Names: The Complete List of the Passengers and Crew

Previous page

Titanic docked at Southampton, April 9, 1912.

This page

Titanic departs Southampton, April 10, 1912.

Table of Contents

Titanic in Belfast, April 2, 1912. Preparing for sea trials and voyage to Southampton.

Preface

In early 1999, Savas Publishing Company published *1912 Facts About Titanic*, my interpretation of the *Titanic* story. It was the culmination of more than thirty-five years of fact gathering and research. In a stroke of pure good fortune, the book hit the shelves about one year after James Cameron's blockbuster movie. Sales were brisk and *1912 Facts About Titanic* went through several printings.

In 2000, I traveled to Las Vegas, Nevada, to visit "Titanic: The Artifact Exhibition," put on by RMS Titanic, Inc. My book was prominently displayed in the Exhibition gift shop. I happily signed copies for several purchasers and before an hour had passed most of the inventory was sold. They hadn't sold that many books in two weeks. Collecting signed books has been a hobby of mine for many years, but it never occurred to me that someone might want *my* signature! The opportunity that beckoned was obvious even to me. When my book sold out its next printing, I reacquired rights and began publishing the book under my own imprint. Over the past two years I have traveled to nearly every Titanic Exhibition site and other *Titanic* meetings across the country. Thanks to all the readers of *Titanic* lore, sales have been outstanding, the book has gone through several additional printings, and I have met many wonderful people and made many lasting friendships that I treasure greatly.

Many readers have a deep interest in the people who were on the ship during that fateful voyage, a fact I rediscovered over and over during my travels. The Titanic Exhibition satisfies some of this interest and curiosity by providing a card to each visitor that lists the name of a passenger or crewmember. After experiencing the very moving display of artifacts and just before exiting the exhibit, each cardholder scans a posted list of names to determine whether the person listed on their card survived the disaster. The randomness of the sudden icy death so many innocent people experienced sends chills down modern-day spines, especially after having placed their hands on the "ice wall" and experiencing first hand how cold the water was that night. Families—especially the children—often learn that the person whose name is on the card survived the sinking, but that their siblings or parents were not so lucky.

Many visitors see their current family name or the names of ancestors posted on the large board. Natural curiosity bubbles to the surface. Who was this person? Where were they from? What was their final destination? If they perished, was their body ever recovered? Although some of this information has been published (almost as an afterthought) in other books, finding it and trying to read through the incomplete presentation is laborious and often unsatisfying. Because of this fact and numerous requests from readers across the nation, I determined to write *Titanic Names,* the book you now hold in your hands. It is a complete listing of every known passenger and crewmember (published listings of the latter are particularly difficult to locate).

A few observations on using this list are in order. Most similar lists I have seen do not include the names of maids, servants, and other domestic help employed by First Class passengers except as a subset under their employer's name. In other words, it was difficult to find the entry for Miss Rosalie Bidois unless you knew she was the maid for Mrs. John J. Astor. Now, Miss Bidois and others like her are included in the alphabetical listing of passengers.

Likewise, finding a married woman was also a problem if you only knew her maiden name. For example, most lists present the married name followed by the maiden name—"Mrs. John J. Astor (Madeleine Force)." In an attempt to make this list as user friendly as possible, I have listed both names under separate entries in every case where a married woman's maiden name is known.

Another problem commonly encountered has to do with family groups. Lists published in strict alphabetical order guarantee that families are sometimes not listed together. That, in turn, makes it difficult to determine with confidence who belongs to which family. In order to overcome this problem, I decided to keep families together—even if it means each separate listing is not in strict alphabetical order. I hope all of the purists using this book will forgive me. It is my sincere hope that the end result of my efforts is a useable, accurate, and interesting reference guide for everyone interested in researching family members (or others), or just learning more about the human side of the tragic *Titanic* saga.

* * *

As usual, there are many people to thank for their assistance with this work. Any errors or omissions are mine alone. Paul Williams, who collects *Titanic* "stuff", helped me fill numerous gaps with information I did not have or could not find. As usual, Theodore P. "Ted" Savas of the wild outback known as El Dorado Hills, California, gets almost top billing for his outstanding insight into book publishing and his technical help with the layout of *Titanic Names*. Ted introduced me to his cover designer, Jim Zach, who lives in Mason City, Iowa. The *Titanic* image on the front cover is actually a photograph of a 1:350 scale model I built several years ago as a visual aide for my talks. Jim worked his magic so well that several people have asked me where I was able to find a color photo of the real ship! Ross Mehan of Sunnyvale, California, shot the model for me. Through the wonders of the Internet and e-mail, Ross and Jim were able to communicate each other's needs to get the cover done. Bill Haley of Huntington Beach, California, and Connie Silveria of Tracy, California, handled the editing and proofreading duties. Both saved me from making several embarrassing mistakes.

Finally, I want to thank my mother, Eleanore Merideth. She has been demanding for several years that I slow down (I am on a plane almost every weekend to attend some *Titanic*-related event). I promised her that once *Titanic Names* was completed, I would take a break. Five years later, I still haven't taken that break.

However, someday I will.

Lee William Merideth
Sunnyvale, California
November 2007

TITANIC
Names

**A COMPLETE LIST OF THE
PASSENGERS AND CREW**

Second Edition

How to Use This Book

Titanic Names: A Complete List of the Passengers and Crew contains two sections: starting on page 7 is the listing of the passengers and starting on page 59 is the list of the crew. The lists are slightly different in that the crew list does not list destination since it is assumed all were going to New York City and then back home. Also, the crew list indicates the type of job the person performed and not a class of accommodations.

The Passenger List

The Passenger List is in alphabetical order except in those cases where families are kept together in which case some of the names may be slightly out of order. All names in *italic* indicate that person survived. A name in parenthesis ( ) is the maiden name of the married woman (i.e. Mrs. John J. Astor (Madeleine T. Force) where Madeleine Force was her maiden name. Names in brackets [ ] is an additional name a person might use.

The second column (AGE) is the age, if known, of the passenger. Ages with "mo" indicate the child was only that many months old.

The third column (RESIDENCE) is the passenger's home, if known.

The forth column (Class) is the class of accommodations the person was traveling (1st, 2nd or 3rd).

The fifth column (E) is where the person embarked: B is for Belfast, Ireland; S is for Southampton, England; C is for Cherbourg, France and Q is for Queenstown, Ireland, (today known as Cobh).

The sixth column (DESTINATION) lists the person's destination, if known.

The seventh column (L/B) indicates the lifeboat(s) the survivor was on, if known.

The eighth column (BODY #, WHERE RECOVERED) shows in which order the body was recovered by the *MacKay-Bennett* and other recovery vessels, and where they were buried.

The ninth column (NOTES) allows for a brief description of who the passenger was, why they were making the trip, etc. If the description is too extensive, then it moves to the lines below the name and at that time it becomes highlighted in dark shade.

Families of three or more are kept together and also highlighted in he dark shade. The lighter shade is used only to help visually guide your eye across the page to make it easier to read without lines.

The Crew List

The Crew List is in strict alphabetical order since there are no family affiliations. A name in parenthesis ( ) is the maiden name of the married woman and names in [ ] is an additional name.

The second column (AGE) is the age, if known.

The third column (TITLE/FUNCTION) indicates the job the person had. A glossary of the job titles follows the Crew List.

The fourth column (Department) indicates which department aboard the ship the person worked for.

The fifth column (RESIDENCE) indicates where the person lived. Note almost 700 of them called Southampton home.

The sixth column (E) indicates were the person embarked: S is for Southampton, B is for Belfast

The remaining columns follow the format as the Passenger List.

Facts and Statistics

Who were the 2,208 people who left Queenstown, Ireland on April 11, 1912 on *Titanic's* maiden voyage? There were 1,317 passengers who were traveling to America, some on business and a few on vacation, but most of them were returning home or were emigrating. Then there were 891 crewmembers doing their jobs who felt fortunate that, during the long British coal strike, they had a job for another two weeks.

There are probably as many "counts" of the actual numbers of people on *Titanic* the night it struck the iceberg as there are people counting. Counting names would seem to be relatively easy, but this hasn't been an exact science. Passengers boarded *Titanic* in four different ports (Belfast, Southampton, Cherbourg and Queenstown) and some only made a cross-channel voyage (Southampton to Cherbourg or Queenstown or Cherbourg to Queenstown.) There may have been some young children who weren't counted.

Several crewmembers signed on the days before voyage but failed to appear and substitutes were hired on as the ship was leaving Southampton. At least one crewman is unknown because he was working with another person's identification. At least one went AWOL (absent without leave) in Queenstown.

The best number that I have come up with, which mirrors most of the other credible estimates, is the number of 2,208. Of that number, 705 survived (some lists show 712, which probably includes those who disembarked in Queenstown) which means 1,503 people died that night.

Passengers

There were 324 First Class, 283 Second Class and 710 Third Class passengers on *Titanic* when it sank. Thirty-two percent of the passengers (including 75 percent of First Class passengers) were residents or citizens of the United States or Canada, most of whom were returning home from vacation in Europe or visiting family in their former homelands. Fifteen percent (108 of 710) Third Class passengers were residents of the United States.

Of the 324 First Class passengers, 244 made up the 75% of United States or Canadian citizens returning home. The remaining 80 First Class passengers were mostly traveling from Great Britain or France on business. Virtually all of the 602 Third Class passengers who weren't U.S. citizens were emigrating to start a new life in a new country.

The passengers represented forty-six countries from six continents. Some of those countries constituted more than one language, and there were probably 60 plus languages spoken by the passengers.

Four First Class women (1.23%) and one First Class child (.32%) were lost. Down in Third Class there were 94 children 15 years or younger. Of these, 63 were lost (67%). The Sage family of eleven (father, mother and nine children) from Peterborough, England was emigrating to St. Petersburg, FL. None survived, making the Sage family the largest family lost. The Andersson family from Sweden lost all seven members and the Goodwin family from England lost all eight. All four members of the Boulos family from Lebanon and the five members of the Ford family from England were lost. Other losses of entire families include the Lefebre family (five members) from France, the Paulson family from Sweden (five members) the Panula family form Pennsylvania (six members), the Rice family from Ireland (six members) and the six members of the Skoog family form Michigan.

There were 140 Third Class passengers from Scandinavian countries (Finland, Sweden and Norway) and of those, 104 or 74.2% did not survive. Worse odds yet were for the 63 Third Class passengers from southeastern Europe (Bulgaria, Bosnia and Croatia). There were only 2 survivors, or a 96.8% loss rate.

But it even gets worse. Of the 11 First and Second Class Irish male passengers, there were no survivors, or 100% loss.

* * *

There were 127 Male First Class adult passengers that were U.S. or Canadian residents of which 87 (68.5%) were lost. This is an interesting number because one would think that the ratio of survivors would be higher since these passengers had easier access to the Boat deck. Only four of 110 adult female First Class U.S. or Canadian passengers were lost which means 96.4% survived.

Countries Represented by Passengers on *Titanic*

Argentina	Bosnia	Cuba	France	Ireland	Mexico	Portugal	Spain	Turkey
Armenia	Bulgaria	Denmark	Germany	Italy	Netherlands	Russia	Sweden	Uruguay
Australia	Canada	Egypt	Greece	Japan	Norway	Scotland	Switzerland	USA
Austria	China	England	Hong Kong	Lebanon	Peru	Slovenia	Syria	Wales
Belgium	Croatia	Finland	India	Lithuania	Poland	So. Africa	Thailand	

I have a theory that the high loss of First Class male passengers is due more to selfish reasons than trying to be heroic. During the Victorian Era, a persons' social status and maintaining that status was at least as important as life itself. There is the distinct possibility that some of the First Class male passengers chose to remain behind because they were afraid of being ostracized for surviving when so many others didn't. They didn't want to be seen getting onto a lifeboat by their peers. Several of the survivors were, in fact, ostracized. Bruce Ismay, Arthur Peuchen and Cosmo Duff-Gordon all suffered the loss of social standing, income and business and all were vilified in the press which called them cowards and worse. It could be that passengers chose to go down with Titanic because they didn't want to face a vengeful public. They were all rich, their families were well provided for, and so what better way to go to your end but as a hero?

There were at least 13 newly wed couples aboard *Titanic*, either starting out on their honeymoon or returning home from their honeymoon. Four of the husbands survived but nine were lost. At least three couples were engaged to be married and in every case the men were lost. There were also at least five male passengers (and three more male crewmen) who had been married less than two weeks who made the trip without their wives. All eight of them were lost. Married couples as a whole did not fair well on this voyage. There were 107 married couples (and a few unmarried couples) on *Titanic*. Only 22 of the married couples survived intact with both members making it into a lifeboat. Another 65 couples had the husband fail to survive and a further 20 couples had both members lost.

Children were considered as children until the age of five, at which time they became "boys" and "girls" until the age of 15 at which time they were considered adults. When the order came to load "women and children first" it was assumed to include all females of any age and male children under five. Boys between five and fifteen, on the other hand, weren't expected to be included in "women and children first" group. This was apparent when Second Officer Lightoller exclaimed "no more boys" after First Class passenger

Passenger Statistics

FIRST CLASS	Male		Female		6-15 Years		<5 Years		Total	Percent
	Saved	Lost	Saved	Lost	Saved	Lost	Saved	Lost		
From USA	37	71	96	2	4		1		211	65.12%
Scandinavia		1	1						2	0.62%
England	7	17	12						36	11.11%
Lebanon/Syria									0	0.00%
Other	12	10	17	1					40	12.35%
Canada	3	16	11	1			1	1	33	10.19%
Ireland		2							2	0.62%
Bulgaria/Bosnia/Croatia									0	0.00%
Belgium									0	0.00%
Total	59	118	136	4	4	0	2	1	**324**	
Percent	18.21%	36.11%	42.28%	1.23%	1.23%	0.00%	0.62%	0.31%		

First Class Saved   201   62.35%

First Class Lost   123   37.65%

SECOND CLASS	Male		Female		6-15 Years		<5 Years		Total	Percent
	Saved	Lost	Saved	Lost	Saved	Lost	Saved	Lost		
From USA	2	27	16	3	2		1		51	18.02%
Scandinavia		6	4	1			1		12	4.24%
England	8	82	41	6	6	1	6		150	53.00%
Lebanon/Syria					1				1	0.35%
Other	4	16	12	3	1		8		44	15.55%
Canada		10	5				1		16	5.65%
Ireland		9							9	3.18%
Bulgaria/Bosnia/Croatia									0	0.00%
Belgium									0	0.00%
Total	14	150	78	13	10	1	17	0	**283**	
Percent	4.95%	53.00%	27.56%	4.59%	3.53%	0.35%	6.01%	0.00%		

Second Class Saved   119   42.05%
Second Class Lost   164   57.95%

THIRD CLASS	Male		Female		6-15 Years		<5 Years		Total	Percent
	Save	Lost	Save	Lost	Save	Lost	Save	Lost		
From USA	14	41	14	17		8	6	8	108	15.21%
Scandinavia	15	73	18	18	2	6	1	7	140	19.72%
England	6	83	12	10	5	11	2	5	134	18.87%
Lebanon/Syria	4	29	7	6	7	4	6		63	8.87%
Other	10	50	2	7	1	5	1	2	78	10.99%
Canada		2	1						3	0.42%
Ireland	6	43	29	20		3		2	103	14.51%
Bulgaria/Bosnia/Croatia	1	56	1	5					63	8.87%
Belgium	3	10		3		2			18	2.54%
Total	59	387	83	87	15	39	16	24	**710**	
Percent	8.31%	54.51%	11.83%	12.11%	2.11%	5.49%	2.25%	3.38%		

Third Class Saved   173   24.51%
Third Class Lost   537   75.49%

Alfred Ryerson insisted that his 13-year old son be allowed access to a lifeboat with his mother.

Only one child in First Class was lost. Two-year old Helen Loraine Allison was with her parents as they tried to locate baby Hudson Allison who had been carried into a lifeboat without the parents knowledge. Searching too long, the Allison's missed getting into a lifeboat and Helen and her parents were lost. Only one "boy" in Second Class was lost, 14-year old George Sweet who was traveling with his adoptive parents.

Third Class children faired badly because so many of the large Third Class families were lost. Sixteen of 40 children five years or younger were lost as were 39 of 54 boys and girls aged six through 15.

* * *

The story about Third Class passengers being prevented from leaving the lower decks by armed crewmen as perpetrated by the James Cameron movie is totally fiction. There were doors and gates located on *Titanic* to prevent Third Class passengers from accessing the First and Second Class areas because of an American Immigration Law that stated all passengers had to be disease free and all ships had to have barriers to prevent the classes from mixing (it was assumed that Third Class passengers would transmit diseases that First and Second Class passengers would not). Regardless of how politically incorrect this might be today, it was the law in 1912.

Only one surviving passenger ever

CREW	Male		Female			
	Saved	Lost	Saved	Lost	Total	Percent
Crew	191	608	18	1	818	91.81%
a la Carte	2	64	1	1	68	7.63%
Postal	0	5	0	0	5	0.56%
Total	193	677	19	2	**891**	
Percent	21.66%	75.98%	2.13%	0.22%		

Crew Saved	212	23.79%
Crew Lost	679	76.21%

reported finding a locked gate. Once the order to launch the lifeboats was given, orders were passed to the crew to awaken the Third Class passengers and to open the doors and gates, which was done. Three crewmembers were credited with saving 58 Third Class passengers by leading them up to the Boat Deck.

The problem the Third Class passengers had was two-fold: one was the language barrier caused by the large number of languages spoken among the passengers and the lack of interpreters and the difficulty they had in navigating their way from the Third Class spaces up to the Boat Deck. It certainly didn't help that a majority of the survivors stated that they didn't even realize the ship was sinking until after most of the lifeboats had been launched. Once the Third Class passengers realized that they needed to find their way to the Boat Deck, getting lost in the corridors and stairwells prevented them from getting out. However, many of those who made it to the open Shelter Deck (Third Class open deck at the bow and stern of the ship), were able to get up to the Boat Deck by climbing the stairs and over the low gate on B Deck. Many of the male passengers in Third Class also climbed up the cargo cranes on the shelter deck then walked across the cargo boom to A Deck then up to the Boat Deck.

Although members of the crew had been sent into the Third Class areas to wake the passengers and have them report to the Boat Deck with their lifebelts on, most of the survivors couldn't tell the ship was sinking until almost two hours after striking the iceberg.

Crew

The crew of Titanic consisted of 891 men and women. This number includes the staff of the à la Carte restaurant (68) and the postal clerks (5). Of this, 212 were saved and 679 (over 76.2%) were lost. The loss rate among the crew was almost 15% higher than the loss rate among passengers (62.4%).

The question arises about why even this number of crew survived if their responsibility was to the passengers first. Taking out the 18 women crew who were part of the "women and children first" concept leaves 194 crew men who survived.

As the lifeboats were being manned, there was supposed to be a nine-man crew for each one, eight to row and one to man the rudder. Considering none of the crew knew rescue was only a couple hours away, it makes sense that there should be enough trained crew on each lifeboat to man the oars. That isn't what happened, but it was attempted on the earlier lifeboats that were launched.

About half of the crew that survived were ordered into the lifeboats by the ships' officers. The remaining for the most part boarded on the starboard side where First Officer Murdoch allowed men to enter the lifeboats if there weren't any women or children around. With few exceptions, the survivors were married and had families who were totally dependent upon the meager salaries of the head of household. It's understandable, then that they tried to find places on the lifeboats. The 589 lost crew from Southampton left 232 widows and 1,897 orphaned children.

* * *

If the numbers prove anything it's that 71% of the survivors were passengers and 29% were crew, and that in raw numbers, almost as many Third Class (174) passengers survived as did First Class (202) and crew (212). As a percentage there was a higher survival rate of First Class passengers which would be expected since their cabins were for the most part located near the Boat Deck. Other than "women or children first", there wasn't any attempt to save one class of passengers over another or crew over passengers. It was just luck, and a little fate, that those 705 people who survived happened to be at the right place at the right time.

Passenger Listing

Name *(Maiden Name)[Other Name]* *Names in italic indicate survivors*	Age	Residence	Class	E	Destination	L/B	Body # Recovered / Where Buried	Notes
A								
Abbing, Mr. Anthony	42	Cincinnati, OH	3rd	S	Cincinnati, OH			
Abbott Family								
Abbott, Master Eugene J.	13	East Providence, RI	3rd	S	East Providence, RI			
Abbott, Mr. Rossmore E.	16	East Providence, RI	3rd	S	East Providence, RI			
Abbott, Mrs. Stanton (Rosa Hunt)	35	East Providence, RI	3rd	S	East Providence, RI	A		

Mrs. Stanton Abbott, divorced wife of a former middleweight boxer in England, was returning to East Providence with her two sons Rossmore and Eugene. As *Titanic* was sinking, all three waited until the end, then jumped into the water. Mrs. Abbott managed to get into the half-submerged Collapsible Lifeboat A and had to stand for several hours in water up to her knees until picked up by Fifth Officer Lowe in Collapsible Lifeboat D. The two boys were never seen again after they jumped into the water.

Abelseth, Miss Karen Marie	16	Alesund, Norway	3rd	S	Minneapolis, MN	16		

Karen Abelseth traveled with Olaus Abelseth (no relation), Adolf Humblen, Sigrid Moen, Anna Salkjelsvik and Peter Soholt.

Abelseth, Mr. Olaus J.	25	Perkins County, SD	3rd	S	Perkins County, SD	A		

Olaus Abelseth traveled with Karen Abelseth (no relation), Adolf Humblen, Sigrid Moen, Anna Salkjelsvik and Peter Soholt.

Name	Age	Residence	Class	E	Destination	L/B	Body / Buried	Notes
Abelson, Mr. Samuel	30	Russia	2nd	C	New York City, NY			
Abelson, Mrs. Samuel (Hannah Wizosky)	28	Russia	2nd	C	New York City, NY	12		
Abraham, Mrs. Joseph (Mary Easu)	18	Greensburg, PA	3rd	C	Greensburg, PA	C		
Abrahamsson, Mr. August	20	Kimito Island, Finland	3rd	S	Hoboken, NJ	15		
Achem, Adele								see Mrs. Nicholas Nasser
Ådahl, Mr. Mauritz Nils M.	30	Sweden	3rd	S	Brooklyn, NY		#72, buried at sea	
Adams, Mr. John [Richard May]	26	Bournemouth, England	3rd	S	Indiana		#103, buried at sea	

John Adams had acquired that name shortly before leaving Southampton. He was born Richard May, but had decided to bail out on a failing marriage, so he changed his name to John Adams.

Name	Age	Residence	Class	E	Destination	L/B	Body / Buried	Notes
Ahlin, Mrs. Johan (Johanna P. Larsson)	40	Akeley, MN	3rd	S	Akeley, MN			Traveled with brother Johan Petterson.
Aks Family								
Aks, Master Frank Philip	10 mo	London, England	3rd	S	Norfolk, VA	11		
Aks, Mrs. Samuel (Leah Rosen)	18	London, England	3rd	S	Norfolk, VA	13		

Leah Aks was traveling with her baby to Norfolk to meet her husband. The night *Titanic* sank, she was standing on the Boat deck with the baby who had been wrapped up in a shawl given her by Madeleine Astor. While she was waiting by Lifeboat 11, someone grabbed the baby and tossed it, football style, into the lifeboat. Elizabeth Nye, who initially thought the object being tossed her way was someone's luggage, caught the baby. Leah Aks was prevented from getting into the lifeboat, but eventually she made her way into Lifeboat 13 and was reunited with her son on board *Carpathia*.

Name	Age	Residence	Class	E	Destination	L/B	Body / Buried	Notes
Albimona, Mr. Nassef Cassem	26	Lebanon	3rd	C	Fredericksburg, VA	15?		Traveled with Master Houssien Hassan.
Aldworth, Mr. Charles A.	30	Bryn Mawr, PA	2nd	S	Bryn Mawr, PA			Chauffeur to William E. Carter.
Alexander, Amenia								see Mrs. George Moubarek
Alexander, Mr. William	23	Norfolk, England	3rd	S	Albion, NY			

Name *(Maiden Name)[Other Name]* *Names in italic indicate survivors*	Age	Residence	Class	E	Destination	L/B	Body # Recovered / Where Buried	Notes
Alhomäki, Mr. Ilmari Rudolf	20	Salo, Finland	3rd	S	Astoria, OR			
Ali, Mr. Ahmed	24	Syria	3rd	S	unknown			
Ali, Mr. William	25	Argentina	3rd	S	Argentina		#79, buried in Mt. Olivet Cemetery, Halifax	
Allen, Mr. William Henry	35	Middlesex, England	3rd	S	unknown			
Allen, Miss Elisabeth Walton	29	St. Louis, MO	1st	S	St. Louis, MO	2		Traveling with her aunt Mrs. Edward Robert and cousin Georgette Madill
Allison Family								
Allison, Mr. Hudson Joshua C.	30	Montreal, Quebec, Canada	1st	S	Montreal, Quebec, Canada		#135, buried in Ontario, Canada	
Allison, Mrs. Hudson (Bess Waldo Daniels)	25	Montreal, Quebec, Canada	1st	S	Montreal, Quebec, Canada			
Allison, Miss Helen Loraine	2	Montreal, Quebec, Canada	1st	S	Montreal, Quebec, Canada			
Allison, Master Hudson Trevor	11mo	Montreal, Quebec, Canada	1st	S	Montreal, Quebec, Canada	11		

On this night of so much tragedy, the **Allison** family story is especially so. Returning home from England after a business meeting, the family traveled with Alice Cleaver, a nurse for young Hudson; Sarah Daniels, a nursemaid for Helen; chauffeur George Swane and Amelia "Mildred" Brown, a cook. After striking the iceberg, Alice Cleaver took her charge, 11-month old Hudson up to the Boat deck and got into Lifeboat 11 and survived. She didn't bother to tell anyone where she was going. Consequently, Mr. and Mrs. Allison, young Helen and the three employees spent the next two hours looking for Alice and the baby. Sarah Daniels and Mildred Brown survived. Mr. and Mrs. Allison, baby Helen and George Swain did not survive. Baby Hudson was raised by his aunt and uncle. Young Helen was the only child in First or Second Class who was lost, and Mrs. Allison only one of four First Class women to die. Mr. Allison's body was the only body recovered.

Allum, Mr. Owen George	18	Berkshire, England	3rd	S	New York City, NY		#259, buried in Berkshire, England	
Andersen, Mr. Thor								see Mr. Thor A. Olsvigan
Anderson, Mr. Albert Karvin	32	Bergen, Norway	3rd	S	New York City, NY		#260, buried in Fairview Cemetery, Halifax	
Anderson, Mr. Harry	47	New York City, NY	1st	S	New York City, NY	3		His pet Chow dog did not survive.
Andersson Family								
Andersson, Mr. Anders Johan	39	Ostergotland, Sweden	3rd	S	Winnipeg, Mantoba, Canada			
Andersson, Mrs. Anders (Alfrida K. Brogren)	39	Ostergotland, Sweden	3rd	S	Winnipeg, Mantoba, Canada			
Andersson, Miss Ebba Iris	6	Ostergotland, Sweden	3rd	S	Winnipeg, Mantoba, Canada			
Andersson, Miss Ellis Anna Maria	2	Ostergotland, Sweden	3rd	S	Winnipeg, Mantoba, Canada			
Andersson, Miss Ingeborg C.	9	Ostergotland, Sweden	3rd	S	Winnipeg, Mantoba, Canada			
Andersson, Miss Sigrid Elizabeth	11	Ostergotland, Sweden	3rd	S	Winnipeg, Mantoba, Canada			
Andersson, Master Sigvard Harald Elias	4	Ostergotland, Sweden	3rd	S	Winnipeg, Mantoba, Canada			

The **Andersson** family was emigrating to Canada. The Ernst Danbom family, Ernst being the brother-in-law of Mr. Andersson, accompanied them. All seven members of the Andersson family and three members of the Danbom family were lost.

Andersson, Anna Elisabeth Judith								see Mrs. Adolf Dyker
Andersson, Mr. August E.								See August Wennerström
Andersson, Miss Erna	17	Stromfors, Finland	3rd	S	New York City, NY	D		
Andersson, Miss Ida Augusta M.	38	Vadsbro, Sweden	3rd	S	Ministee, MI			
Andersson, Mr. Johan Samuel	20	Hartford, CT	3rd	S	Hartford, CT			
Andreasson, Mr. Paul Edvin	20	Smaland, Sweden	3rd	S	Chicago, IL			
Andrew, Mr. Edgar Samuel	18	Buenos Aires, Argentina	2nd	S	Trenton, NJ			
Andrew, Mr. Frank T.	25	Cornwall, England	2nd	S	Houghton, MI			
Andrews, Anna								see Mrs. John C. Hogeboom
Andrews, Miss Kornelia Theodosia	63	Hudson, NY	1st	S	Hudson, NY	10		

Kornelia Andrews traveled with Mrs. John C. Hogeboom and Miss Gretchen F. Longley.

Name *(Maiden Name)[Other Name]* *Names in italic indicate survivors*	Age	Residence	Class	E	Destination	L/B	Body # Recovered / Where Buried	Notes
Andrews, Mr. Thomas, Jr.	39	Belfast, Ireland	1st	B				

Mr. **Thomas Andrews** was the Managing Director of the Harland & Wolff Shipyard and was a nephew of Lord Pirrie, owner of H&W. Andrews was also the principal designer of *Titanic*, and no detail of its construction was done without his approval. Andrews had been instrumental in putting the new Welin Lifeboat Davits on *Titanic*, which would have allowed the ship to carry three times as many lifeboats. In the end, the White Star Line decided not to install the lifeboats. Andrews always traveled on the maiden voyage of a new WSL ship and *Titanic* was no exception. Once Andrews determined that *Titanic* would sink, he helped load people into lifeboats and helped secure their lifebelts. He was last seen in the First Class Smoking Room staring at a painting, making no attempt to save himself. See Harland & Wolff Group Notes.

Name	Age	Residence	Class	E	Destination	L/B	Body # Recovered / Where Buried	Notes
Angheloff, Mr. Minko	26	Bulgaria	3rd	S	Chicago, IL			
Angle, Mr. William A.	34	New York City, NY	2nd	S	New York City, NY			
Angle, Mrs. William A. (Florence A. Hughes)	36	New York City, NY	2nd	S	New York City, NY	11		
Annan, Dorothy								see Mrs. George A. Harder
Appleton, Mrs. Edward D. (Charlotte Lamson)	53	Bayside, Queens, NY	1st	S	Bayside, Queens, NY	2		Traveled with sisters Mrs. John M. Brown and Mrs. Robert C. Cornell.
Arman, Ellen Truelove								see Mrs. Benjamin Howard
Arnold, Mr. Josef	25	Switzerland	3rd	S	New Glarus, WI			Cousin of Miss Aloisia Haas.
Arnold, Mrs. Josef (Josefine Franchi)	18	Switzerland	3rd	S	New Glarus, WI			
Aronsson, Mr. Ernst Axel A.	24	Smaland, Sweden	3rd	S	Joliet, IL			
Artagaveytia, Mr. Ramon	71	Garamini, Argentina	1st	C	Garamini, Argentina		#22, buried in Montevideo, Uruguay	

Mr. **Ramon Artagaveytia** survived the sinking of the steamship *America* off Uruguay in 1871. The ship had burned and he survived by jumping into the water. He was haunted by the event the rest of his life, and would wake up at night shouting *"Fire!, Fire!"*. He wasn't looking forward to the voyage on *Titanic,* but was assured by the WSL staff that the powerful Marconi system would prevent loss of life if something happened to the ship. He did not survive, dying from exposure and freezing water and not by the dreaded fire which had haunted him for so many years.

Name	Age	Residence	Class	E	Destination	L/B	Body # Recovered / Where Buried	Notes
Ashby, Mr. John	57	West Hoboken, NJ	2nd	S	West Hoboken, NJ			
Asim, Mr. Adola	35	Syria	3rd	S	unknown			
Asplund Family								
Asplund, Master Carl Edgar	5	Worcester, MA	3rd	S	Worcester, MA			
Asplund, Mr. Carl Oscar V.G.	40	Worcester, MA	3rd	S	Worcester, MA		#142, buried in Worchester, MA	
Asplund, Mrs. Carl Oscar (Selma A. Johansson)	38	Worcester, MA	3rd	S	Worcester, MA	4/15		
Asplund, Master Clarence Gustaf Hugo	9	Worcester, MA	3rd	S	Worcester, MA			
Asplund, Master Edvin R.F.	3	Worcester, MA	3rd	S	Worcester, MA	4/15		
Asplund, Master Filip Oscar	13	Worcester, MA	3rd	S	Worcester, MA			
Asplund, Miss Lillian Gertrud	5	Worcester, MA	3rd	S	Worcester, MA	4/15		Last American survivor, died in 2006

The **Carl Asplund** family had lived in Worcester for several years then returned to Sweden for a couple years. The family was emigrating back to Worcester, MA. Of seven family members, only Mrs. Asplund and two children survived. Lillian Asplund died in 2006, the last American survivor to pass away. She seldom spoke to anyone about events that night.

Name	Age	Residence	Class	E	Destination	L/B	Body # Recovered / Where Buried	Notes
Asplund, Mr. Johan Charles	23	Oskarshamn, Sweden	3rd	S	Minneapolis, MN	13		
Assaf, Mr. Gerios	21	Syria	3rd	C	Ottawa, Ontario, Canada			Cousin of Mariana Assaf Khalil.
Assam, Mr. Ali	23	Syria	3rd	S	unknown			
Astor, Colonel John Jacob IV	47	New York City, NY	1st	C	New York City, NY		#124, buried in Trinity Cemetery, New York City, NY	
Astor, Mrs John J. (Madeleine T. Force)	19	New York City, NY	1st	C	New York City, NY	4		

John Jacob Astor was the wealthiest passenger on *Titanic*. He traveled with his 19-year old wife Madeleine, his manservant Victor Robbins, Madeleine's maid Rosalie Bidois, her nurse Caroline Endres, and the family pet, an Airedale dog called "Kitty". Mrs. Astor was pregnant. They were returning home from an extended honeymoon to face the wrath Mr. Astor was to expect for having divorced his wife and marrying Madeleine (as opposed to remaining married and keeping Madeleine as a mistress, which was perfectly acceptable in Victorian society.) Madeleine survived, had a child, John Jacob Astor V, married twice more and died in her early 40's. Rosalie Bidoisa and Caroline Endres survived, John Jacob Astor, Robbins and Kitty did not.

Name	Age	Residence	Class	E	Destination	L/B	Body # Recovered / Where Buried	Notes
Atkinson, Anna S.								see Mrs. Frank M. Warren
Attala, Mr. Sleiman [Solomon]	27	Ottawa, Ontario, Canada	3rd	C	Ottawa, Ontario, Canada			
Attalah, Miss Malaki	17	Syria	3rd	C	unknown			

Name (Maiden Name)[Other Name] *Names in italic indicate survivors*	Age	Residence	Class	E	Destination	L/B	Body # Recovered / Where Buried	Notes
Aubart, Mme. Léontine Pauline	24	Paris, France	1st	C	New York City, NY	9		.

Mme. Leontine Aubart was a cabaret singer from Paris. She was also the mistress of Benjamin Guggenheim, traveling back to New York where presumably his wife was awaiting his return. After *Titanic* sank, Mme. Aubart returned to Paris where in later years she was noted for the wild parties she threw.

Name (Maiden Name)[Other Name]	Age	Residence	Class	E	Destination	L/B	Body # Recovered / Where Buried	Notes
Augustsson, Mr. Albert	23	Smaland, Sweden	3rd	S	Bloomington, IL			
Ayoub, Miss Banoura	14	Lebanon	3rd	C	Ontario, Canada	C		

B

Name	Age	Residence	Class	E	Destination	L/B	Body # Recovered / Where Buried	Notes
Baccos, Mr. Rafoul	20	Syria	3rd	C	unknown			
Backstrom, Mr. Karl Alfred	32	Ruotsinphyhtaa, Finland	3rd	S	New York City, NY			see Backstrom-Gustafsson Notes.
Backström, Mrs. Karl A. (Maria M. Gustafsson)	33	Ruotsinphyhtaa, Finland	3rd	S	New York City, NY	D		She was pregnant. See Backstrom-Gustafsson Group Notes.
Baclini Family								
Baclini, Miss Eugenie	3	Syria	3rd	C	Brooklyn, NY	C		
Baclini, Miss Helene Barbara	9 mo	Syria	3rd	C	Brooklyn, NY	C		
Baclini, Miss Maria Catherine	5	Syria	3rd	C	Brooklyn, NY	C		
Baclini, Mrs. Solomon (Latifa Qurban)	24	Syria	3rd	C	Brooklyn, NY	C		

Mrs. Solomon Baclini was emigrating to America. She was going to meet up with her husband who was already there, but he didn't know his wife and family were on *Titanic*. Traveling with them was Miss Adele Najib, whom Mrs. Baclini was chaperoning and who was getting married in New York. Mrs. Baclini and the children were in Collapsible Lifeboat C, but Adele could not be found. Not wanting to have to tell the family that she survived but Adele did not, Mrs. Baclini was getting out of the lifeboat when Adele Najib was found, and she, too got into Collapsible Lifeboat C and was saved.

Name	Age	Residence	Class	E	Destination	L/B	Body # Recovered / Where Buried	Notes
Badman, Miss Emily Louisa	18	Somerset, England	3rd	S	Skanteales, NY	C		
Badt, Mr. Mohamed	40	Syria	3rd	C	unknown			
Bailey, Mr. Andrew Percy	18	Cornwall, England	2nd	S	Akron, OH			
Baimbrigge, Mr. Charles Robert	23	Guernsey, England	2nd	S	St. Paul, MN			
Balkic, Mr. Cerin	26	Batic, Bosnia	3rd	S	Harrisburg, PA			
Ball, Mrs. Martin Luther (Ada E. Hall)	36	Somerset, England	2nd	S	Jacksonville, FL	14		Traveled with brother-in-law Reverend Robert Bateman
Banfield, Mr. Frederick James	28	Plymouth, England	2nd	S	Houghton, MI			Traveled with Samuel Sobey and Joseph Fillbrook
Banoura, Miss Ayout								see Miss Banoura Ayoub
Barbara, Miss Saiide	18	Syria	3rd	C	Ottawa, Ontario, Canada			
Barbara, Mrs. Catherine	45	Syria	3rd	C	Ottawa, Ontario, Canada			
Barber, Edith Martha Bowerman								see Mrs. Alfred B. Chibnall
Barber, Miss Ellen	26	Stafford, England	1st	S	Chicago, IL	6		Maid to Mrs. Tyrell Cavendish.
Barkworth, Mr. Algernon H.W.	48	Yorkshire, England	1st	S	New York City, NY	B		
Barrett, Elizabeth L.								see Mrs. Martin Rothschild
Barron, Margaret Welles								see Mrs. Frederick J. Swift
Barry, Miss Julia	27	New York City, NY	3rd	Q	New York City, NY			
Barton, Mr. David John	22	Wicken, England	3rd	S	New York City, NY			
Bateman, Reverend Robert James	51	Jacksonville, FL	2nd	S	Jacksonville, FL		#174, buried in Jacksonville, FL	Traveled with sister-in-law Mrs. Martin Luther Ball, who survived.
Baumann, Mr. John D.		New York City, NY	1st	S	New York City, NY			
Baumgardner, Nellie E.								see Mrs. Allen O. Becker
Baxter, Mary Hélène Jane								see Mrs. Frederick C. Douglas
Baxter, Mrs. James (Hélène Chaput De Laudenière)	50	Montreal, Quebec, Canada	1st	C	Montreal, Quebec, Canada	6		
Baxter, Mr. Quigg Edmond	32	Montreal, Quebec, Canada	1st	C	Montreal, Quebec, Canada			

Mr. Quigg Baxter was a former star football and hockey player until an eye injury forced him to retire. He was traveling back to Canada with his mother Hélène, his sister Mary Douglas and his girlfriend Bertha Mayné. His mother didn't approve of his girlfriend and because Ms. Mayné was a cabaret singer (or, not of a social level for her first-class passenger son), Quigg booked her a room under the name Madame Bertha de Villiers. All three women survived, Quigg did not.

Name *(Maiden Name)[Other Name]* *Names in italic indicate survivors*	Age	Residence	Class	E	Destination	L/B	Body # Recovered / Where Buried	Notes
Bazzani, Miss Albina	32	Philadelphia, PA	1st	C	Philadelphia, PA	8		Maid to Mrs. William Bucknell.
Beane, Mr. Edward	32	New York City, NY	2nd	S	New York City, NY	13		Newly-wed on honeymoon.
Beane, Mrs. Edward (Ethel Clarke)	19	Norwich, England	2nd	S	New York City, NY	13		Newly-wed on honeymoon.
Beattie, Mr. Thomson	36	Winnipeg, Manatoba, Canada	1st	C	Winnipeg, Manitoba, Canada		Buried at sea	

Mr. **Thomson Beattie** and his friends Thomas McCaffry and John H. Ross had been vacationing in Europe and were returning home to Canada. As *Titanic* was sinking, Thomson went into the water but managed to get into Collapsible Lifeboat A. This boat was half full of water and several of the passengers, including Beattie who made it aboard, died during the night from exposure. When Officer Lowe eventually rescued the survivors from Collapsible Lifeboat A, he left three bodies remaining in the lifeboat. Lowe cut the canvas siding, expecting it to sink. However, a month later and 300 miles from where *Titanic* sank, the steamer *Oceanic* came across the lifeboat and the three bodies. They were all buried at sea.

Beauchamp, Mr. Henry James	28	London, England	2nd	S	New York City, NY		#194, buried at sea	
Beaven, Mr. William Thomas	19	Kent, England	3rd	S	unknown			
Becker Family								
Becker, Mrs. Allen Oliver (Nellie E. Baumgardner)	36	Guntur, India	2nd	S	Benton Harbor, MI	11		
Becker, Miss Marion Louise	4	Guntur, India	2nd	S	Benton Harbor, MI	11		
Becker, Master Richard F.	1	Guntur, India	2nd	S	Benton Harbor, MI	11		
Becker, Miss Ruth Elizabeth	12	Guntur, India	2nd	S	Benton Harbor, MI	13		

Mrs. Allen Becker, married to a missionary stationed in India, was traveling to Michigan with her children to receive medical treatment for young Richard. Ruth Becker got separated from her mother when loading the lifeboats, and although Ruth knew her family had made it to a lifeboat, Mrs. Becker did not know Ruth was saved until they found each other on *Carpathia*. Ruth Becker Blanchard died in 1990. She is seen and interviewed on many of the *Titanic* television shows and videos.

Beckwith, Mr. Richard Leonard	37	New York City, NY	1st	S	New York City, NY	5		Traveled with wife and daughter.
Beckwith, Mrs. Richard L. (Sallie Monypeny)	47	New York City, NY	1st	S	New York City, NY	5		Traveled with husband Richard and married daughter Helen Newsom.
Beesley, Mr. Lawrence	34	London, England	2nd	S	Toronto, Ontario, Canada	13		

Lawrence Beesley was a science teacher in England, traveling to America on vacation. He chose *Titanic* because it was on its maiden voyage. Beesley wanted to *"stand some distance away to take in a full view of her beautiful proportions, which the narrow approach to the dock made impossible"* He decided he would have to wait until *Titanic* reached New York. Beesley managed to get into Lifeboat 13, and survived. Later he wrote a book about his experiences in a book titled *"The Loss of the SS Titanic."*

Behr, Mr. Karl Howell	26	New York City, NY	1st	C	New York City, NY	5		He was courting Helen M. Newsom.
Bengtsson, Agnes Charlotta								see Mrs. Hjalmar Sandstrom
Bengtsson, Mr. Johan Viktor	26	Krakudden, Sweden	3rd	S	Moune, IL			
Bennett, Claire								see Mrs. J. Frank Karnes
Bentham, Miss Lillian W.	19	Holley, NY	2nd	S	Rochester, NY	12		
Berglund, Miss Alma Cornelia								see Mrs. Nils Palsson
Berglund, Mr. Karl Ivar S.	22	Tranvik, Finland	3rd	S	unknown			
Berriman, Mr. William J.	23	Cornwall, England	2nd	S	Calumet, Michigan			
Bessette, Miss Amelia	35	New York City, NY	1st	C	New York City, NY	8		Maid to Mrs. John S. White.
Betros, Masterr Seman	9	Syria	3rd	C	unknown			
Betros, Mr. Tannous	20	Syria	3rd	C	unknown			
Bidois, Miss Rosalie	42	New York City, NY	1st	C	New York City, NY	4		Maid to Mrs. John J. Astor.
Bing, Mr. Lee	32	Hong Kong	3rd	S	New York City, NY	C/13		see Donaldson Line's Group Notes
Bird, Miss Ellen	31	Norfolk, England	1st	S	New York City, NY	8		Maid to Mrs. Isidor Straus.
Birkeland, Mr. Hans M.M.	21	Brennes, Norway	3rd	S	New York City, NY			
Birnbaum, Mr. Jakob	25	San Francisco, CA	1st	C	San Francisco, CA		#148, buried in Putte, Holland	
Bishop, Mr. Dickinson H.	25	Dowagiac, MI	1st	C	Dowagiac, MI	7		
Bishop, Mrs. Dickinson H. (Helen Walton)	19	Dowagiac, MI	1st	C	Dowagiac, MI	7		

The **Bishop's** were returning from a four-month honeymoon in Europe, accompanied by their dog "Frou-Frou". Mrs. Bishop was pregnant, and when the baby was born in December 1912 it only lived two days. Mrs. Bishop later was seriously injured in an automobile accident, then in January 1916 Mr. Bishop divorced her. She died in March 1916 from complications from the auto accident. The day after she died, the local newspaper announced her death. Ironically, on the same page as the death notice was the announcement that Mr. Bishop had remarried. The dog did not survive the sinking.

Bjorklund, Mr. Ernst Herbert	18	Stockholm, Sweden	3rd	S	New York City, NY			
Björnström-Steffansson, Mr. Mauritz H.	28	Washington, DC	1st	S	Washington, DC	D		
Blackwell, Mr. Stephen Weart	45	Trenton, NJ	1st	S	Trenton, NJ			see Caroline Bonnell Notes

Name *(Maiden Name)[Other Name]* *Names in italic indicate survivors*	Age	Residence	Class	E	Destination	L/B	Body # Recovered / Where Buried	Notes
Blank, Mr. Henry	39	Glen Ridge, NJ	1st	C	Glen Ridge, NJ	7		
Bloomfield, Esther Ada								see Mrs. Benjamin Hart
Blun, Ida								see Mrs. Isidor Straus
Boeson, Pauline C.								see Mrs. Leonard Gibson
Bone, Ada Julia								see Mrs. John T. Doling
Bonnell, Miss Caroline	30	Youngstown, OH	1st	S	Youngstown, OH	8		
Bonnell, Miss Elizabeth	58	Birkdale, England	1st	S	Youngstown, OH	8		

Elizabeth Bonnell was the aunt of **Caroline Bonnell**. They were traveling to Youngstown with the George Wick family and friends Washington Roebling and Stephen Blackwell.

Name	Age	Residence	Class	E	Destination	L/B	Body #	Notes
Borebank, Mr. John James	42	Toronto, Ontario, Canada	1st	S	Toronto, Ontario, Canada			
Borie, Emily Maria								see Mrs. Arthur L. Ryerson
Bostandyeff, Mr. Guentcho	26	Bulgaria	3rd	S	New York City, NY			
Botsford, Mr. William Hull	25	Elmira, NY	2nd	S	Elmira, NY			
Boulos Family								
Boulos, Master Akar	6	Lebanon	3rd	C	Kent, Ontario, Canada			
Boulos, Mr. Hanna	18	Lebanon	3rd	C	Kent, Ontario, Canada			
Boulos, Mrs. Joseph	40	Lebanon	3rd	C	Kent, Ontario, Canada			
Boulos, Miss Nourelian	9	Lebanon	3rd	C	Kent, Ontario, Canada			
Bourke Family								
Bourke, Miss Mary	25	County Mayo, Ireland	3rd	Q	Chicago, IL			
Bourke, Mr. John	28	County Mayo, Ireland	3rd	Q	Chicago, IL			
Bourke, Mrs John (Catherine McHugh)	32	County Mayo, Ireland	3rd	Q	Chicago, IL			

Miss **Mary Bourke** was sister of John Bourke. Both Mary and Mrs. John Bourke were in Lifeboat 16, but got out to remain with Mr. Bourke, and all three died.

Name	Age	Residence	Class	E	Destination	L/B	Body #	Notes
Bowen, Mr. David John	26	Rhondda, Wales	3rd	S	unknown			
Bowen, Miss Grace Scott	45	Cooperstown, NY	1st	C	Cooperstown, NY	4		Governess to Jack Ryerson.
Bowenur, Mr. Solomon	42	London, England	2nd	S	New York City, NY			
Bowerman, Miss Elsie Edith	22	Sussex, England	1st	S	New York City, NY	6		
Bracken, Mr. James H.	27	Lake Arthur, NM	2nd	S	Lake Arthur, NM			
Bradley, Miss Bridget Delia	18	County Cork, Ireland	3rd	Q	Glens Falls, NY	13		see Irish Contingent Group Notes
Bradley, Mr. George A.								see George A. Brereton
Brady, Mr. John Bertram	40	Pomeroy, WA	1st	S	Pomeroy, WA			
Braf, Miss Elin Ester M.	20	Smaland, Sweden	3rd	S	Chicago, IL			
Brailey, W. Theodore R.		London, England	2nd	S				*Titanic* Musician. See Musicians Group Notes.
Brandeis, Mr. Emil	48	Omaha, NB	1st	C	Omaha, NB		#208, buried in Omaha	
Braund, Mr. Lewis R.	29	Devon, England	3rd	S	Saskatchewan, Canada			see Braund-Dennis Group Notes
Braund, Mr. Owen H.	22	Launceston, England	3rd	S	Saskatchewan, Canada			see Braund-Dennis Group Notes
Brereton, [Brady, Bradley, Brayton] Mr. George Andrew	37	Los Angeles, CA	1st	S	New York City, NY	9/15		He was a gambler, traveling under several names.
Brewe, Dr. Arthur J.		Philadelphia, PA	1st	C	Philadelphia, PA			
Bricoux, Mr. Roger Marie	21	Lille, France	2nd	S				*Titanic* Musician. See Musicians Group Notes.
Brobeck, Mr. Karl Rudolf	22	Ostergotland, Sweden	3rd	S	Worcester, MA			
Brocklebank, Mr. William A.	35	Chelmsford, England	3rd	S	New York City, NY			
Brogren, Alfrida K.								see Mrs. Anders Andersson
Brogren, Anna Sigrid Maria								see Mrs. Ernst G. Danbom
Brown, Emily A.								see Mrs. Frank J. Goldsmith
Brown, Miss Amelia Mary "Mildred"	24	Montreal, Quebec, Canada	2nd	S	Montreal, Quebec, Canada	11		Amilia Brown was the cook for the Allison family.

Name *(Maiden Name)[Other Name]* *Names in italic indicate survivors*	Age	Residence	Class	E	Destination	L/B	Body # Recovered / Where Buried	Notes
Brown, Mrs. James Joseph "Molly" (Margaret Tobin)	44	Denver, CO	1st	C	Denver, CO	6		

Margaret Brown, wife of one of the world's wealthiest goldminers, was involved in the early feminist movements. She also ran for political office before women were allowed to vote and she was an early human rights activist. She was returning from a tour of Europe and Africa, traveling with her daughter (who remained in France) and Mr. and Mrs. John Jacob Astor. After *Titanic* sank, she commanded the lifeboat, threatening to toss its nominal captain into the water if he didn't act more civil to the survivors. While on *Carpathia*, Margaret established a Survivor's Committee, which raised over $10,000 for the survivors. She was never known as "Molly" or "The Unsinkable Molly Brown" while she was alive, and the names came from a fictional play that was produced in the 1940's.

Name	Age	Residence	Class	E	Destination	L/B	Body # / Buried	Notes
Brown, Mrs. John M. (Caroline Lamson)	59	Belmont, MA	1st	S	Belmont, MA	D		Traveled with her sisters Mrs. E. Appleton and R. Cornell. Edith Evans gave up her lifebo at seat to her.

Brown Family

Name	Age	Residence	Class	E	Destination	L/B		Notes
Brown, Miss Edith E.	15	Cape Town, South Africa	2nd	S	Seattle, WA	14		
Brown, Mr. Thomas William S.	60	Cape Town, South Africa	2nd	S	Seattle, WA			
Brown, Mrs. Thomas (Elizabeth Ford)	40	Cape Town, South Africa	2nd	S	Seattle, WA	14		

Thomas W.S. Brown, his wife and daughter were traveling from their home in South Africa, going to Seattle to relocate. Edith Brown and her mother survived. Edith, in later years known as Edith Haisman, was a popular guest on many of the television and video shows. She died in 1997 at 101 years of age.

Name	Age	Residence	Class	E	Destination	L/B	Body/Buried	Notes
Bryhl, Miss Dagmar Jenny Ingeborg	20	Skara, Sweden	2nd	S	Rockford, IL			Fiancé of Ingvar Enander and sister of Kurt A. Bryhl
Bryhl, Mr Kurt Arnold G.	25	Skara, Sweden	2nd	S	Rockford, IL			Brother of Dagmar Bryhl.
Buckley, Mr. Daniel	21	County Cork, Ireland	3rd	Q	New York City, NY	4/11		see Irish Contingent Group Notes
Buckley, Miss Katherine	20	County Cork, Ireland	3rd	Q	Roxbury, MA		#299, buried in Boston	
Bucknell, Mrs. William R. (Emma Ward)	60	Philadelphia, PA	1st	C	Philadelphia, PA	8		

Mrs. William Bucknell was traveling home to Philadelphia accompanied by her maid Albina Bazzani and friend Margaret Brown. Mrs. Bucknell's husband William Bucknell was the founder of Bucknell University in Pennsylvania.

Name	Age	Residence	Class	E	Destination	L/B	Body/Buried	Notes
Burke, Mr. Jeremiah	19	County Cork, Ireland	3rd	Q	Charleston, MA			
Burns, Miss Elizabeth Margaret	41	Tuxedo Park, NJ	1st	C	Tuxedo Park, NJ	3		Nanny to Robert D. Spedden.
Burns, Miss Mary Delia	18	County Sligo, Ireland	3rd	Q	New York City, NY			
Buss, Miss Kate	36	Sittingbourne, England	2nd	S	San Diego, CA	9		
Butler, Mr. Reginald F.	25	Hampshire, England	2nd	S	New York City, NY		#97, buried in Fairview Cemetery, Halifax	
Butt, Major Archibald W.	45	Washington, DC	1st	S	Washington, DC			

Major **Archibald Butt** was a senior military aide to both President Theodore Roosevelt and William Howard Taft. A veteran of the Spanish American War in Cuba, he later served in the Philippines. As friend to both Roosevelt and Taft, he ended up in the middle of the personal quarrel they had, so Butt took six-weeks leave and went to Europe to rest, traveling with his good friend Francis Millet.

Name	Age	Residence	Class	E	Destination	L/B		Notes
Byles, Rev. Thomas Roussel D.	42	London, England	2nd	S	Brooklyn, NY			

The Reverend **Thomas Byles** was a highly respected minister and a Roman Catholic Rector. He was traveling to New York to conduct his brother's wedding ceremony. Father Byles was last seen giving last rites and hearing confessions of those who knew they wouldn't be saved. His brother had the wedding as planned, then the newly-wed couple went home, changed into their mourning clothes and returned to the church for a memorial mass.

Name	Age	Residence	Class	E	Destination	L/B		Notes
Byström, Mrs. Karolina	42	New York City, NY	2nd	S	New York City, NY			

C

Name	Age	Residence	Class	E	Destination	L/B		Notes
Cacic, Mr. Jego	18	Croatia	3rd	S	Chicago, IL			
Cacic, Mr. Luka	38	Croatia	3rd	S	Chicago, IL			
Cacic, Miss Manda	21	Croatia	3rd	S	Chicago, IL			
Cacic, Miss Marija	30	Croatia	3rd	S	Chicago, IL			

It is not known if the four passengers with the last name **Cacic** were related. However, they all bought tickets at the same time from the same agent, so probably they were part of an extended family.

Name *(Maiden Name)[Other Name]* *Names in italic indicate survivors*	Age	Residence	Class	E	Destination	L/B	Body # Recovered / Where Buried	Notes
Cairns, Mr. Alexander		Bryn Mawr, PA	1st	S	Bryn Mawr, PA			Manservant to Mr. William E. Carter.
Calderhead, Mr. Edward P.	42	New York City, NY	1st	S	New York City, NY	5		
Caldwell Family								
Caldwell, Master Alden G.	10 mo	Bangkok, Thailand	2nd	S	Roseville, IL	13		Returning home to Roseville after
Caldwell, Mr. Albert Francis	26	Bangkok, Thailand	2nd	S	Roseville, IL	13		teaching at the Bangkok Christian
Caldwell, Mrs. Albert (Sylvia Harbaugh)	26	Bangkok, Thailand	2nd	S	Roseville, IL	13		College for Boys
Calic, Mr. Jovo	17	Croatia	3rd	S	Sault Ste. Marie, MI			Sometimes listed as Jovo Uzelas.
Calic, Mr. Peter	17	Croatia	3rd	S	Sault Ste. Marie, MI			
Cameron, Miss Clear Annie	35	London, England	2nd	S	Mamaroneck, NY	10		
Campbell, Mr. William		Belfast, Ireland	2nd	B	New York City, NY			Joiner Apprentice: see H&W Guarantee Group Notes.
Canavan, Miss Mary	21	County Mayo, Ireland	3rd	Q	New York City, NY			
Canavan, Mr. Patrick	21	County Mayo, Ireland	3rd	Q	Philadelphia, PA			
Candee, Mrs. Edward (Helen Churchill Hungerford)	53	Washington, D.C.	1st	C	Washington, D.C.	6		

Mrs. Candee was a well-known author and had written a book titled "How a Woman May Earn a Living" which gave advice to women on how to get along without a man to support them.

Cann, Mr. Ernest C.	28	Cornwall, England	3rd	S	unknown			
Caram, [Kareem] Mr. Joseph	28	Lebanon	3rd	C	Ottawa, Ontario, Canada			
Caram, [Kareem] Mrs. Joseph (Maria Elias)	18	Lebanon	3rd	C	Ottawa, Ontario, Canada			
Carbines, Mr. William	19	Cornwall, England	2nd	S	Calumet, MI		#18, buried in St. Ives, England	
Cardeza, Mr. Thomas Drake M.	36	Germantown, PA	1st	C	Germantown, PA	3		
Cardeza, Mrs. James W.M. (Charlotte Wardle Drake)	58	Germantown, PA	1st	C	Germantown, PA	3		

Mrs. James W.M. Cardeza, her son Thomas, maid Anna Ward and manservant Gustave Lesueur were returning from vacation and occupied the second "Promenade Suite" (J. Bruce Ismay had the other). All four members of the entourage would survive. Mrs. Cardeza later filed a claim totaling $177,000 for the 14 steamer trunks, three crates and four suitcases of clothing they lost. She eventually settled for much less.

Carlsson, Mr. August S.	28	Sweden	3rd	S	Fower, MN			
Carlsson, Mr. Carl R.	24	Sweden	3rd	S	Huntley, IL			
Carlsson, Mr. Frans Olof	33	New York City, NY	1st	S	New York City, NY			
Carr, Miss Helen								see Helen Corr
Carr, Miss Jane [Jeannie]	47	County Sligo, Ireland	3rd	Q	Windsor Locks, CT			
Carrau, Mr. Francisco M.	28	Montevideo, Uruguay	1st	S	Montevideo, Uruguay			
Carrau, Mr. Jose Pedro	17	Montevideo, Uruguay	1st	S	Montevideo, Uruguay			
Carter, Rev. Ernest C.	54	London, England	2nd	S	New York City, NY			
Carter, Mrs. Ernest C. (Lilian Hughes)	44	London, England	2nd	S	New York City, NY			
Carter Family								
Carter, Master William Thornton II	11	Bryn Mawr, PA	1st	S	Bryn Mawr, PA	4		
Carter, Miss Lucile Polk	14	Bryn Mawr, PA	1st	S	Bryn Mawr, PA	4		
Carter, Mr. William Ernest	36	Bryn Mawr, PA	1st	S	Bryn Mawr, PA	C		
Carter, Mrs. William E. (Lucile Polk)	36	Bryn Mawr, PA	1st	S	Bryn Mawr, PA	4		

The **Carter** family was returning home from vacation. Traveling with them was Mrs. Carter's maid Auguste Serraplan, Mr. Carter's manservant Alexander Cairns and chauffeur Charles Aldworth. In the cargo hold was Mr. Carter's 25 hp Renault automobile and in the kennel two dogs, breed and names unknown. Mr. Carter managed to get his wife, children and Miss Serreplan into Lifeboat 4, but was refused permission to get in by 2nd Officer Lightoller. So, he moved to the starboard side of the ship and found space in Collapsible Lifeboat C. William Carter knew his family was safe, however, they didn't know he survived until they met up on the *Carpathia.* The dogs did not survive.

Carver, Mr. Alfred J.	28	Southampton, England	3rd	S	New York City, NY			see American Line Group Notes
Case, Mr. Howard B.	48	Ascot, England	1st	S	Rochester, NY			
Cassebeer, Mrs. Henry A. (Genevieve Fosdick)	37	New York City, NY	1st	C	New York City, NY	5		

Name (Maiden Name)[Other Name] *Names in italic indicate survivors*	Age	Residence	Class	E	Destination	L/B	Body # Recovered / Where Buried	Notes
Catavelas, Mr. Vassilios								see Katavelas, Mr. Vassilios
Cavendish, Mr. Tyrell W.	36	Staffordshire, England	1st	S	New York City, NY		# 172, buried in Staffordshire, England	
Cavendish, Mrs. Tyrell W. (Julia F. Siegel)	25	Staffordshire, England	1st	S	New York City, NY	6		
Cazaly, Annie Elizabeth								see Mrs. John G. Sage
Celotti, Mr. Francesco	24	London, England	3rd	S	unknown			
Chaffee, Mr. Herbert F.	46	Amenia, ND	1st	S	Amenia, ND			
Chaffee, Mrs. Herbert F. (Carrie C. Toogood)	47	Amenia, ND	1st	S	Amenia, ND	4		
Chambers, Mr. Norman C.	27	New York City, NY	1st	S	New York City, NY	5		
Chambers, Mrs. Norman C. (Bertha Griggs)	31	New York City, NY	1st	S	New York City, NY	5		
Chapman, Mr. Charles H.	52	Bronx, NY	2nd	S	Bronx, NY		#130, buried in Bronx, NY	
Chapman, Mr. John H.	37	Cornwall, England	2nd	S	Spokane, WA		#17, buried in Fairview Cemetery, Halifax	
Chapman, Mrs. John H. (Sara E. Lawry)	29	Cornwall, England	2nd	S	Spokane, WA			
Charters, [Chartens] Mr. David	21	County Longford, Ireland	3rd	Q	New York City, NY			
Chaudanson, Miss Victorine	36	Haverford, PA	1st	C	Haverford, PA	4		Maid to Mrs. Emily Ryerson.
Chehab, Mr. Emir Farres								see Chehab Emir-Farres
Cherry, Miss Gladys	30	London, England	1st	S	New York City, NY	8		Cousin to Countess of Rothes.
Chevré, Mr. Paul R.	45	Paris, France	1st	C	Ottawa, Ontario, Canada	7		

Mr. **Paul Chevre** was a famous Canadian sculptor, and several of his works are located throughout the country. Charles Hays, a passenger on *Titanic,* and General Manager of the Grand Trunk Pacific Railroad had commissioned Chevre to do a bust of the Canadian Prime Minister Sir Wilfred Laurier to be placed in the lobby of the Grand Trunk's new hotel in Ottawa, the Château Laurier. Hays and Chevre were returning to Ottawa for the grand unveiling of the statue. Chevre survived but Hays did not.

Name (Maiden Name)[Other Name]	Age	Residence	Class	E	Destination	L/B	Body # Recovered / Where Buried	Notes
Chibnall, Mrs. Alfred (Edith Bowerman)	47	Sussex, England	1st	S	Cleveland, OH	6		
Chip, Mr. Chang	32	Hong Kong, China	3rd	S	New York City, NY	?		see Donaldson Line's Group Notes.
Chisholm, Mr. Roderick R.C.		Liverpool, England	1st	B	New York City, NY			Chief Ships Draftsman, see H&W Guarantee Group Notes.
Christian, Lulu Thorne								see Mrs. James V. Drew
Christmann, Mr. Emil	29	London, England	3rd	S	unknown			
Christy [Cohen], Amy Francis								see Mrs. Sidney S. Jacobsohn
Christy, Mrs. Alice F.	45	London, England	2nd	S	Montreal, Quebec, Canada	12		Mother of Julie Christy.
Christy, Miss Julie R.	25	London, England	2nd	S	Montreal, Quebec, Canada	12		Daughter of Alice Christy.
Chronopoulos, Mr. Apostolos	26	Greece	3rd	C	unknown			
Chronopoulos, Mr. Demetrios	18	Greece	3rd	C	unknown			
Clark, Mr. Walter M.	27	Los Angeles, CA	1st	C	Los Angeles, CA			
Clark, Mrs. Walter M. (Virginia E. McDowell)	26	Los Angeles, CA	1st	C	Los Angeles, CA	4		
Clarke, Mr. Charles V.	29	Netley Abbey, England	2nd	S	San Francisco, CA			
Clarke, Mrs. Charles V. (Ada Maria Winfield)	28	Netley Abbey, England	2nd	S	San Francisco, CA	14		
Clarke, Mr. John Frederick P.		Liverpool, England	2nd	S			#202, buried in Mount Olivet Cemetery, Halifax	see Musicians Group Notes.
Clarke, Miss Ethel								see Mrs. Edward Beane
Cleaver, Miss Alice C.	22	London, England	1st	S	Montreal, Quebec, Canada	11		see Allison Family Notes
Clifford, Mr. George Q.	40	Stoughton, MA	1st	S	Stoughton, MA			
Coelho, Mr. Domingos F.	20	Madeira Island, Portugal	3rd	S	New York City, NY			

Name *(Maiden Name)[Other Name]* *Names in italic indicate survivors*	Age	Residence	Class	E	Destination	L/B	Body # Recovered / Where Buried	Notes
Cohen, Amy Francis "Christy"								see Mrs. Sidney S. Jacobsohn
Cohen, Mr. Gurshon	19	London, England	3rd	S	New York City, NY	12		
Colbert, Mr. Patrick	24	County Limerick, Ireland	3rd	Q	Sherbrooke, Quebec, Canada			
Colcheff, Mr. Peju								see Mr. Peyo Coleff
Coleff, Mr. Fotio	24	Bulgaria	3rd	S	Chicago, IL			Might be Fatio Coleff.
Coleff, Mr. Peyo	36	Bulgaria	3rd	S	Chicago, IL			see Gumostnik, Bulgaria, Group Notes
Coleridge, Mr. Reginald C.	29	Huntingdonshire, England	2nd	S	Detroit, MI			
Collander, Mr. Erik G.	27	Helsinki, Finland	2nd	S	Ashtabula, OH			
Collett, Mr. Sidney C. Stuart	24	London, England	2nd	S	Fort Bryon, NY	9		
Colley, Mr. Edward P.	37	Vancouver, BC, Canada	1st	S	Vancouver, BC, Canada			
Collyer Family								
Collyer, Mr. Harvey	31	Hampshire, England	2nd	S	Payette, ID			
Collyer, Mrs. Harvey (Charlotte Tate)	31	Hampshire, England	2nd	S	Payette, ID	14		
Collyer, Miss Marjorie Charlotte	8	Hampshire, England	2nd	S	Payette, ID	14		
Colvin, Irene								see Mrs. Walter H. Corbett
Compton Family								
Compton, Mr. Alexander T. Jr.	37	Lakewood, NJ	1st	C	Lakewood, NJ			
Compton, Mrs. Alexander T. (Mary E.Ingersoll)	64	Lakewood, NJ	1st	C	Lakewood, NJ	14		
Compton, Miss Sara Rebecca	39	Lakewood, NJ	1st	C	Lakewood, NJ	14		
Conlon, Mr. Thomas H.	31	Philadelphia, PA	3rd	Q	Philadelphia, PA			
Connaghton, Mr. Michael	31	Brooklyn, NY	3rd	Q	Brooklyn, NY			
Connolly, Miss Kate	30	County Caven, Ireland	3rd	Q	unknown			
Connolly, Miss Katherine [Kate]	22	County Tipperary, Ireland	3rd	Q	New York City, NY	13		
Connors, Mr. Patrick	28	County Cork, Ireland	3rd	Q	unknown		#171, buried at sea	
Cook, Mrs. Arthur (Selena Rogers)	22	Oxford, England	2nd	S	New York City, NY	14		
Cook, Mr. Jacob	43	Russia	3rd	S	unknown			
Cor, Mr. Bartol	35	Croatia	3rd	S	Great Falls, MT			
Cor, Mr. Ivan	27	Croatia	3rd	S	Great Falls, MT			
Cor, Mr. Liudevit [Ludovik]	19	Croatia	3rd	S	Great Falls, MT			

It is unknown if the three passengers with the last name **Cor** were related. However, they all bought tickets at the same time from the same agent, so probably they were part of an extended family.

Corbett, Mrs. Walter H. (Irene Colvin)	30	Provo, UT	2nd	S	Provo, UT			
Corey, Mrs. Percy C. (Mary P. Miller)		India	2nd	S	Pittsburgh, PA			
Corn, Mr. Harry	30	London, England	3rd	S	unknown			
Cornell, Mrs. Robert C. (Malvina H. Lamson)	55	New York City, NY	1st	S	New York City, NY	2		Traveled with sisters Mrs. Edward Appleton and Mrs. John M. Brown. Her husband founded Cornell Univ.
Corr, [Carr] Miss Helen	16	County Longford, Ireland	3rd	Q	New York City, NY	14/16		
Cotterill, Mr. Henry	21	Penzance, England	2nd	S	Akron, OH			
Coutts Family								
Coutts, Master Neville L.	3	Southampton, England	3rd	S	Brooklyn, NY	2		
Coutts, Master William L.	9	Southampton, England	3rd	S	Brooklyn, NY	2		
Coutts, Mrs. William (Winnie Trainer)	36	Southampton, England	3rd	S	Brooklyn, NY	2		

The **Coutts** family is another rare instance where an entire family traveling Third Class managed to survive.

Coxon, Mr. Daniel	59	London, England	3rd	S	Merrill, WI			
Crafton, Mr. John B.	59	Roachdale, IN	1st	S	Roachdale, IN			
Crease, Mr. Ernest J.	19	Bristol, England	3rd	S	Cleveland, OH			Traveled with Edward R. Stanley.

Name *(Maiden Name)[Other Name]* *Names in italic indicate survivors*	Age	Residence	Class	E	Destination	L/B	Body # Recovered / Where Buried	Notes
Cribb, Mr. John H.	44	Newark, NJ	3rd	S	Newark, NJ			
Cribb, Miss Laura Alice	17	Newark, NJ	3rd	S	Newark, NJ	12		
Crosby Family								
Crosby, Captain Edward G.	67	Milwaukee, WI	1st	S	Milwaukee, WI		#269, buried in Milwaukee, WI	
Crosby, Mrs. Edward G. (Catherine E. Halstead)	65	Milwaukee, WI	1st	S	Milwaukee, WI	5/7		
Crosby, Miss Harriette R.	36	Paris, France	1st	S	Milwaukee, WI	5/7		
Cumings, Mr. John B.	39	New York City, NY	1st	C	New York City, NY			
Cumings, Mrs. John B. (Florence Briggs Thayer)	38	New York City, NY	1st	C	New York City, NY	4		
Cunningham, Mr. Alfred F.		Belfast, Ireland	2nd	B	New York City, NY			Fitter Apprentice. See H&W Guarantee Group Notes.

D

Daher, Mr. Shedid [Tannous]	19	Syria	3rd	C	Kulpmont, PA		#9, buried in Pennsylvania	
Dahl, Mr. Charles E. [Karl]	45	Adelaide, Australia	3rd	S	Fingal, ND	15		
Dahlberg, Miss Gerda Ulrika	22	Stockholm, Sweden	3rd	S	Chicago, IL			
Dakic, Mr. Branko	19	Austria	3rd	S	unknown			
Daly, Mr. Eugene Patrick	29	County Westmeath, Ireland	3rd	Q	New York City, NY	B		No relation to Margaret Daly.
Daly, Miss Margaret Marcella	30	County Westmeath, Ireland	3rd	Q	New York City, NY	15		No relation to Eugene Daly.
Daly, Mr. Peter Dennis	51	Lima, Peru	1st	S	Lima, Peru	A		
Danbom Family								
Danbom, Mr. Ernst G.	34	Stanton, IA	3rd	S	Stanton, IA		#197, buried in Stanton, IA	
Danbom, Mrs. Ernst G. (Anna S.M. Brogren)	28	Stanton, IA	3rd	S	Stanton, IA			
Danbom, Master Gilbert Sigvard E.	4 mo	Stanton, IA	3rd	S	Stanton, IA			

The **Ernst Danbom** family was emigrating to Canada. The Anders Andersson family, Ernst being the brother-in-law of Mr. Andersson, accompanied them. All seven members of the Andersson family and three members of the Danbom family were lost.

Daniel, Mr. Robert W.	27	Philadelphia, PA	1st	S	Philadelphia, PA	3?		

Mr. **Robert Daniel's** pet French Bulldog named "Gamin de Pycombe" did not survive. While on *Carpathia,* Daniel met Mrs. Lucian P. Smith, who had lost her husband when *Titanic* sank. In later years, Daniel and Mrs. Smith would marry.

Daniels, Bessie Waldo								see Mrs. Hudson Allison
Daniels, Miss Sarah	33	London, England	1st	S	Montreal, Quebec, Canada	8		Maid to Mrs. Hudson Allison.
Danoff, Mr. Yoto	27	Bulgaria	3rd	S	Chicago, IL			
Dantchoff [Dantcheff], Mr. Kristo	25	Bulgaria	3rd	S	Chicago, IL			
Davidson, Mr. Thornton	31	Montreal, Quebec, Canada	1st	S	Montreal, Quebec, Canada			see Charles M. Hays Family Notes
Davidson, Mrs. Thornton (Orian Hays)	27	Montreal, Quebec, Canada	1st	S	Montreal, Quebec, Canada	3		see Charles M. Hays Family Notes
Davies, Mr. Alfred J.	24	West Bromwich, England	3rd	S	Pontiac, MI			
Davies, Mr. John S.	21	West Bromwich, England	3rd	S	Pontiac, MI			
Davies, Mr. Joseph	17	West Bromwich, England	3rd	S	Pontiac, MI			

Mr. **Alfred Davies** was traveling with his brothers John S. Davies and Joseph Davies and his Uncle James Lester to jobs they had secured in Michigan. Alfred was married two days prior to *Titanic's* sailing. He left his wife in England, and she would follow along at a later time. All four men were lost.

Davies, Mr. Charles H.	18	Hampshire, England	2nd	S	unknown			see Hickman Group Notes
Davies, Mr. Evan	22	South Wales	3rd	S	unknown			

Name *(Maiden Name)[Other Name]* *Names in italic indicate survivors*	Age	Residence	Class	E	Destination	L/B	Body # Recovered / Where Buried	Notes
Davies, Mrs. John M. (Elizabeth A. White)	48	Cornwall, England	2nd	S	Hancock, MI	14		
Davies, Master John M. Jr.	10	Cornwell, England	2nd	S	Hancock, MI	14/3		
Mrs. John M. Davies was emigrating to America with her sons Joseph Nicholls and John Junior and family friend Maude Sincock. All except Joseph survived.								
Davis, Miss Mary	28	London, England	2nd	S	Staten Island, NY	13		Died in 1987, lived to 104 years old.
Davison, Mr. Thomas H.		Liverpool, England	3rd	S	Bedford, OH			
Davison, Mrs. Thomas H. (Mary Finck)		Liverpool, England	3rd	S	Bedford, OH	?		
de Brito, Mr. Jose Joaquim	32	London, England	2nd	S	Sao Paulo, Brazil			
De Laudenière, Helene Chaput								see Mrs. James Baxter
De Messemaeker, Mr. William J.	36	Tampico, MT	3rd	S	Tampico, MT	13		
De Messemaeker, Mrs. William J.	36	Tampico, MT	3rd	S	Tampico, MT	13		
De Mulder, Mr. Theodore	30	Aspelare, Belgium	3rd	S	Detroit, MI	?		Traveled with Mr. Jules Sap and Mr. Jean Scheerlinckx
De Pelsmaeker, Mr. Alphonse	16	Heldergem, Belgium	3rd	S	Gladstone, MI			
de Villiers, Berthe								Traveling under assumed name. See Berthe Antonine Mayné.
Deacon, Mr. Percy	17	Hampshire, England	2nd	S	Boston, MA			see Hickman Group Notes
Dean Family								
Dean, Mr. Bertram F.	25	Devon, England	3rd	S	Wichita, KS			
Dean, Mrs. Bertram F. (Eva G. Light)	32	Devon, England	3rd	S	Wichita, KS	10/13		
Dean, Master Bertram Vere	1	Devon, England	3rd	S	Wichita, KS	10/13		
Dean, Miss Elizabeth G. (Millvina)	9 wks	Devon, England	3rd	S	Wichita, KS	10/13		
Millvina Dean is still alive as of November 2007, and is the last survivor of the *Titanic* disaster. She has been very popular on the television and video circuit for several years.								
del Carlo, Mr. Sebastiano	29	Lucca, Italy	2nd	C	California		#295, buried in Italy	
del Carlo, Mrs. Sebastiano (Argene Genovese)	24	Lucca, Italy	2nd	C	California	11		She was pregnant.
Delalic, Mr. Regyo (Redjo)	25	Bosnia	3rd	S	Harrisburg, PA			
Demetri, Mr. Marinko	23	Austria	3rd	S	unknown			
Denbury, Mr. Herbert	25	Guernsey, England	2nd	S	Elizabeth, NJ			
Herbert Denbury, brothers Clifford and Ernest Jefferys, their sister Lillian Renouf and her husband Peter H. Renouf were all traveling together to Elizabeth, NJ. All except Lillian Renouf were lost.								
Denkoff, Mitto	30	Bulgaria	3rd	S	Coon Rapids, IA			
Dennis, Mr. Samuel	23	Cornwall, England	3rd	S	Saskatchewan, Canada			see Braund-Dennis Group Notes
Dennis, Mr. William	26	Cornwall, England	3rd	S	Saskatchewan, Canada			see Braund-Dennis Group Notes
Devaney, Miss Margaret	19	County Sligo, Ireland	3rd	Q	New York City, NY	C		
Dewan [Dwan], Mr. Frank	67	County Waterford, Ireland	3rd	Q	Morris Plains, NJ			
Dibden, Mr. William	18	New Forest, England	2nd	S	unknown			see Hickman Group Notes
Dibo, Mr. Elias								see Mr. Dibo Elias
Dick, Mr. Albert A.	31	Calgary, Alberta, Canada	1st	C	Calgary, Alberta, Canada	3		
Dick, Mrs. Albert A. (Vera Gillespie)	17	Calgary, Alberta, Canada	1st	C	Calgary, Alberta, Canada	3		
Dika, Mr. Mirko	17	Croatia	3rd	S	Vancouver, BC, Canada			
Dimic, Mr. Jovan	42	Croatia	3rd	S	Red Lodge, MT			
Dintcheff, Mr. Valtcho	43	Bulgaria	3rd	S	unknown			
Dodge Family								
Dodge, Dr. Washington	53	San Francisco, CA	1st	S	San Francisco, CA	13		Died by suicide in 1919.
Dodge, Master Washington Jr.	4	San Francisco, CA	1st	S	San Francisco, CA	5		
Dodge, Mrs. Washington (Ruth Vidaver)	34	San Francisco, CA	1st	S	San Francisco, CA	5		
Doharr, Mr. Tannous		Syria	3rd	C	Youngstown, OH			
Dolck, Elin Matilda								see Mrs. Pekka Hakkarainen
Doling, Miss Elsie	19	Southampton, England	2nd	S	New York City, NY			
Doling, Mrs. John T. (Ada J. Bone)	32	Southampton, England	2nd	S	New York City,NY			
Donohoe, Miss Bridget	21	County Mayo, Ireland	3rd	Q	Chicago, IL			

Name *(Maiden Name)[Other Name]* *Names in italic indicate survivors*	Age	Residence	Class	E	Destination	L/B	Body # Recovered / Where Buried	Notes
Dooley, Mr. Patrick	32	County Limerick, Ireland	3rd	Q	New York City, NY			
Dorking, Mr. Edward A.	19	Hampshire, England	3rd	S	Oglesby, IL	B		
Dougherty, John								see Mr. James Moran
Douglas Family								
Douglas, Mrs. Frederick C. (Mary Hélène Jane Baxter)	27	Montreal, Quebec, Canada	1st	C	Montreal, Quebec, Canada	6		Traveled with mother Hélène Baxter and brother Quigg Baxter.
Douglas, Mr. Walter D.	50	Deephaven, MN	1st	C	Deephaven, MN		#62, buried in Cedar Rapids, IA	
Douglas, Mrs. Walter D. (Mahala Dutton)	48	Deephaven, MN	1st	C	Deephaven, MN	2		

Mr. and Mrs. **Walter Douglas** and their daughter-in-law Mary were returning from a vacation in Europe. Their son did not accompany them. Mary's mother Mrs. James Baxter and brother Quigg Baxter were also on *Titanic*, along with Quigg's girlfriend Bertha Mayné. See Baxter Family Notes.

Name	Age	Residence	Class	E	Destination	L/B	Body # Recovered / Where Buried	Notes
Dowdell, Miss Elizabeth	30	Union Hill, NJ	3rd	S	New York City, NY	13		Nurse to Virginia Emanuel.
Downton [Douton], Mr. William J.	54	Holley, NY	2nd	S	Holley, NY			
Doyle, Miss Elizabeth	24	County Wexford, Ireland	3rd	Q	New York City, NY			
Drake, Charlotte Wardle								see Mrs. James W.M. Cardeza
Drazonovic, Mr. Josef	33	Croatia	3rd	C	New York City, NY		#51, buried at sea	
Drew Family								
Drew, Mr. James V.	42	Greenport, NY	2nd	S	Greenport, NY			
Drew, Mrs. James V. (Lulu T. Christian)	34	Greenport, NY	2nd	S	Greenport, NY	10		
Drew, Master Marshall B.	8	Greenport, NY	2nd	S	Greenport, NY	10		Adopted nephew of James and Lulu Drew.
Driscoll, Miss Bridget								see Miss Bridget O'Driscoll
Dropkin [Drapkin], Miss Jennie	23	London, England	3rd	S	Brooklyn, NY			
Duff-Gordon, Lady Cosmo (Lucy C. Sutherland)	48	London, England	1st	C	New York City, NY	1		
Duff-Gordon, Sir Cosmo Edmund	49	London, England	1st	C	New York City, NY	1		

Sir Cosmo and **Lady Duff-Gordon** were an interesting couple. Cosmo had represented Great Britain as a fencer in the 1908 Olympics. He doesn't seem to have had a job. Lady Duff-Gordon was a fashion designer and owned her own business, rather unusual in the early 1900's for a woman to do so. They were traveling to America for business, but were traveling under assumed names of Mr. and Mrs. Morgan. They had separate cabins on *Titanic* that were not located together. They were on the first lifeboat launched, and there were only five passengers and seven crewmen in a lifeboat designed to hold 40 people. Sir Cosmo made a generous offer to pay the crewmen of the lifeboat for the personal equipment they lost. Later, this was construed that he paid the crewmen not to go back to pick up survivors. Untrue, but the public believed it, and he had to defend himself at the Court of Inquiry.

Name	Age	Residence	Class	E	Destination	L/B	Body # Recovered / Where Buried	Notes
Dulles, Mr. William C.	39	Philadelphia, PA	1st	C	Philadelphia, PA		#113, buried in Philadelphia, PA	
Duquemin, Mr. Joseph	24	Guernsey, England	3rd	S	Albion, NY	D		
Duran y More, Miss Asuncion	27	Barcelona, Spain	2nd	C	Havana, Cuba	12		
Duran y More, Miss Florentina	30	Barcelona, Spain	2nd	C	Havana, Cuba	12		
Dutton, Mahala								see Mrs. Walter D. Douglas
Dwan, Frank								see Frank Dewan
Dyer-Edwards, Noël Martha, Countess of Rothes	33	Kensington, England	1st	S	Vancouver, BC, Canada	8		Traveled with cousin Gladys Cherry and maid Roberta Maioni.
Dyker, Mr. Adolf F.	23	New Haven, CT	3rd	S	New Haven, CT			
Dyker, Mrs. Adolf F. (Anna E. Andersson)	22	New Haven, CT	3rd	S	New Haven, CT	16		

Name *(Maiden Name)[Other Name]* *Names in italic indicate survivors*	Age	Residence	Class	E	Destination	L/B	Body # Recovered / Where Buried	Notes
E								
Earnshaw, Mrs. Boulton (Olive Potter)	23	Mt. Airy, PA	1st	C	Mt. Airy, PA	7		
Ecimovic [Culumovic], Mr. Jeso	17	Croatia	3rd	S	Hammond, IN			
Edvardson, Mr. Gustaf Hjalmar	18	Smaland, Sweden	3rd	S	Joliet, IL			
Eitemiller, Mr. George F.	23	London, England	2nd	S	Detroit, MI			
Eklund, Mr. Hans Linus	16	Narke, Sweden	3rd	S	Jerome Junction, AZ			
Ekstrom, Mr. Johan	45	Effington Rut, SD	3rd	S	Effington Rut, SD			Traveled with father Johan Svensson.
Elias, Dibo	29	Lebanon	3rd	C	unknown			
Elias, Maria								see Mrs. Joseph Caram
Elias, Mr. Joseph	39	Syria	3rd	C	Ottawa, Ontario, Canada			
Elias, Mr. Joseph Jr.	17	Syria	3rd	C	Ottawa, Ontario, Canada			
Elias, Mr. Tannous	17	Syria	3rd	C	Ottawa, Ontario, Canada			

Mr. **Joseph Elias** was emigrating to America with his two sons Joseph, Jr. and Tannous. None of them survived.

Name	Age	Residence	Class	E	Destination	L/B	Body # Recovered / Where Buried	Notes
Elkins, Eleanor								see Mrs. George D. Widener
Elsbury, Mr. James	47	Gurnee, IL	3rd	S	Gurnee, IL			
Emanuel, Miss Virginia E.	5	New York City, NY	3rd	S	New York City, NY	13		Traveled with nurse Elizabeth Dowell to visit grandparents.
Emir-Farres, Mr. Chehab/Shihab	29	Lebanon	3rd	C	unknown			Could be Mr. Emir Farres Chehab
Enander, Mr. Ingvar	21	Gothenburg, Sweden	2nd	S	Rockford, IL			Fiancé of Dagmar Bryhl.
Endres, Miss Caroline Louise	38	New York City, NY	1st	C	New York City, NY	4		Nurse for Madeleine Astor.
Estanslau, Mr. Manuel Goncalves	38	Portugal	3rd	S	New York City, NY			
Eugenie, Marie								see Mrs. William A. Spencer
Eustis, Miss Elizabeth Mussey	54	Brookline, MA	1st	C	Brookline, MA	4		
Eustis, Martha								see Mrs. Walter B. Stephenson
Evans, Miss Edith Corse	36	New York City, NY	1st	C	New York City, NY			

Edith Evans was single and traveling alone. She met up with several passengers, including Mrs. John M. Brown who although was much older, had young children at home. Miss Evans and Mrs. Brown managed to get up to Collapsible Lifeboat D, the last lifeboat, but it was full and only had room for one more person. Edith Evans, who was closest to the lifeboat, stepped back and told Mrs. Brown to get in, telling her *"you go first, you have children waiting at home"*. Mrs. Brown was saved, but Miss Evans was not. She was one of four First Class women who were lost.

Name	Age	Residence	Class	E	Destination	L/B	Body # Recovered / Where Buried	Notes
Everett, Mr. Thomas J.	36	Somerset, England	3rd	S	New York City, NY		#187, buried in Fairview Cemetery, Halifax	
F								
Fahlstrøm, Mr. Arne J.	19	Oslo, Norway	2nd	S	New York City, NY			
Fardon, Mr. Charles	38	Southampton, England	3rd	C	Canada			Traveled, for some reason, as "Charles Franklin".
Farnham, Alice								see Dr. Alice Leader
Farquarson, Mary Graham Carmichael								see Mrs. Daniel W. Marvin
Farrell, Mr. James	26	County Longford, Ireland	3rd	Q	New York City, NY		#68, buried at sea	
Farthing, Mr. John		New York City, NY	1st	S	New York City, NY			Manservant to Mr. Isidor Straus.
Faunthorpe, Mr. Harry	40	Liverpool, England	2nd	S	Philadelphia, PA		#286, buried in Philadelphia, PA	Traveled with mistress Elizabeth Wilkinson.
Faunthorpe, Mrs. Harry (Elizabeth Wilkinson)						16		She was a Harry Faunthorpe's mistress, traveling under his name.
Fillbrook, Mr. Joseph Charles	18	Cornwall, England	2nd	S	Houghton, MI			Traveled with Frederick Banfield and Samuel Sobey.
Finck, Mary								see Mrs. Thomas H. Davison
Finoli, Mr. Luigi	35	Philadelphia, PA	3rd	S	Philadelphia, PA	15		
Fischer, Mr. Eberhard Telander	18	Skane, Sweden	3rd	S	unknown			
Fischer, Ida Sophia								see Mrs. Louis A. Hippach

Name *(Maiden Name)[Other Name]* *Names in italic indicate survivors*	Age	Residence	Class	E	Destination	L/B	Body # Recovered / Where Buried	Notes
Flegenheim, Mrs. Alfred (Antoinette *Liche)*	48	Manhattan, NY	1st	C	Manhattan, NY	7		
Fleming, Miss Honora	21	County Mayo, Ireland	3rd	Q	New York City, NY			
Fleming, Miss Margaret		Haverford, PA	1st	C	Haverford, PA	4		Maid to Mrs. John B. Thayer.
Flynn, Mr. James	28	County Mayo, Ireland	3rd	Q	New York City, NY			
Flynn, Mr. John Irwin	48	County Galway, Ireland	3rd	Q	Pittsburgh, PA			
Flynn, Mr. John Irwin	36	Brooklyn, NY	1st	S	Brooklyn, NY	5		
Foley, Mr. Joseph	26	Ireland	3rd	Q	Chicago, IL			
Foley, Mr. William	20	County Cork, Ireland	3rd	Q	unknown			
Foo, Mr. Choong		Hong Kong	3rd	S	New York City, NY	?		see Donaldson Line's Group Notes
Forby, Jane Ann								see Mrs. Frederick M. Hoyt
Force, Madeleine Talmadge								see Mrs. John Jacob Astor
Ford, Mr. Arthur	22	Somerset, England	3rd	S	Elmira, NY			
Ford, Elizabeth Catherine								see Mrs. Thomas William Brown
Ford Family								
Ford, Mrs. Edward (Margaret Watson)	48	Sussex, England	3rd	S	Massachusetts			
Ford, Miss Dollina Margaret	21	Sussex, England	3rd	S	Massachusetts			
Ford, Mr. Edward Watson	18	Sussex, England	3rd	S	Massachusetts			
Ford, Miss Robina Maggie	7	Sussex, England	3rd	S	Massachusetts			
Ford, Mr. William Neal Thomas	16	Sussex, England	3rd	S	Massachusetts			

Edward Ford had deserted his wife and five children, one of whom was living in America. **Mrs. Ford** was emigrating, traveling with four remaining children and several other family members and friends. See Ford – Johnston – Harknett Group Notes.

Foreman, Mr. Benjamin L.	30	New York City, NY	1st	C	New York City, NY			
Fortune Family								
Fortune, Miss Alice Elizabeth	24	Winnipeg, Manitoba, Canada	1st	S	Winnipeg, Manitoba, Canada	10		
Fortune, Mr. Charles Alexander	19	Winnipeg, Manitoba, Canada	1st	S	Winnipeg, Manitoba, Canada			
Fortune, Miss Ethel Flora	28	Winnipeg, Manitoba, Canada	1st	S	Winnipeg, Manitoba, Canada	10		
Fortune, Miss Mabel	23	Winnipeg, Manitoba, Canada	1st	S	Winnipeg, Manitoba, Canada	10		
Fortune, Mr. Mark	64	Winnipeg, Manitoba, Canada	1st	S	Winnipeg, Manitoba, Canada			
Fortune, Mrs. Mark (Mary McDougald)	60	Winnipeg, Manitoba, Canada	1st	S	Winnipeg, Manitoba, Canada	10		
Fosdick, Genevieve								see Mrs. Henry A. Cassebeer
Fox, Mr. Patrick	23	County Westmeath, Ireland	3rd	Q	New York City, NY			
Fox, Mr. Stanley H.	38	Rochester, NY	2nd	S	Rochester, NY		#236, buried in Rochester, NY	A stranger tried to claim his body for insurance fraud!
Francatelli, Miss Laura M.	30	London, England	1st	C	New York City, NY	1		Secretary to Lady Duff-Gordon.
Franchi, Josefine								see Mrs. Josef Arnold
Franklin, Mr. Charles								see Charles Fardon
Franklin, Mr. Thomas P.		London, England	1st	S	New York City, NY			
Frauenthal Family								
Frauenthal, Dr. Henry W.	49	New York City, NY	1st	S	New York City, NY	5		Traveling on honeymoon with wife and brother, died by suicide in 1927.
Frauenthal, Mrs. Henry W. (Clara *Heinsheimer)*	42	New York City, NY	1st	S	New York City, NY	5		Traveling on honeymoon.
Frauenthal, Mr. Isaac G.	44	New York City, NY	1st	C	New York City, NY	5		Brother of Dr. Henry Frauenthal..
Frolicher-Stehli Family								
Frölicher, Miss Hedwig Margaritha	22	Zurich, Switzerland	1st	C	New York City, NY	5		
Frölicher-Stehli, Mr. Maxmilian J.	61	Zurich, Switzerland	1st	C	New York City, NY	5		
Frölicher-Stehli, Mrs. Maxmilian *(Margaretha Stehli)*	48	Zurich, Switzerland	1st	C	New York City, NY	5		

Name (Maiden Name)[Other Name] *Names in italic indicate survivors*	Age	Residence	Class	E	Destination	L/B	Body # Recovered / Where Buried	Notes
Frost, Mr. Anthony W.	37	Belfast, Ireland	2nd	B	New York City, NY			Outside Foreman Manager. See H&W Guarantee Group Notes.
Fry, Mr. John R.		Liverpool, England	1st	S	New York City, NY			Valet to J. Bruce Ismay.
Funk, Miss Annie C.	38	India	2nd	S	Bally, PA			Mennonite missionary in India.
Futrelle, Mr. Jacques H.	37	Scituate, MA	1st	S	Scituate, MA			
Futrelle, Mrs. Jacques, (Lily May Peel)	35	Scituate, MA	1st	S	Scituate, MA	D		

Mr. **Jacques Futrelle** was a famous novelist during his lifetime. He had been a reporter for the *Atlanta Journal* and *New York Herald*. His early works may have been the inspiration for the Agatha Christie detective novels. He and Mrs. Futrelle were traveling back to Massachusetts after an extended vacation in Europe.

Fynney, Mr. Joseph J.	35	Liverpool, England	2nd	S	Montreal, Quebec, Canada		#322, buried in Montreal, Canada	Traveling with Alfred Gaskell.

G

Gale, Mr. Harry	38	Cornwall, England	2nd	S	Clear Creek, CO			Brother of Shadrach Gale.
Gale, Mr. Shadrach	34	Cornwall, England	2nd	S	Clear Creek, CO			Brother of Harry Gale.
Gallagher, Mr. Martin	29	Rye, NY	3rd	Q	Rye, NY			
Garfirth, Mr. John		Northamptonshire, England	3rd	S	unknown			
Garside, Miss Ethel	34	Liverpool, England	2nd	S	Brooklyn, NY	12		
Garvey, Mr. Lawrence	26	Guernsey, England	2nd	S	Elizabeth, NJ			
Gaskell, Mr. Alfred	16	Liverpool, England	2nd	S	Montreal, Quebec, Canada			Traveling with Joseph Fynney.
Gastafsson, Mr. Karl G.	19	Myren, Sweden	3rd	S	New York City, NY			
Gee, Mr. Arthur H.	47	Lancashire, England	1st	S	Mexico City, Mexico		#275, buried in Manchester, England	
Genovese, Argene								see Mrs. Sebastiano del Carlo
George [Whabee], Mrs. Shawneene [Shahini]	38	Youngstown, OH	3rd	C	Youngstown, OH	C		

Mrs. **George** was returning home from Lebanon. She traveled with cousins Tannous Doharr, Tannous Thomas and Gerios Yousseff. Her last name is sometimes listed as "Whabee".

Gerda, Elin								see Mrs. Edvard Lindell
Gerios, Mr. Youssiff								see Mr. Gerios Youssiff
Gheorgheff, Mr. Stanio		Bulgaria	3rd	C	Butte, MT			
Gibson, Miss Dorothy	22	New York City, NY	1st	C	New York City, NY	7		

Dorothy Gibson was a well-known artist's model and a little-known silent film actress who was returning from vacation in France with her mother Pauline. Both were saved. One month after the disaster, Dorothy acted in a one-reel, ten-minute silent movie titled *"Saved From the Titanic"*, which was a moderate hit when it was released only 29 days after *Titanic* sank. Dorothy, in order to lend some authenticity to the story, wore the same dress she was wearing the night *Titanic* sank. Dorothy Gibson is NOT the inspiration for the "Gibson Girl."

Gibson, Mrs. Leonard (Pauline C. Boeson)	45	New York City, NY	1st	C	New York City, NY	7		
Gieger, Miss Amalie H.	35	Germany	1st	C	Elkins Park, PA	4		Maid to Mrs. George Widener.
Giglio, Mr. Victor	23	New York City, NY	1st	C	New York City, NY			Valet to Mr. Benjamin Guggenheim.
Gilbert, Mr. William	47	Cornwall, England	2nd	S	Butte, MT			
Giles, Mr. Edgar	21	Cornwall, England	2nd	S	Camden, NJ			Brother of Frederick Giles.
Giles, Mr. Frederick E.	21	Cornwall, England	2nd	S	Camden, NJ			Brother of Edgar Giles.
Giles, Mr. Ralph	25	London, England	2nd	S	unknown		#297, buried in Fairview Cemetery, Halifax	
Giles, Mrs. Marvin (Harriette Crosby)								see Miss Harriette Crosby
Gilinski [Gilinsky], Mr. Edward	22	South Wales	3rd	S	unknown		#47, buried at sea	
Gill, Mr. John William	24	Somerset, England	2nd	S	unknown		#155, buried at sea	
Gillespie, Vera								see Mrs. Albert A. Dick
Gillespie, Mr. William H.	34	Ireland	2nd	S	Vancouver, BC. Canada			
Gilnagh, Miss Mary Katherine	16	County Longford, Ireland	3rd	Q	New York City, NY	16		

Name *(Maiden Name)[Other Name]* *Names in italic indicate survivors*	Age	Residence	Class	E	Destination	L/B	Body # Recovered / Where Buried	Notes
Givard, Mr. Hans C.	30	Argentina	2nd	S	unknown		#305, buried in Fairview Cemetery, Halifax	
Glynn, Miss Mary A.	19	County Clare, Ireland	3rd	Q	Washington, DC	13		
Godfrey, Johanna [Hannah]								see Mrs. Thomas O'Brien
Goldenberg, Mr. Samuel L.	49	Paris, France	1st	C	New York City, NY	5		
Goldenberg, Mrs. Samuel L. (Nella Wiggins)	32	Paris, France	1st	C	New York City, NY	5		
Goldschmidt, Mr. George B.	71	New York City, NY	1st	C	New York City, NY			
Goldsmith Family								
Goldsmith, Master Frank J.W.	9	Kent, England	3rd	S	Detroit, MI	C		
Goldsmith, Mr. Frank J.	33	Kent, England	3rd	S	Detroit, MI			
Goldsmith, Mrs. Frank J. (Emily A. Brown)	31	Kent, England	3rd	S	Detroit, MI	C		

The **Goldsmith** family was emigrating to Detroit, traveling with his friends Thomas Theobald and Alfred Rush. As Thomas Theobald realized he would not survive the sinking, he gave his wedding ring to Mrs. Goldsmith to give to his wife. Frank Goldsmith, Theobald and Rush were all lost. Mrs. Goldsmith did give Thomas Theobald's wedding ring to his wife.

Goldsmith, Mr. Nathan	41	Bryn Mawr, PA	3rd	S	Bryn Mawr, PA			
Goncalves, Mr. Manuel Estanslas								see Mr. Manuel G. Estanslau
Goodwin Family								
Goodwin, Master Harold V.	9	Wiltshire, England	3rd	S	Niagara Falls, NY			
Goodwin, Master Sidney L.	2	Wiltshire, England	3rd	S	Niagara Falls, NY			
Goodwin, Master William F.	11	Wiltshire, England	3rd	S	Niagara Falls, NY			
Goodwin, Miss Jesse A.	10	Wiltshire, England	3rd	S	Niagara Falls, NY			
Goodwin, Miss Lillian Amy	16	Wiltshire, England	3rd	S	Niagara Falls, NY			
Goodwin, Mr. Charles E.	14	Wiltshire, England	3rd	S	Niagara Falls, NY			
Goodwin, Mr. Frederick	40	Wiltshire, England	3rd	S	Niagara Falls, NY			
Goodwin, Mrs. Frederick (Augusta Tyler)	43	Wiltshire, England	3rd	S	Niagara Falls, NY			

Mr. **Frederick Goodwin**, his wife and their six children were emigrating to America. The entire family was lost.

Goransson, Mr. Nils Johan								see Mr. Nils Johan Olsson
Govaert, Rosalie								see Mrs. Jean B. Van Impe
Grabowsko, Edwiga								She was NOT on Titanic
Gracie, Colonel Archibald IV	54	Washington, D.C.	1st	S	Washington, D.C.	B		

Colonel **Archibald Gracie** was extremely wealthy. His ancestors had built Gracie Mansion, home of the mayor of New York City. His father was a famous Confederate Civil War general. Gracie had recently published a book titled *The Truth About Chickamauga* and had gone to Europe for vacation. Gracie and several first class men helped load about a dozen women into various lifeboats. As *Titanic* sank, Gracie went into the water but was able to climb onto the overturned Collapsible Lifeboat B and was eventually rescued by the *Carpathia*. Gracie wrote a book about his adventures that night, but before *The Truth About The Titanic* was published in late 1912, Gracie died from the affects of his exposure to the cold and freezing water the night *Titanic* sank.

Graham, Mr. George E.	38	Winnipeg, Manitoba, Canada	1st	S	Winnipeg, Manitoba, Canada		#147, buried in St. Mary's Cemetery, Ontario, Canada	
Graham, Miss Margaret E.	19	Greenwich, CT	1st	S	Greenwich, CT	3		Traveled with Mrs. W.T. Graham and governess Elizabeth Schutes
Graham, Mrs. William T. (Edith W. Junkins)	48	Greenwich, CT	1st	S	Greenwich, CT	3		Traveled with her daughter Margaret E. Graham
Green, Mr. George H.	40	Surrey, England	3rd	S	Lead City, SD			
Greenberg, Mr. Samuel	52	Bronx, NY	2nd	S	Bronx, NY		#19, buried in the Bronx, NY	
Greenfield, Mr. William B.	23	New York City, NY	1st	C	New York City, NY	7		Son of Mrs. Leo D. Greenfield.
Greenfield, Mrs. Leo D. (Blanche Strouse)	45	New York City, NY	1st	C	New York City, NY	7		Traveled with son William B. Greenfield.
Gregg, Clara Jennings								see Mrs. Charles M. Hays
Griggs, Bertha								see Mrs. Norman C. Chambers

Name (Maiden Name)[Other Name] Names in italic indicate survivors	Age	Residence	Class	E	Destination	L/B	Body # Recovered / Where Buried	Notes
Grønnestad, Mr. Daniel D.	32	Portland, ND	3rd	S	Portland, ND			
Guest, Mr. Robert	23	London, England	3rd	S	unknown			Traveled with friend Percival Thorneycroft.
Guggenheim, Mr. Benjamin	46	New York City, NY	1st	C	New York City, NY			

Mr. **Benjamin Guggenheim** was traveling with his mistress Mme. Leontine Aubart, his valet Victor Giglio and chauffer Rene Pernot. As *Titanic* sank, he saw Mrs. Aubart into a lifeboat, and then he and Giglio returned to their stateroom. They both dressed in their best evening wear and then returned to the First Class lounge, where they sat in chairs and watched the events unfolding around them. At some point during the evening, Bruce Ismay asked if he wasn't going to try to get into a lifeboat, and Mr. Guggenheim answered *"we are dressed in our best and are prepared to go down like gentlemen."* Later, Guggenheim handed a note to a steward that stated *"If anything should happen to me, tell my wife I've done my best in doing my duty."* Guggenheim, Giglio and Pernot went down with the ship.

Name	Age	Residence	Class	E	Destination	L/B	Body # Recovered / Where Buried	Notes
Gustafsson, Mr. Alfred O.	20	Waukegan, IL	3rd	S	Waukegan, IL			
Gustafsson, Mr. Anders V.	37	Stromfors, Finland	3rd	S	New York City, NY		#98, buried at sea	see Backstrom-Gustafsson Group Notes
Gustafsson, Mr. Johan B.	28	Stromfors, Finland	3rd	S	New York City, NY			see Backstrom-Gustafsson Group Notes
Gustafsson, Maria Mathilda								see Mrs. Karl Alfred Backstrom

H

Name	Age	Residence	Class	E	Destination	L/B	Body # Recovered / Where Buried	Notes
Haas, Miss Aloisia	24	Switzerland	3rd	S	Chicago, IL			Cousin of Josef Arnold-Franchi.
Hagland, Mr. Ingvald O.O.	28	Skaare, Norway	3rd	S	New Jersey			Brother-in-law of Konrad Hagland.
Hagland, Mr. Konrad M.R.	19	Skaare, Norway	3rd	S	New Jersey			Brother-in-law of Ingvald Hagland.
Hakkarainen, Mr. Pekka P.	28	Helsinki, Finland	3rd	S	Monessen, PA			Traveling on honeymoon.
Hakkarainen, Mrs. Pekka P. (Elin Dolck)	24	Helsinki, Finland	3rd	S	Monessen, PA	15		Traveling on honeymoon.
Hale, Mr. Reginald	30	Auburn, NY	2nd	S	Auburn, NY		#75, buried at sea	
Hall, Ada E.								see Mrs. Martin Luther Ball
Hall, Imanita Parrish								see Mrs. William Shelley
Halstead, Catherine E.								see Mrs. Edward G. Crosby
Hämäläinen, Master Viljo	8 m	Finland	2nd	S	Detroit, MI	4		
Hämäläinen, Mrs. William	24	Finland	2nd	S	Detroit, MI	4		
Hampe, Mr. Leo J.	19	Westrozebeke, Belgium	3rd	S	unknown			Often listed as Leo Mampe.
Hanna, Mr. Mansour	35	Lebanon	3rd	C	Ottawa, Ontario, Canada		#188, buried in Mt. Olivet Cemetery, Halifax	Often listed as Hanna Mansour (Mansour being a last name)
Hannah, Mr. Borak	20	Lebanon	3rd	C	Port Huron, MI	15		Often listed as Hanna Moubarek, Moubarek being a last name.
Hansen, Mr. Henrik J.	26	Denmark	3rd	S	Racine, WI			Brother of Peter C. Hansen.
Hansen, Mr. Henry D.	21	Jutland, Denmark	3rd	S	unknown		#69, buried at sea	
Hansen, Mr. Peter Claus	41	Racine, WI	3rd	S	Racine, WI			Brother of Henrik Hansen.
Hansen, Mrs. Peter C. (Jennie Howard)	45	Racine, WI	3rd	S	Racine, WI	11		Traveled with husband Peter and Brother-in-law Henrik Hansen.
Harbaugh, Sylvia Mae								see Mrs. Albert F. Caldwell
Harbeck, Mr. William H.	44	Vancouver, Canada	2nd	S	New York City, NY		#35, buried in Toledo, OH	Famous filmmaker, traveling with mistress Henriette Yrois.
Harder, Mr. George A.	25	Brooklyn, NY	1st	C	Brooklyn, NY	5		
Harder, Mrs. George A. (Dorothy Annan)	21	Brooklyn, NY	1st	C	Brooklyn, NY	5		
Hargadon, Miss Catherine	17	County Sligo, Ireland	3rd	Q	unknown			
Harknett, Miss Alice Pheobe	21	Surrey, England	3rd	S	unknown			See Ford-Johnston-Harknett Group Notes
Harmer, Mr. Abraham								This was an assumed name, see Mr. David Livshin.

Name *(Maiden Name)[Other Name]* *Names in italic indicate survivors*	Age	Residence	Class	E	Destination	L/B	Body # Recovered / Where Buried	Notes
Harper, Mr. Henry Sleeper	48	New York City, NY	1st	C	New York City, NY	3		
Harper, Mrs. Henry Sleeper (Myra Haxtun)	49	New York City, NY	1st	C	New York City, NY	3		

Mr. **Henry Sleeper Harper** and his wife Myra were returning from an extended trip to Egypt. In 1902 Harper had been on another ship that collided with an iceberg off Nova Scotia. Traveling with the Harper's was a dragoman (interpreter of Egyptian languages) named Hammad Hassab, whose presence caused some amount of rumors by the First Class passengers. Harper also had his pet Pekinese Sun Yat-Sen with him. Everyone, including the dog survived.

Harper, Rev. John	28	Surrey, England	2nd	S	Chicago, IL			
Harper, Miss Annie Jessie [Nina]	6	Surrey, England	2nd	S	Chicago, IL	11		

The Reverend **John Harper** was an extremely popular minister in England who drew huge crowds to his sermons. His wife died days after their daughter Annie was born, and Harper had almost drowned twice in earlier years. Harper was traveling to Chicago to preach for three months. He took Annie and Jessie Leitch, his adult niece who was Annie's nanny, with him. Harper conducted services every day while on *Titanic,* and was last seen holding onto a stanchion on the afterdeck, with a large crowd of people gathered around while Harper lead them in prayer. Annie and her cousin Jessie survived, but Reverend John Harper did not. One of the more famous surviving photographs of *Titanic* is of Reverend Harper and his daughter walking along the Boat deck.

Harrington, Mr. Charles H.		Washington, DC	1st	S	Washington, DC			Manservant to Clarence B. Moore.
Harris, Mr. George	62	London, England	2nd	S	New York City, NY	15		
Harris, Mr. Henry B.	45	New York City, NY	1st	S	New York City, NY			World famous theatrical director.
Harris, Mrs. Henry B. (Irene Wallach)	36	New York City, NY	1st	S	New York City, NY	D		

Mr. **Henry B. Harris** was a famous theater and traveling entertainment manager. He owned the Harris Theater in New York City and the Follies Bergere. He also managed Lillie Langtry and other personalities. For all his money, after he died on *Titanic* it was discovered he was insolvent. **Mrs. Harris** took over the business and built it up into a multi-million dollar enterprise, and helped many young actresses get their start on the stage, including Judith (later Dame) Anderson and Barbara Stanwyck.

Harris, Mr. Walter	30	Walthamstow, England	2nd	S	unknown			
Harrison, Mr. William H.	40	Cheshire, England	1st	S	New York City, NY		#110, buried in Fairview Cemetery, Halifax	Personal secretary to J. Bruce Ismay.

Hart Family

Hart, Mr. Benjamin	43	Essex, England	2nd	S	Winnipeg, Manitoba, Canada			
Hart, Mrs. Benjamin (Esther Bloomfield)	45	Essex, England	2nd	S	Winnipeg, Manitoba, Canada	14		
Hart, Miss Eva M.	7	Essex, England	2nd	S	Winnipeg, Manitoba, Canada	14		

Benjamin Hart was a successful builder in England who was moving to Canada to start a new construction company. Esther Hart did not want to make the trip, having serious doubts about the ship and afraid something serious would happen. She was so eccentric that other passengers even commented on it. Afraid the ship would sink while everyone was asleep, she sat up all night while her husband and daughter slept, then she would sleep all day. When *Titanic* struck the iceberg, Benjamin Hart managed to get his family onto a lifeboat, but as happened so often that night, he did not survive.

Hart, Mr. Henry	27	County Sligo, Ireland	3rd	Q	Boston, MA			
Hartley, Mr. Wallace H.	33	Dewsbury, England	2nd	S			#224, buried in Colne, England	see Musician's Group Notes
Hassab, Mr. Hammad	27	Cairo, Egypt	1st	C	New York City, NY	3		Dragoman (Eqyptian guide or interpreter) for Henry Harper.
Hassan, Master Houssien G.N.	11	Lebanon	3rd	C	unknown			Traveled with Mr. Nassef C. Albimona.
Haven, Harry ["E"]								see Mr. Harry Homer
Hawksford, Mr. Walter J.		Surrey, England	1st	S	New York City, NY	3		

Hays Family

Hays, Mr. Charles M.	55	Montreal, Quebec, Canada	1st	S	Montreal, Quebec, Canada		#307, buried in Mount Royal Cemetery, Montreal, Canada	
Hays, Mrs. Charles M. (Clara J. Gregg)	52	Montreal, Quebec, Canada	1st	S	Montreal, Quebec, Canada	3		
Hays, Orian								see Mrs. Thornton Davidson

Mr. **Charles M. Hays** was the General Manager of the Grand Trunk Pacific Railroad of Canada. He had been in England on business, part of which was to establish a connection to the Orient using White Star Line ships and Grand Trunk Railroad passenger cars. Hays also built the beautiful Château Laurier Hotel in Ottawa. Traveling back to Ottawa for the grand opening of the hotel as a guest of J. Bruce Ismay, chairman of the White Star Lines, Hays was accompanied by his wife Clara, daughter Orian and son-in-law Thornton Davidson, a maid Miss Mary Anne Perreault, and Mr. Hays' secretary Mr. Vivian Payne. Also traveling with the Hays group was Mr. Paul R. Chevre, a famous sculptor who did the bust of Sir Wilfrid Laurier that still stands in the lobby of the Château Laurier Hotel. Three men (Mr. Hays, Mr. Davidson, and Mr. Payne) went down with the ship while the women and Mr. Chevre survived. Also traveling with the family was their pet dog, a Pomeranian, who survived the voyage.

Name *(Maiden Name)[Other Name]* *Names in italic indicate survivors*	Age	Residence	Class	E	Destination	L/B	Body # Recovered / Where Buried	Notes
Hays, Miss Margaret B.	24	New York City, NY	1st	C	New York City, NY	7		
Margaret Hays, accompanied by her pet Pomeranian dog, was the first passenger to enter a lifeboat. She is also the person who took responsibility for the two orphaned children that no one knew who they belonged to (see Navratil Family).								
Head, Mr. Christopher	42	Middlesex, England	1st	S	New York City, NY			
Healy, Miss Hanora	29	County Galway, Ireland	3rd	Q	New York City, NY	16		
Hedman, Mr. Oscar	27	Sioux Falls, SD	3rd	S	Sioux Falls, SD	15?		
Hee, Mr. Ling	24	Hong Kong	3rd	S	New York City, NY	?		see Donaldson Line's Group Notes
Hegarty, Miss Hanora	18	County Cork, Ireland	3rd	Q	Charlestown, MA			
Heikkinen, Miss Laina	26	Helsinki, Finland	3rd	S	New York City, NY	14		
Heilmann, Luise								see Mrs. Luise Kink
Heininen, Miss Wendla M.	23	Laitila, Finland	3rd	S	New York City, NY		#8, buried in Fairview Cemetery, Halifax	
Heinsheimer, Clara								see Mrs. Henry Frauenthal
Hellström, Miss Hilda M.	22	Stora Tuna, Sweden	3rd	S	Evanston, IL	C		
Hemming, Miss Nora	21	unknown	3rd	Q	unknown			
Hendekovic, Mr. Ignjac	28	Croatia	3rd	S	Harrisburg, PA		#306, buried in Mt. Olivet Cemetery, Halifax	
Henery [Henry], Miss Delia	23	County Westmeath, Ireland	3rd	Q	unknown			
Henriksson, Miss Jenny L.	28	Stockholm, Sweden	3rd	S	Iron Mountain, MI			
Jenny Henricksson was emigrating to America, along with her friend Ellen Petterson. She was also aquainted with Kurt Gottfrid and Dagmar Bryhl, relatives of her previous employer. They all met up with the Skoog family, also friends. All ten members of the group were lost.								
Herman Family								
Herman, Miss Alice	24	Somerset, England	2nd	S	Bernardsville, NJ	9		
Herman, Miss Kate	24	Somerset, England	2nd	S	Bernardsville, NJ	9		
Herman, Mr. Samuel	49	Somerset, England	2nd	S	Bernardsville, NJ			
Herman, Mrs. Samuel (Jane Laver)	48	Somerset, England	2nd	S	Bernardsville, NJ	9		
Mr. and Mrs. **Herman** and their two children and adopted son 14-year George Sweet were traveling to America to visit family in New Jersey. Mr. Herman and George Sweet did not survive.								
Hewlett, Mrs. Frederick R. (Mary D. Kingcome)	56	India	2nd	S	Rapid City, SD	13		
Hickman Family								
Hickman, Mr. Leonard M.	24	Eden, Manitoba, Canada	2nd	S	Eden, Manitoba, Canada			see Hickman Group Notes
Hickman, Mr. Lewis	32	London, England	2nd	S	Eden, Manitoba, Canada		#256, buried in Manitoba, Canada	see Hickman Group Notes
Hickman, Mr. Stanley G.	21	London, England	2nd	S	Eden, Manitoba, Canada			see Hickman Group Notes
Hill, Margaret Annie								see Mrs. Stephen Hold
Hilliard, Mr. Herbert H.	44	Brighton, MA	1st	S	Brighton, MA			
Hiltunen, Miss Marta	18	Kontiolahti, Finland	2nd	S	Detroit, MI			Traveled with Anna and Viljo Hamalainen.
Hipkins, Mr. William E.	55	London, England	1st	S	New York City, NY			Well-known English businessman.
Hippach, Miss Jean Gertrude	16	Chicago, IL	1st	C	Chicago, IL	4		
Hippach, Mrs. Louis A. (Ida S. Fischer)	46	Chicago, IL	1st	C	Chicago, IL	4		
Ida Hippach, wife of a wealthy plate glass manufacturer in Chicago, was returning from Europe where she was trying to recover from the loss of two sons in the famous Iroquois Theatre fire in Chicago in 1903. Two years after *Titanic* sank, her third and last son was killed in an automobile accident.								
Hirvonen, Mrs. Alexander (Helga E. Lindqvist)	22	Taalintehdas, Finland	3rd	S	Monessen, PA	15?		Traveled with daughter Hildur and brother Eino Lindvquist.
Hirvonen, Miss Hildur E.	2	Taalintehdas, Finland	3rd	S	Monessen, PA	15?		
Hitchcock, Mary								see Mrs. George D. Wick
Hocking, Mr. Samuel J.M.	36	Devon, England	2nd	S	Middletown, CT			

Name *(Maiden Name)[Other Name]* *Names in italic indicate survivors*	Age	Residence	Class	E	Destination	L/B	Body # Recovered / Where Buried	Notes
Hocking Family								
Hocking, Miss Ellen [Nellie]	31	Penzance, England	2nd	S	Schenectady, NY	4		Enroute to U.S. to get married. See Hocking-Richards Group Notes. see Mrs. George D. Wick
Hocking, Miss Emily								
Hocking, Mr. Richard G.	23	Akron, OH	2nd	S	Akron, OH			see Hocking-Richards Group Notes
Hocking, Mrs. William R. (Eliza [Elizabeth] Needs)	54	Penzance, England	2nd	S	Akron, OH	4	14	see Hocking-Richards Group Notes
Hodges, Mr. Henry P.	50	Southampton, England	2nd	S	New York City, NY		#149, buried in Fairview Cemetery, Halifax	
Hoffman Family								
Hoffman, Master Edmond R.								see Edmond R. Navratil
Hoffman, Master Michel M.								see Michel M. Navratil
Hoffman, Mr. Michel								see Mr. Michel Navratil
Hogeboom, Mrs. John C. (Anna Andrews)	51	Hudson, NY	1st	S	Hudson, NY	10		

Anna Hogeboom was returning from vacation in Europe. Traveling with her were her sister Kornellia Andrews and her niece Gretchen Longley. They all survived.

Name	Age	Residence	Class	E	Destination	L/B	Body # Recovered / Where Buried	Notes
Hold, Mr. Stephen	42	Sacramento, CA	2nd	S	Sacramento, CA			
Hold, Mrs. Stephen (Margaret Annie Hill)	36	Sacramento, CA	2nd	S	Sacramento, CA	10		
Holm, Mr. John F.A.	43	Karlshamn, Sweden	3rd	S	New York City, NY			
Holmes, Ella								see Mrs. John S. White
Holthen, Mr. Johan M.	28	Horten, Norway	3rd	S	New York City, NY			
Holverson, Mr. Alexander O.	42	New York City, NY	1st	S	New York City, NY		#38, buried in the Bronx, NY	
Holverson, Mrs. Alexander (Mary A. Towner)	35	New York City, NY	1st	S	New York City, NY	8		
Homer, Mr. Harry	35	Indianapolis, IN	1st	C	New York City, NY	15		Professional gambler traveling under the name Harry or "E" Haven.
Honkanen, Miss Eluna [Eliina]	27	Finland	3rd	S	New York City, NY	?		
Hood, Mr. Ambrose Jr.	21	New Forest, England	2nd	S	unknown			see Hickman Group Notes
Horgan, Mr. John [Landers]	22	unknown	3rd	Q	unknown			
Hosono, Mr. Masabumi	42	Tokyo, Japan	2nd	S	New York City, NY	13		

Mr. Hosono was a government worker from Tokyo and the only Japanese passenger. He survived, either by being pulled from the water, rescued from a floating door, or by getting into a lifeboat as it was being lowered (we don't know which version is correct). When he got home, he was ostracized for surviving when so many women and children had died. He was fired from his job, labeled a coward by the newspapers and public, schoolbooks referred to his "shameful" behavior. He was called immoral, and a derogatory term "hosono" was used for many years to refer to a coward.

Name	Age	Residence	Class	E	Destination	L/B	Body # Recovered / Where Buried	Notes
Howard, Mr. Benjamin	63	Swindon, England	2nd	S	Idaho			
Howard, Mrs. Benjamin (Ellen T. Arman)	60	Swindon, England	2nd	S	Idaho			
Howard, Miss May E.	27	Norfolk, England	3rd	S	Toronto, Ontario, Canada	C		
Howard, Jennie L.								see Mrs. Peter C. Hansen
Hoyt, Mr. Frederick M.	38	New York City, NY	1st	S	New York City, NY	D		
Hoyt, Mrs. Frederick M. (Jane A. Forby)	35	New York City, NY	1st	S	New York City, NY	D		
Hoyt, Mr. William F.		New York City, NY	1st	C	New York City, NY			

Mr. William F. Hoyt was pulled from the water by Lifeboat 14, but died from exposure while on the lifeboat. The crew of the *Carpathia* buried his body at sea.

Name	Age	Residence	Class	E	Destination	L/B	Body # Recovered / Where Buried	Notes
Hughes, Florence Agnes								see Mrs. William A. Angle
Hughes, Lilian								see Mrs. Ernest C. Carter
Hughes, Mary Eloise								see Mrs. Lucien Philip Smith
Humblen, Mr. Adolf M.N.O.	42	Alesund, Norway	3rd	S	New York City, NY			

Adolf Humblen traveled with friends Olaus Abelseth and Sigrid Moen and his cousins Karen Abelseth, Anna Salkjelsvik and Peter A.L.A. Solholt. Some of them, but not Adolf Humblen, would survive.

Name	Age	Residence	Class	E	Destination	L/B	Body # Recovered / Where Buried	Notes
Hume, Mr. John Law	21	Dumfries, England	2nd	S			#193, buried in Fairview Cemetery, Halifax	see Musicians Group Notes

Key: **Names** are in alphabetical order except where family members are grouped together. Names listed in italic were survivors. Names in parenthesis (name) are the maiden (or birth) name of the person. Names in brackets [name] are other names the passenger used. **Age** is the person's age at the time of the sinking. **Residence** is where the person's home was located. **Class** indicates the class the person was traveling. **"E"** indicates where the person embarked Titanic (**B** is for Belfast, Ireland; **C** is for Cherbourg, France; **S** is for Southampton, England and **Q** is for Queenstown (now Cobh) Ireland. **Destination** is where the passenger was traveling. **L/B** indicates which Lifeboat the person escaped on, if known. **Body Recovered / Where Buried** indicates in what sequence the body was recovered and where it was buried. **Family** groups are kept together and have dark shade fore easy reference and if there are any family notes they are listed after the last family name. Individuals with notes have the note after the name. Listings in light shade are designed only to assist the reader in following the text across the page.

Name *(Maiden Name)[Other Name]* *Names in italic indicate survivors*	Age	Residence	Class	E	Destination	L/B	Body # Recovered / Where Buried	Notes
Hungerford, Helen Churchill								see Mrs. Edward Candee
Hunt, Amelia "Millie"								see Mrs. James Lemore
Hunt, Mr. George H.	33	Philadelphia, PA	2nd	S	Philadelphia, PA			
Hunt, Rosa								see Mrs. Stanton Abbott
Huxtun, Myra								see Mrs. Henry Sleeper Harper
Hyman, Mr. Abraham	34	Manchester, England	3rd	S	Springfield, MA	C		

I

Ibrahim-Shawah, Mr. Yousseff								see Mr. Yousseff Ibrahim Shawah, last name Shawah
Icard, Miss Amelie "Amelia"	38	Cincinnati, OH	1st	S	Cincinnati, OH	6		Maid to Mrs. George N. Stone.
Ilett, Miss Bertha	17	Guernsey, England	2nd	S	New York City, NY			
Ilieff, Mr. Ylio			3rd	S				
Ilmakangas, Miss Ida L.	27	New York City, NY	3rd	S	New York City, NY			Traveled with sister Pieta.
Ilmakangas, Miss Pieta S.	25	Paavola, Finland	3rd	S	New York City, NY			Traveled with sister Ida.
Ingersoll, Mary Eliza								see Mrs. Alexander T. Compton
Isham, Miss Ann Elizabeth	50	Paris, France	1st	C	New York City, NY			One of four First Class women lost.
Ismay, Mr. Joseph Bruce	49	Liverpool, England	1st	S	New York City, NY	C		

Mr. **J. Bruce Ismay** was President of the White Star Line, the company that owned and built RMS *Titanic.* Ismay was instrumental in the design and development of the ship, working directly with the owner of the Harland and Wolff shipyard to sketch out the plans for the ship (and it's sister ships *Olympic* and *Britannic*). Ismay always traveled on the maiden voyage of WSL ships, and he occupied one of the two "Grand Promenade" suites (the Cardeza's occupied the other). Ismay helped load several lifeboats, and when one of the last was ready to launch and had seats available, he got in. Ismay was ostracized by the American public for having survived; however, he wasn't blamed in Great Britain. He gave up his position as president of White Star Line, the company his father had founded, and retired to his farm in Great Britain.

Ivanoff, Mr. Konio		Bulgaria	3rd	S	unknown			

J

Jacobsohn, Mr. Sidney S.	42	London, England	2nd	S	Montreal, Quebec, Canada			
Jacobsohn, Mrs. Sidney S. (Amy F. *"Christy" Cohen)*	24	London, England	2nd	S	Montreal, Quebec, Canada	12		Also often listed as Amy F. Christy
Jalšĕvac, Mr. Ivan	29	Croatia	3rd	C	Galesburg, IL	15		
James, Elizabeth Lindsey								see Mrs. Ernest H. Lines
Jansson, Mr. Carl O.	21	Orebro, Sweden	3rd	S	Swedeburg, NE	A		
Jardim [Jardin], Mr. José Netto	21	Maderia Island, Portugal	3rd	S	New York City, NY			
Jarvis, Mr. John D.	47	Leicester, England	2nd	S	unknown			
Jefferys Family								
Jefferys, Mr. Clifford T.	24	Guernsey, England	2nd	S	Elizabeth, NJ			
Jefferys, Mr. Ernest	22	Guernsey, England	2nd	S	Elizabeth, NJ			
Jefferys, Lillian								see Mrs. Peter H. Renouf.

Brother's **Clifford** and **Ernest Jefferys**, their sister Lillian Renouf, her husband Peter H. Renouf and family friend Herbert Denbury were all traveling together to Elizabeth, NJ. Everyone except Lillian Renouf was lost.

Jenkin, Mr. Stephen C.	32	Painesdale, MI	2nd	S	Painesdale, MI			
Jensen Family								
Jensen, Miss Carla Christine N.	19	Odense, Denmark	3rd	S	Portland, OR	16		
Jensen, Mr. Hans Peder	20	Fyn, Denmark	3rd	S	Portland, OR			
Jensen, Mr. Niels Peder	48	Portland, OR	3rd	S	Portland, OR			
Jensen, Mr. Svend L.	17	Odense, Denmark	3rd	S	Portland, OR			

Mr. **Niels Peder Jensen** lived in Portland, Oregon. He went to Denmark for a visit, and offered to help his niece Carla Jensen, her fiancé Hans Peder Jensen and his nephew Svend L. Jensen with their move to America. Of the four, only Carla Jensen survived.

Name *(Maiden Name)[Other Name]* *Names in italic indicate survivors*	Age	Residence	Class	E	Destination	L/B	Body # Recovered / Where Buried	Notes
Jermyn, Miss Annie	22	County Cork, Ireland	3rd	Q	East Lynn, MA	D		
Jerwan, Mrs. Amin S. (Marie Thuillard)	23	New York City, NY	2nd	C	New York City, NY	11		
Johannessen, Mr Bernt J.	29	Eiko, Norway	3rd	S	New York City, NY	13		
Johanson, Mr. Jakob A.	34	Uusikaarlepyy, Finland	3rd	S	Olympia, WA		#143, buried in Fairview Cemetery, Halifax	
Johansson, Mr. Erik	22	Frostensmala, Sweden	3rd	S	unknown		#156, buried at sea	
Johansson, Mr. Gustaff J.	33	Bockebo, Sweden	3rd	S	Sheyenne, ND		#285, buried in Fairview Cemetery, Halifax	
Johansson, Mr. Karl Johan	32	Duluth, MN	3rd	S	Duluth, MN			
Johansson, Mr. Nils	29	Chicago, IL	3rd	S	Chicago, IL			Traveled with fiancé Olga Lundin.
Johansson, Mr. Oskar L.	26	Milwaukee, WI	3rd	S	Milwaukee, WI	15		Murdered in 1928 by husband of woman he was having an affair with.
Johansson, Selma A.								see Mrs. Carl Oscar Asplund
Johnson, Mr. Alfred	49	Southampton, England	3rd	S	New York City, NY			see American Lines Group Notes
Johnson, Mr. Malkolm J.	33	Minneapolis, MN	3rd	S	Minneapolis, MN		#37, buried in Fairview Cemetery, Halifax	

Johnson, Oscar Family

Name	Age	Residence	Class	E	Destination	L/B	Body # Recovered / Where Buried	Notes
Johnson, Mrs. Oscar W. (Alice Burg)	24	St. Charles, IL	3rd	S	St. Charles, IL	13/15		
Johnson, Master Harold T.	4	St. Charles, IL	3rd	S	St. Charles, IL	13/15		
Johnson, Miss Eleanor Ileen	1	St. Charles, IL	3rd	S	St. Charles, IL	13/15		
Johnson, Mr. William C. Jr.	19	Hawthorne, NJ	3rd	S	New York City, NY			see American Lines Group Notes

Johnston, Andrew Family

Name	Age	Residence	Class	E	Destination	L/B	Body # Recovered / Where Buried	Notes
Johnson, Mr. Andrew E.	35	Surrey, England	3rd	S	unknown			
Johnson, Mrs. Andrew E. (Eliza Watson)	34	Surrey, England	3rd	S	unknown			
Johnson, Miss Catherine N.	7	Surrey, England	3rd	S	unknown			
Johnson, Master William A.	9	Surrey, England	3rd	S	unknown			

See additional information about the **Johnson** family in the Ford-Johnston-Harknett Group Notes.

Name	Age	Residence	Class	E	Destination	L/B	Body # Recovered / Where Buried	Notes
Jones, Mr. Charles C.	46	Bennington, VT	1st	S	Bennington, VT		#80, buried in Bennington, VT	
Jonkoff, Mr. Lazor [Lilio]	23	Bulgaria	3rd	S	unknown			see Gumostnik, Bulgaria Group Notes
Jonsson, Mr. Carl	32	Huntley, IL	3rd	S	Huntley, IL	A/15		
Jönsson, Mr. Nils H.	27	Halland, Sweden	3rd	S	unknown			Traveled with Carl R. Carlsson.

Joseph Family

Name	Age	Residence	Class	E	Destination	L/B	Body # Recovered / Where Buried	Notes
Joseph, Miss Anna [Mary]	2	Detroit, MI	3rd	C	Detroit, MI	C		AKA Miss Anna Peter
Joseph, Master Michael	5	Detroit, MI	3rd	C	Detroit, MI	D		AKA Master Michael J. Peter
Joseph, Mrs. Peter	24	Detroit, MI	3rd	C	Detroit, MI	C		AKA Mrs. Joseph Peter

Mrs. Peter Joseph (sometimes listed at Mrs. Joseph Peter) had lived in Detroit for several years, and was returning from a visit to Lebanon. As *Titanic* was sinking, Mrs. Joseph lost track of her son Michael, and she thought he was lost until they were reunited on *Carpathia*. This is one of the few 3rd class families that escaped without a loss. However, survival wasn't kind to the family. A year later another son died after childbirth, and Anna was killed in a house fire in 1914. Mrs. Joseph herself died in 1915 of disease.

Name	Age	Residence	Class	E	Destination	L/B	Body # Recovered / Where Buried	Notes
Julian, Mr. Henry F.	51	London, England	1st	S	San Francisco, CA			World famous metalurgist, scientist and inventor.
Junkins, Edith Ware								see Mrs. William T. Graham
Jussila, Miss Aina Maria	21	Paavola, Finland	3rd	S	New York City, NY			Sister of Katriina Jussila.
Jussila, Miss Katriina	20	Paavola, Finland	3rd	S	New York City, NY			Sister of Aina Maria Jussila.
Jussila, Mr. Erik	32	Michigan	3rd	S	Monessen, PA	15		

Name *(Maiden Name)[Other Name]* *Names in italic indicate survivors*	Age	Residence	Class	E	Destination	L/B	Body # Recovered / Where Buried	Notes
K								
Kallio, Mr. Nikolai E.	17	Finland	3rd	S	Sudbury, Ontario, Canada			
Kalvig [Kalvik], Mr. Johannes H.	21	Norway	3rd	S	Iowa			
Kantor, Mr. Sinai	34	Moscow, Russia	2nd	S	Bronx, NY		#283, buried in Queens, NY	
Kantor, Mrs. Sinai (Miriam Sternin)	34	Moscow, Russia	2nd	S	Bronx, NY	12		
Karajic, Mr. Milan	30	Croatia	3rd	S	Youngstown, OH			
Karlsson, Anna								see Mrs. William Skoog
Karlsson, Mr. Einar G.	21	Oskarshamn, Sweden	3rd	S	Brooklyn, NY	13		
Karlsson, Mr. Julius Konrad E.	23	Goteborg, Sweden	3rd	S	New York City, NY			
Karlsson, Mr. Nils A.	22	Narke, Sweden	3rd	S	Palmer, MA			
Karnes, Mrs. J. Frank (Claire Bennett)	22	Pittsburgh, PA	2nd	S	Pittsburgh, PA			

Mrs. Karnes was newly married to a missionary in India. She did not know that her husband had died in India from smallpox several days prior to *Titanic's* sailing.

Karun, Mr. Franz	39	Galesburg, IL	3rd	C	Galesburg, IL	15		
Karun, Miss Manca [Anna]	4	Galesburg, IL	3rd	C	Galesburg, IL	15		
Kassem, Mr. Fared			3rd	C				
Katavelas, Mr. Vassilios	18	Peloponnes, Greece	3rd	C	Milwaukee, WI		#58, buried at sea	Last name could be Catavelas or Vassilios.
Keane, Mr. Andrew	20	County Cork, Ireland	3rd	Q	Auburndale, MA			
Keane, Mr. Daniel	35	Limerick, Ireland	2nd	Q	unknown			No relation to Nora Keane.
Keane, Miss Nora A.		Harrisburg, PA	2nd	Q	Harrisburg, PA	10		No relation to Daniel Keane.
Keefe, Mr. Arthur	39	Rahway, NJ	3rd	S	Rahway, NJ			
Keeping, Mr. Edward H.	32	Elkins Park, PA	1st	C	Elkins Park, PA		#45, buried at sea	Valet to George D. Widener.
Kelly, Miss Anna Katherine	21	County Mayo, Ireland	3rd	Q	Chicago, IL	16		
Kelly, Mrs. Florence	45	London, England	2nd	S	New York City, NY	9		
Kelly, Mr. James	19	Ireland	3rd	S	unknown			
Kelly, Mr. James	41	County Kildare, Ireland	3rd	Q	New Haven, CT		#70, buried at sea	
Kelly, Miss Mary	21	County Westmeath, Ireland	3rd	Q	New York City, NY	D		
Kennedy, Mr. John	24	County Limerick, Ireland	3rd	Q	New York City, NY	15		
Kent, Mr. Edward A.	58	Buffalo, NY	1st	C	Buffalo, NY		#258, buried in Buffalo, NY	
Kenyon, Mr. Frederick R.	41	Noank, CT	1st	S	Noank, CT			
Kenyon, Mrs. Frederick R. (Marion Stauffer)	31	Noank, CT	1st	S	Noank, CT	8		

The **Kenyon's** traveled with Dr. Alice Leader and Mrs. Frederick J. Swift. Of the four, only Mr. Kenyon did not survive.

Khalil, Mr. Betros	25	Syria	3rd	C	Wilkes-Barre, PA			
Khalil, Mrs. Betros (Zahie "Maria" Elias	20	Syria	3rd	C	Wilkes-Barre, PA			
Khalil, Mrs. Mariana Assaf	45	Ottawa, Ontario, Canada	3rd	S	Ottawa, Ontario, Canada	C		Traveled with cousin Gerios Assef and nephew Solomon Khalil.
Khalil, Mr. Solomon [Saad]	25	Syria	3rd	S	Ottawa, Ontario, Canada			Traveled with aunt Mariana Khalil and cousin Gerios Assef.
Kiernan, Mr. John	25	Jersey City, NJ	3rd	Q	Jersey City, NJ			
Kiernan, Mr. Philip	22	County Longford, Ireland	3rd	Q	Jersey City, NJ			

John and **Philip Kiernan** were brothers, John having convinced Philip to emigrate to America. They were traveling with their cousin Tom McCormack. Tom survived, the two brothers did not.

Kilgannon, Mr. Thomas	21	County Galway, Ireland	3rd	Q	New York City, NY			
Kimball, Mr. Edwin N., Jr.	42	Boston, MA	1st	S	Boston, MA	5		
Kimball, Mrs. Edwin N., (Gertrude Parsons)	45	Boston, MA	1st	S	Boston, MA	5		

Name *(Maiden Name)[Other Name]* *Names in italic indicate survivors*	Age	Residence	Class	E	Destination	L/B	Body # Recovered / Where Buried	Notes
Kink Family								
Kink, Mr. Anton	29	Zurich, Switzerland	3rd	S	Milwaukee, WI	2		
Kink, Mrs. Anton (Luise Heilmann)	26	Zurich, Switzerland	3rd	S	Milwaukee, WI	2		
Kink, Miss Luise Gretchen	4	Zurich, Switzerland	3rd	S	Milwaukee, WI	2		
Kink, Miss Maria	22	Zurich, Switzerland	3rd	S	Milwaukee, WI			
Kink, Mr. Vincenz	26	Zurich, Switzerland	3rd	S	Milwaukee, WI			

Mr. **Anton Kink,** his wife Luise, daughter Luise, his brother Vincenz and sister Maria were emigrating to America. As *Titanic* sank, Anton lost track of his brother and sister, who were subsequently lost. The Kink family was one of the few in Third Class where everyone of the immediate family (father — mother — child) survived.

Name	Age	Residence	Class	E	Destination	L/B	Body # Recovered / Where Buried	Notes
Kirkland, Rev. Charles L.	57	Glasgow, Scotland	2nd	Q	Bangor, ME			
Klaber, Mr. Herman		San Francisco, CA	1st	S	San Francisco, CA			
Klasén, Miss Gertrud Emilia	2	Grimshult, Sweden	3rd	S	unknown			Traveled with brother Klas A. Klasen.
Klasén, Mrs. Hulda K. (Hulda Löfqvist)	36	Los Angeles, CA	3rd	S	Los Angeles, CA			Traveled with niece Hulda Vestrom.
Klasén, Mr. Klas Albin	18	Grimshult, Sweden	3rd	S	unknown			Traveled with sister Gertrude E. Klasen.
Knight, Mr. Robert	38	Belfast, Ireland	2nd	B	New York City, NY			Leading Hand Fitter Engineer. See H&W Guarantee Group Notes.
Kraeff, Mr. Theodor			3rd	C				
Krekorian, Mr. Neshan	25	Turkey	3rd	C	Hamilton, Ontario, Canada	10		
Kreuchen, Miss Emilie	29	Oldisleben, Germany	1st	S	St. Louis, MO	2		Maid to Mrs. Edward S. Robert.
Krins, Mr. Georgas A.	23	London, England	2nd	S				see Musicians Group Notes
Kvillner, Mr. Johan Henrik J.	31	Gothenburg, Sweden	2nd	S	Arlington, NJ		#165, buried in Fairview Cemetery, Halifax	

L

Name	Age	Residence	Class	E	Destination	L/B	Body # Recovered / Where Buried	Notes
LaFargue, Juliette Marie Anna								see Mrs. Joseph L.L. LaRoche
Lahoud, Mr. Sarkis	30	Turkey	3rd	C	unknown			
Lahtinen, Rev. William	30	Minneapolis, MN	2nd	S	Minneapolis, MN			Traveled with wife Anna and friend Lyyli Silven.
Lahtinen, Mrs. William (Anna Sylfven)	26	Minneapolis, MN	2nd	S	Minneapolis, MN			Originally in a lifeboat, she got out to remain with her husband.
Laitinen, Miss Kristina Sofia	37	New York City, NY	3rd	S	New York City, NY			
Laleff, Mr. Kristo	23	Bulgaria	3rd	S	Chicago, IL			
Lam, Mr. Ali	37	Hong Kong	3rd	S	New York City, NY	?		see Donaldson Line's Group Notes
Lam, Mr. Len	23	Hong Kong	3rd	S	New York City, NY			see Donaldson Line's Group Notes
Lamb, Mr. John J.		Ireland	2nd	Q	Providence, RI			
Lamore, Mrs. Amelia								see Lemore, Mrs. Amelia
Lamson, Caroline Lane								see Mrs. John Murray Brown
Lamson, Charlotte								see Mrs. Edward D. Appleton
Lamson, Malvina H.								see Mrs. Robert C. Cornell
Landergren, Miss Aurora Adelia	22	Karlshamn, Sweden	3rd	S	New York City, NY	13		Traveled with John Holm and Mauritz Adahl.
Lane, Mr. Patrick	20	County Limerick, Ireland	3rd	Q	New York City, NY			
Lang, Mr. Fang	26	Hong Kong	3rd	S	New York City, NY	?		see Donaldson Line's Group Notes

Name *(Maiden Name)[Other Name]* *Names in italic indicate survivors*	Age	Residence	Class	E	Destination	L/B	Body # Recovered / Where Buried	Notes
LaRoche Family								
LaRoche, Mr. Joseph L.L.	26	Paris, France	2nd	C	Haiti			
LaRoche, Mrs. Joseph L.L. (Juliette LaFargue)	22	Paris, France	2nd	C	Haiti	14		
LaRoche, Miss Louise	1	Paris, France	2nd	C	Haiti	14		
LaRoche, Miss Simonne Marie A.A.	3	Paris, France	2nd	C	Haiti	14		

Mr. Joseph LaRoche was the only person of color on *Titanic*. Born in Haiti, he lived in France and studied to become an engineer. Married to a French woman, they had two children and Mrs. LaRoche was pregnant again. They left France because of racial discrimination, and were returning to Haiti where his expertise and family connections would get him a good job. Originally they planned to take a French liner to New York, but at that time children could not accompany parents to the dining room, so Mr. and Mrs. LaRoche decided to take *Titanic* instead.

Name	Age	Residence	Class	E	Destination	L/B	Body #	Notes
Larrson, Johanna Persdotter								see Mrs. Johan Ahlin
Larsson, Mr. August V.	29	Stamford, CT	3rd	S	Stamford, CT			
Larsson, Mr. Bengt E.	29	Stockholm, Sweden	3rd	S	Hartford, CT			
Larsson-Rondberg, Mr. Edvard	22	Missoula, MT	3rd	S	Missoula, MT			Traveled with fiancé Berta Nilsson.
Laury, Grace Charity								see Mrs. Alexander Robins
Laver, Jane								see Mrs. Samuel Herman
Lawry, Sarah Elizabeth								see Mrs. John H. Chapman
Leader, Dr. Alice F. (Alice Farnham)	50	New York City, NY	1st	S	New York City, NY	8		

Dr. **Alice Leader** was traveling with Mr. and Mrs. Frederick Kenyon and Mrs. Frederick Swift.

Name	Age	Residence	Class	E	Destination	L/B	Body #	Notes
Leeni, Mr. Fahim								see Fahim [Philip] Zenni
Lefebre Family								
Lefebre, Mrs. Frank (Francis Marie)	39	France	3rd	S	Mystic, IA			
Lefebre, Master Henry	4	France	3rd	S	Mystic, IA			
Lefebre, Miss Ida	2	France	3rd	S	Mystic, IA			
Lefebre, Miss Jennie	6	France	3rd	S	Mystic, IA			
Lefebre, Miss Mathilde	11	France	3rd	S	Mystic, IA			
Lehmann, Miss Bertha	17	Berne, Switzerland	2nd	S	Central City, IA	12		
Leinonen, Mr. Antti G.	32	Valitaipale, Finland	3rd	S	New York City, NY			
Leitch, Miss Jessie W.	32	London, England	2nd	S	New York City, NY	11		Niece of Rev. John Harper. See John Harper Family Notes.
Lellyet, Emma								see Mrs. Samuel B. Risien
Lembereopolous, Mr. Peter L.	30	Greece	3rd	C	Stamford, CT		#196, buried in Mt. Olivet Cemetery, Halifax	
Lemon [Lennon], Mr. Denis	21	County Longford, Ireland	3rd	Q	New York City, NY			Brother of Mary Lemon.
Lemon [Lennon], Miss Mary	21	County Longford, Ireland	3rd	Q	New York City, NY			Sister of Denis Lemon.
Lemore, Mrs. James (Amelia Hunt)	34	Chicago, IL	2nd	S	Chicago, IL	14		
Leonard, Mr. Lionel	36	Southampton, England	3rd	S	New York City, NY			see American Line Group Notes
Leroy, Miss Berthe	28	Compiegne, France	1st	C	Deephaven, MN	2		Maid to Mrs. Walter Douglas.
Leslie, Mrs. Norman Evelyn [19th Earl of Rothes]								see Dyer-Edwards, Mrs. Noel Lucy Martha
Lester, Mr. James	39	Staffordshire, England	3rd	S	Pontiac, MI			Traveled with three relatives, Alfred, John and Joseph Davies.
Lesueur, Mr. Gustave J.	35	Germantown, PA	1st	C	Germantown, PA	3		Manservant to Mr. Thomas Cardeza.
Lévy, Mr. René Jacques	36	Montreal, Quebec, Canada	2nd	C	Montreal, Quebec, Canada			
Lewy, Mr. Ervin G.		Chicago, IL	1st	C	Chicago, IL			
Leyson, Mr. Robert W.N.	24	Swansea, Wales	2nd	S	New York City, NY		#108, buried at sea	
Liche, Antoinette								see Mrs. Alfred Flegenheim
Lievens [Zievens], Mr. Rene Aime	24	Heldergem, Belgium	3rd	S	unknown			Sometimes listed as René Zievens.
Light, Eva Georgette								see Mrs. Bertram F. Dean
Lindahl, Miss Agda V.	25	Saranac Lake, NY	3rd	S	Saranac Lake, NY			
Lindbolm, Miss Augusta C.	45	Stockholm, Sweden	3rd	S	Stratford, CT			

Name *(Maiden Name)[Other Name]* *Names in italic indicate survivors*	Age	Residence	Class	E	Destination	L/B	Body # Recovered / Where Buried	Notes
Lindeberg-Lind, Mr. Erik G.	42	Stockholm, Sweden	1st	S	unknown			Traveled under name Edward Lingrey to hide from his ex-wife.
Lindell, Mr. Edvard B.	36	Stockholm, Sweden	3rd	S	Hartford, CT			
Lindell, Mrs. Edvard B. (Elin Gerda)	30	Stockholm, Sweden	3rd	S	Hartford, CT			

The **Lindell's** were emigrating to America. They were traveling with friends Gunnar Tenglin and August Wennerstrom. They all ended up in the water near Collapsible Lifeboat A. Tenglin and Wennerstrom managed to get into the half-flooded lifeboat, and they pulled Edvard Lindell in with them. The three men were too weak to pull Mrs. Lindell into the lifeboat, so she hung onto the side, and eventually died from the cold. Mr. Lindell also died during the night from exposure, and his body was tossed overboard to improve buoyancy. A month after *Titanic* sank, Collapsible Lifeboat A was found with three bodies in it, and in the bottom of the lifeboat was Mrs. Lindell's wedding ring.

Name	Age	Residence	Class	E	Destination	L/B	Body # Recovered / Where Buried	Notes
Lindqvist, Mr. Eino W.	20	Dals, Finland	3rd	S	Hoboken, NJ	?		

Mr. **Eino Lindqvist** was emigrating to America. He was traveling with his sister Helga Hirvonen and niece Hildur Hirvonen. All three survived.

Name	Age	Residence	Class	E	Destination	L/B	Body # Recovered / Where Buried	Notes
Lindqvist, Helga E.								see Mrs. Alexander Hirvonen
Lindström, Mrs. Carl J. (Sigrid Posse)	55	Stockholm, Sweden	1st	C	New York City, NY	6		
Linehan, Mr. Michael	21	County Cork, Ireland	3rd	Q	unknown			see Irish Contingent Group Notes
Lines, Mrs. Ernest H. (Elizabeth Lindsey James)	50	Paris, France	1st	S	Hanover, NH	9		Wife of President of New York Life Insurance Co.
Lines, Miss Mary Conover	16	Paris, France	1st	C	Hanover, NH	9		
Ling, Mr. Lee	28	Hong Kong	3rd	S	New York City, NY			see Donaldson Line Notes
Lingan [Lingane, Linnana], Mr. John	61	County Cork, Ireland	2nd	Q	New York City, NY			
Lingrey, Mr. Edward								see Mr. Erik G. Lindeberg-Lind
Linhart, Mr. Wenzel	32	Vienna, Austria	3rd	S	unknown		#298, buried in Mount Olivet Cemetery, Halifax	
Lithman, Mr. Simon	20	Edinburgh, Scotland	3rd	S	unknown			
Livshin, Mr. David	25	Manchester, England	3rd	S	unknown			
Lobb, Mr. William A.	30	Scranton, PA	3rd	S	Scranton, PA			
Lobb, Mrs. William A. (Cordelia Stanlick)	26	Scranton, PA	3rd	S	Scranton, PA		#55, buried at sea	Chose to remain with her husband instead of getting into a lifeboat.
Lockyer, Mr. Edward T.	21	London, England	3rd	S	Ontario, NY		#153, buried at sea	
Lofqvist, Hulda Kristina E.								see Mrs. Hulda K. Klasén
Long, Florence L.								see Mrs. John J. Ware
Long, Mr. Milton C.	29	Springfield, MA	1st	S	Springfield, MA		#126, buried in Springfield, MA	
Longley, Miss Gretchen Fiske	21	Hudson, NY	1st	S	Hudson, NY	10		

Gretchen Longley was returning from vacation in Europe. She traveled with her aunt Kornelia Andrews and friend Mrs. John C. Hogeboom. All survived.

Name	Age	Residence	Class	E	Destination	L/B	Body # Recovered / Where Buried	Notes
Loring, Mr. Joseph H.	30	New York City, NY	1st	S	New York City, NY			Traveled with brother-in-law George Rheims.
Louch, Mr. Charles A.	50	Somerset, England	2nd	S	California		#121, buried at sea	
Louch, Mrs. Charles A. (Alice A. Slow)	42	Somerset, England	2nd	S	California	14		
Lovell, Mr. John H.	20	Devon, England	3rd	S	Lakefield, Ontario, Canada			see Braund–Dennis Group Notes
Lulic, Mr. Nicola [Nikola]	27	Chicago, IL	3rd	S	Chicago, IL	15		
Lundahl, Mr. Johan S.	51	Spokane, WA	3rd	S	Spokane, WA			
Lundin, Miss Olga E.	23	Meriden, CT	3rd	S	Meriden, CT	10		

Olga Lundin was returning home from vacation in Sweden. She traveled with fiancé Nils Johansson, brother-in-law Carl Jonsson and friend Paul Andreasson. Olga and Carl survived.

Name	Age	Residence	Class	E	Destination	L/B	Body # Recovered / Where Buried	Notes
Lundstrom, Mr. Thure Edvin	32	China	3rd	S	Los Angeles, CA	15?		Traveled with fiancé Elina Olsson, see Lundstrom Group Notes.
Lurette, Miss Eugenie E.	58	Paris, France	1st	C	New York City, NY	6		Maid to Mrs. William A. Spencer.
Lyntakoff, Mr. Stanko	44	Bulgaria	3rd	S	Coon Rapids, IA			

Name *(Maiden Name)[Other Name]* *Names in italic indicate survivors*	Age	Residence	Class	E	Destination	L/B	Body # Recovered / Where Buried	Notes
M								
Mack, Mrs. Edward	57	Southampton, England	2nd	S	New York City, NY		#52, buried at sea	
Madigan, Miss Margaret	21	County Limerick, Ireland	3rd	Q	New York City, NY	15		
Madill, Miss Georgette A.	15	St. Louis, MO	1st	S	St. Louis, MO	2		Traveled with mother Mrs. Edward Robert and cousin Elisabeth Allen.
Madsen, Mr. Frithiof Arne	24	Trondheim, Norway	3rd	S	Brooklyn, NY	13		
Mäenpää, Mr. Matti A.	22	Finland	3rd	S	Sudbury, Ontario, Canada			
Magnin, Antoinine								see Mrs. Albert Mallet
Maguire, Mr. John E.	30	Brockton, MA	1st	S	Brockton, MA			
Mahon, Miss Bridget D.	20	County Mayo, Ireland	3rd	Q	unknown			
Mahon [Mechan], Mr. John	22	County Sligo, Ireland	3rd	Q	Patterson, NJ			Sometimes listed as John Mechan
Maidment, Elizabeth Anne								see Mrs. Elizabeth Anne Mellinger
Maioni, Miss Roberta Elizabeth M.	20	Surrey, England	1st	S	Vancouver, BC, Canada	8		Maid to the Countess of Rothes
Maisner, Mr. Simon	34	London, England	3rd	S	unknown			
Mäkinen, Mr. Kalle Edvard	29	Ikalis, Finland	3rd	S	Glassport, PA			
Malachard, Mr. Noel		Paris, France	2nd	C	unknown			
Mallet Family								
Mallet, Mr. Albert	31	Montreal, Quebec, Canada	2nd	C	Montreal, Quebec, Canada			Traveled with Mr. Emile Richard
Mallet, Mrs. Albert (Antoinine Magnin)	24	Montreal, Quebec, Canada	2nd	C	Montreal, Quebec, Canada	10		
Mallet, Master André C.	18 m	Montreal, Quebec, Canada	2nd	C	Montreal, Quebec, Canada	10		
Mamee, Mr. Hanna	20	Syria	3rd	C	Philadelphia, PA	15		
Mampe, Leo J.								see Mr. Leo J. Hampe
Mandelbaum, Tillie								see Mrs. Emil Taussig
Mangan, Miss Mary	32	Chicago, IL	3rd	Q	Chicago, IL		#61, buried at sea	Returning to Chicago to get married
Mangiavacchi, Mr. Serafino E.		Paris, France	2nd	C	New York City, NY			
Mannion, Miss Margaret	28	County Galway, Ireland	3rd	Q	New York City, NY	16		
Mansour, Mr. Hanna								see Mr. Mansour Hanna, Hanna being the last name.
Mardirosian, Mr. Sarkis	25	Lyons, France	3rd	C	unknown			
Maréchal, Mr. Pierre		Paris, France	1st	C	New York City, NY	7		
Markoff, Mr. Marin	35	Bulgaria	3rd	S	Chicago, IL			see Gumostnik, Bulgaria Group Notes
Markun [Markim], Mr. Johann	33	Croatia	3rd	C	New York City, NY			
Marshall, Mr. Henry								see Mr. Henry S. Morley
Marshall, Mrs. Henry S.								see Kate Phillips
Marshall, Miss Kate Louise Phillips								see Kate Phillips
Marvin, Mr. Daniel W.	19	New York City, NY	1st	S	New York City, NY			
Marvin, Mrs. Daniel W. (Mary Graham Carmichael Farquarson)	18	New York City, NY	1st	S	New York City, NY	10		

Mr. **Daniel W. Marvin** was the son of the developer of the movie camera. The Marvin's, having been married less than one month, were returning from a honeymoon in Europe.

Masselmany, Mrs. Fatima	17	Dearborn, MI	3rd	C	Dearborn, MI			
Matinoff, Mr. Nicola	35	Bulgaria	3rd	S	unknown			
Matthews, Mr. William J.	30	Cornwall, England	2nd	S	LaSalle, IL			
May, Mr. Richard								see Mr. John Adams
Maybery, Mr. Frank H.	37	Moose Jaw, Saskatchewan, Canada	2nd	S	Moose Jaw, Saskatchewan, Canada			
Mayné, Miss Berthe Antonine [Berthe de Villiers]	24	Brussels, Belgium	1st	C	Montreal, Quebec, Canada	6		

Bertha Mayné was traveling as the girlfriend of Mr. Quigg Baxter. She was a cabaret singer (consequently not of the proper social standing for Quigg's mother's liking) from Belgium. Quigg booked her a room down the hall from his, and booked her under the name "Berthe de Villiers". She did not want to get into the lifeboat without Quigg, and once in the lifeboat, she tried to get out but was restrained (and thus saved) by Mrs. Margaret (Molly) Brown.

Name *(Maiden Name)[Other Name]* *Names in italic indicate survivors*	Age	Residence	Class	E	Destination	L/B	Body # Recovered / Where Buried	Notes
McCaffry, Mr. Thomas F.	46	Vancouver, BC, Canada	1st	C	Vancouver, BC, Canada		#292, buried in Montreal, Canada	Traveled with Thomson Beattie and John Hugo Ross.
McCarthy, Miss Catherine "Katie"	24	County Tipperary, Ireland	3rd	Q	Guttenburg, NJ	15		
McCarthy, Mr. Timothy J.	54	Dorchester, MA	1st	S	Dorchester, MA		#175, buried in Dorchester, MA	Traveled with Mr. Herbert Hilliard.
McCormack, Mr. Thomas J.	19	Bayonne, NJ	3rd	Q	Bayonne, NJ	B		Traveled with cousins John and Philip Kiernan.
McCoy Family								
McCoy, Miss Agnes	28	County Longford, Ireland	3rd	Q	Brooklyn, NY	16		
McCoy, Miss Alice	22	County Longford, Ireland	3rd	Q	Brooklyn, NY	16		
McCoy, Mr. Bernard	21	County Longford, Ireland	3rd	Q	Brooklyn, NY	16		

Bernard McCoy and his sisters Agnes and Alice were emigrating to America. This is another of the rare groups of Third Class passengers who all survived.

McCrae, Mr. Arthur G.	32	Sydney, Australia	2nd	S	Canada		#209, buried in Fairview Cemetery, Halifax	
McCrie, Mr. James M.	30	Sarnia, Ontario, Canada	2nd	S	Sarnia, Ontario, Canada			
McDermott, Miss Bridget Delia	31?	County Mayo, Ireland	3rd	Q	St. Louis, MO	13		
McDougald, Mary								see Mrs. Mark Fortune
McDowell, Virginia Estelle								see Mrs. Walter M. Clark
McElroy [McEvoy], Michael		Dublin, Ireland	3rd	Q	New York City, NY			Traveled with Nora Murphy.
McGough, Mr. James R.	36	Philadelphia, PA	1st	S	Philadelphia, PA	7		
McGovern, Miss Mary	22	County Cavan, Ireland	3rd	Q	New York City, NY	13		
McGowan, Miss Annie [Ann] F.	14	Scranton, PA	3rd	Q	Chicago, IL	13		Traveled with her aunt Katherine McGowan.
McGowan, Miss Katherine	36	Chicago, IL	3rd	Q	Chicago, IL			Traveled with niece Annie McGowan.
McHugh, Catherine								see Mrs. John Bourke
McKane, Mr. Peter D.	46	Guernsey, England	2nd	S	Rochester, NY			
McKay, Mr. George W.	20	London, England	3rd	S	unknown			
McMahon, Mr. Martin	20	County Clare, Ireland	3rd	Q	New York Citiy, NY			
McMillan, Elisabeth Walton								see Mrs. Edward Scott Robert
McNamee, Mr. Neal	27	County Donegal, Ireland	3rd	S	New York City, NY			Newlywed only 3 months.
McNamee, Mrs. Neal (Eileen O'Leary)	19	County Donegal, Ireland	3rd	S	New York City, NY		#53, buried at sea	Newlywed only 3 months.
Meanwell, Miss Marion [Marion Ogden]	63	County Donegal, Ireland	3rd	S	New York City, NY			Final trip in a planned move to NYC
Mechan, John								see Mr. John Mahon
Meek, Mrs. Thomas (Annie L. Rowley)	31	Cardiff, So. Wales	3rd	S	unknown			
Mellinger, Mrs. Elizabeth (Elizabeth Anne Maidment)	41	Surrey, England	2nd	S	New York City, NY	14/12		Au pair for the Colgate family in New York.
Mellinger, Miss Madeleine Violet	13	Surrey, England	2nd	S	New York City, NY	14/12		
Mellors, Mr. William J.	19	Chelsea, England	2nd	S	New York City, NY	B		
Meo, Mr. Alfonso	48	Dorset, England	3rd	S	unknown		#201, buried in Fairview Cemetery, Halifax	
Mernagh [Nemaagh], Mr. Robert	26	County Wexford, Ireland	3rd	Q	Chicago, IL			
Meyer, Mr. August	30	Middlesex, England	2nd	S	unknown			
Meyer, Mr. Edgar J.	28	New York City, NY	1st	C	New York City, NY			
Meyer, Mrs. Edgar J. (Leila Saks)	25	New York City, NY	1st	C	New York City, NY	6		

Mr. **Edgar Meyer** was Vice President of Braden Copper Co. He had an opportunity to get into a lifeboat but remained behind to help several women and children. Mrs. Meyer tried to remain behind with her husband, but she was forcibly placed into a lifeboat, and saved.

Midtsjø, Mr. Karl Albert	21	Oslo, Norway	3rd	S	Chicago, IL	15		
Mihoff [Mionoff], Mr. Stoytcho	28	Bulgaria	3rd	S	unknown			
Miles, Mr. Frank	23	Greenwich, England	3rd	S	unknown			
Miller, Mary Phyllis Elizabeth								see Mrs. Percy C. Corey

Name *(Maiden Name)[Other Name]* *Names in italic indicate survivors*	Age	Residence	Class	E	Destination	L/B	Body # Recovered / Where Buried	Notes
Millet, Mr. Francis D.	65	East Bridgewater, MA	1st	S	East Bridgewater, MA		#249, buried in East Bridgewater, MA	
Mr. **Francis D. Millet** was a Civil War veteran. He was also a famous author and painter whose works appeared in many public buildings. He was traveling with Major Archibald Butt.									
Milling, Mr. Jacob C.	48	Copenhagen, Denmark	2nd	S	unknown		#271, buried in Copenhagen, Denmark	
Milne, Bessie Inglis								see Mrs. James Watt
Minahan Family									
Minahan, Miss Daisy E.	33	Green Bay, WI	1st	Q	Green Bay, WI	14/D		
Minahan, Dr. William E.	44	Fond du Lac, WI	1st	Q	Fond du Lac, WI		#230, buried in Green Bay, WI.	
Minahan, Mrs. William E. (Lillian E. Thorpe)	37	Fond du Lac, WI	1st	Q	Fond du Lac, WI	14/D		
Dr. **Minahan,** his wife Lillian and his sister Daisy were returning from vacation in Europe. Daisy and her brother were very close, and his loss caused Daisy to go into such a deep depression with grief she had to be institutionalized less than a month after *Titanic* sank and she spent most of the remaining seven years of her life there. Dr. Minahan's last words to his wife were *"be brave".*									
Mineff, Mr. Ivan	24	Bulgaria	3rd	S	Coon Rapids, IA			
Minkoff, Mr. Lazar	21	Bulgaria	3rd	S	Coon Rapids, IA			see Gumostnik, Bulgaria Group Notes
Mirko, Mr. Dika								see Mr. Mirko Dika, Dika is the last name
Mitchell, Mr. Henry M.	71	Guernsey, England	2nd	S	Montclair, NJ			
Mitkoff [Mirkoff, Minkoff], Mr. Mito	23	Bulgaria	3rd	S	unknown			see Gumostnik, Bulgaria Group Notes
Mock, Emma								see Mrs. Paul Schabert
Mock, Mr. Philip E.	30	New York City, NY	1st	C	New York City, NY	11		Traveled with sister Emma Schabert.
Mocklare [Mockler], Miss Ellen [Helen] Mary	23	County Galway, Ireland	3rd	Q	New York City, NY	16		
Moen, Mr. Sigurd H.	25	Bergan, Norway	3rd	S	Minneapolis, MN		#309, buried in Norway	
Mr. **Sigurd H. Moen** traveled with friends Karen Abelseth, Olaus Abelseth, Anna Salkjelsvik , Peter Soholt and Adolf Humblen.									
Molson, Mr. Harry M.	55	Montreal, Quebec, Canada	1st	S	Montreal, Quebec, Canada			Member of the Molson Beer family, influential Canadian businessman.
Montvila, Rev. Juozas [Joseph]	27	Lithuania	2nd	S	Worcester, MA			
Monypeny, Sallie								see Mrs. Richard Beckwith
Moor [Moore], Mrs. Bella	27	Russia	3rd	S	Canada	?		
Moor [Moore], Master Meier	6	Russia	3rd	S	Canada	?		
Moore, Mr. Clarence B.	47	Washington, DC	1st	S	Washington, DC			
Moore, Mr. Leonard Charles	19	Hoboken, NJ	3rd	S	Hoboken, NJ			Had been in Ireland to visit his sick mother.
Moran, Miss Bertha B.	28	County Limerick, Ireland	3rd	Q	Bronx, NY	16		Traveled with brother Daniel Moran.
Moran, Mr. Daniel James	27	County Limerick, Ireland	3rd	Q	Bronx, NY			Traveled with sister Bertha Moran.
Moran, Mr. James	22	Ireland	3rd	Q	unknown			Also Traveled under name "John Dougherty".
Moraweck, Dr. Ernest	53	Frankfort, KY	2nd	S	Frankfort, KY			
Morley, Mr. Henry S.	39	Worcester, England	2nd	S	Sacramento, CA			Eloping with Kate Phillips, traveled under the name Mr. Henry Marshall.
Morley, Mr. William	34	Sussex, England	3rd	S	unknown			
Morris, Annie May								see Mrs. Charles Emil H. Stengel
Morris, Marian Longstreth								see Mrs. John B. Thayer
Morrow, Mr. Thomas Rowan	30	County Down, Ireland	3rd	Q	Alberta, Canada			
Moss, Mr. Albert Johan	29	Bergan, Norway	3rd	S	New York City, NY	B		

Name *(Maiden Name)[Other Name]* *Names in italic indicate survivors*	Age	Residence	Class	E	Destination	L/B	Body # Recovered / Where Buried	Notes
Moubarek Family								
Moubarek, Mrs. George (Amenia Alexander)	26	Lebanon	3rd	C	Wilkes-Barre, PA	C		
Moubarek, Master George	7	Lebanon	3rd	C	Wilkes-Barre, PA	C		
Moubarek, Master William	3	Lebanon	3rd	C	Wilkes-Barre, PA	C		
Moubarek [Borak], Mr. Hanna								see Mr. Borak Hannah, Hannah is the last name
Moussa, Mrs. Mantoura B.		Lebanon	3rd	C	Troy, NY	C		
Moutal, Mr. Rahamin	35	London, England	3rd	S	unknown			
Mowad, Mary								see Mrs. Said Nackid
Mudd, Mr. Thomas C.	16	Suffolk, England	2nd	S	unknown			
Mullen [Mullins], Miss Katherine	19	County Longford, Ireland	3rd	Q	New York City, NY	16		
Mulvihill, Miss Bertha E.	24	Providence, RI	3rd	Q	Providence, RI	15		
Munger, Alice								see Mrs. William Baird Silvey
Murdin, Mr. Joseph	22	London, England	3rd	S	unknown			
Murphy, Miss Katherine	19	County Longford, Ireland	3rd	Q	New York City, NY	16		Sister of Margaret Murphy.
Murphy, Miss Margaret J.	26	County Longford, Ireland	3rd	Q	New York City, NY	16		Sister of Katherine Murphy.
Murphy, Miss Nora	28	County Dublin, Ireland	3rd	Q	New York City, NY	16		Traveled with Michael McEvoy.
MUSICIAN'S:								see individual names listings and the Musician's Group Notes.
Myhrman, Mr. Pehr Fabian Oliver M.	18	Kristinehamn, Sweden	3rd	S	New York City, NY			
Myles, Mr. Thomas F.	64	Cambridge, MA	2nd	Q	Cambridge, MA			

N

Name	Age	Residence	Class	E	Destination	L/B	Body # Recovered / Where Buried	Notes
Nackid Family								
Nackid, Mr. Said	20	Syria	3rd	C	Waterbury, CT	C		
Nackid, Mrs. Said (Mary Mowad)	19	Syria	3rd	C	Waterbury, CT	C		
Nackid, Miss Maria	18 m	Syria	3rd	C	Waterbury, CT	C		

The **Said Nackid** family was emigrating to Connecticut. This is one of the few third class families that survived intact, having gotten onto the first collapsible lifeboat launched. Little Maria was the first survivor to die. Having caught meningitis, she died only three months after *Titanic* sank.

Name	Age	Residence	Class	E	Destination	L/B	Body # Recovered / Where Buried	Notes
Naidenoff, Mr. Penko	22	Bulgaria	3rd	S	Chicago, IL			see Gumostnik, Bulgaria, Group Notes
Najib, Miss Adele J.K.	15	Syria	3rd	C	unknown	C		see Baclini Family Notes
Nancarrow, Mr. William H.	33	Yonkers, NY	3rd	S	Yonkers, NY			Traveled with his aunt and uncle, Mr. and Mrs. Alexander Robins.
Nankoff, Mr. Minko	32	Bulgaria	3rd	S	Chicago, IL			
Nasr, Mr. Mustafa			3rd	C	unknown			
Nasser [Nasrallah], Mr. Nicholas		New York City, NY	2nd	C	New York City, NY		#43, buried in New York City	
Nasser [Nasrallah], Mrs. Nicholas (Adele Achem)	14	Lebanon	2nd	C	New York City, NY	?		Newly married (at age 14), she was also pregnant and now a widow.
Natsch, Mr. Charles H.	36	Brooklyn, NY	1st	C	Brooklyn, NY			
Naughton, Miss Hannah	21	County Cork, Ireland	3rd	Q	New York City, NY			She turned 21 on April 10, the day *Titanic* left Southampton.

Name *(Maiden Name)[Other Name]* *Names in italic indicate survivors*	Age	Residence	Class	E	Destination	L/B	Body # Recovered / Where Buried	Notes
Navratil Family								
Navratil [Hoffman], Master Edmond R.	2	Nice, France	2nd	S	unknown	D		
Navratil [Hoffman], Master Michel M.	3	Nice, France	2nd	S	unknown	D		
Navratil [Hoffman], Mr. Michel	32	Nice, France	2nd	S	unknown		#15, buried in Baron de Hirsch Cemetery, Halifax	

Mr. **Michael Navratil** was a tailor living in Nice, France. He was married but separated from his wife, and they had two boys, Michel M. and Edmond. During one weekend when he had the boys, their father disappeared with them, taking them to England. There he changed his name to Hoffman, booked passage to America on *Titanic,* and, when the ship went down, so did Mr. Navratil (Hoffman). He managed to get his sons onto Collapsible Lifeboat D, the last lifeboat launched. Nobody knew who the boys were, and only a couple survivors recalled seeing them with their father, who was using the name Hoffman. Once rescued by *Carpathia, Titanic* survivor Margaret Hays took over the care of the children. Newspapers around America and Europe published their photograph in an attempt to find out who they were. Eventually their mother saw the photographs. White Star Line paid for her to travel to New York City to identify and claim her children, which she did, and return to France. Edmond Navratil died in the mid-50's, but Michel was interviewed on many of the *Titanic* television stories, and he died in January 2001, the last of the male survivors of *Titanic* to die.

Name	Age	Residence	Class	E	Destination	L/B	Body # Recovered / Where Buried	Notes
Needs, Eliza								see Mrs. William R. Hocking
Needs, Ellen								see Mrs. James Wilkes
Nemaugh [Mernagh], Mr. Robert								see Mr. Robert Mernagh
Nenkoff, Mr. Christo	22	Bulgaria	3rd	S	Coon Rapids, IA			
Nesson, Mr. Israel	26	London, England	2nd	S	Boston, MA			
Newell Family								
Newell, Mr. Arthur Webster	58	Lexington, MA	1st	C	Lexington, MA		#122, buried in Springfield, MA	
Newell, Miss Madeleine	31	Lexington, MA	1st	C	Lexington, MA	6		
Newell, Miss Marjorie	23	Lexington, MA	1st	C	Lexington, MA	6		Died 1992, age 103.

Mr. **Arthur Newell** was very wealthy and was the President of the Fourth National Bank of Boston. He and two daughters were returning from a several-months tour of Egypt and Israel and had delayed returning home so they could travel on *Titanic.* His body, when recovered, contained his gold pocket watch, which was returned to the family. Newell's wife, who was not on the trip, slept with the watch under her pillow for the next 45 years until she died at the age of 103. Marjorie also lived to be 103 years old. She died in 1992 and was the last of the First Class passengers to pass on.

Name	Age	Residence	Class	E	Destination	L/B	Body # Recovered / Where Buried	Notes
Newsom, Miss Helen Monypeny	19	New York City, NY	1st	S	New York City, NY	5		Daughter of Mrs. Richard Beckwith. Later married survivor Karl H. Behr.
Nicholls, Mr. Joseph C.	19	Cornwall, England	2nd	S	Hancock, MI		#101, buried at sea	

Joseph Nicholls was emigrating to America where his brother was living. He traveled with his mother Elizabeth Davies, step-brother John M. Davies and family friend Maude Sincock. All except Joseph survived.

Name	Age	Residence	Class	E	Destination	L/B	Body # Recovered / Where Buried	Notes
Nicholson, Mr. Arthur Ernest	64	Isle of Wight, England	1st	S	New York City, NY		#263, buried in Bronx, NY	
Nicola-Yarred [Garrett], Master Elias	12	Lebanon	3rd	C	Jacksonville, FL	C		
Nicola-Yarred [Garrett], Miss Jamila	14	Lebanon	3rd	C	Jacksonville, FL	C		

Jamila and Elias **Nicola-Yarred** were two unaccompanied children traveling to Florida to meet their family, their father having been refused boarding in Cherbourg because of an eye infection. That two children would be allowed to undertake such a voyage is a stunning commentary of how trusting one could be of strangers in the early 20th Century. You wouldn't attempt to do that today.

Name	Age	Residence	Class	E	Destination	L/B	Body # Recovered / Where Buried	Notes
Nieminen, Miss Manta J.	29	Abo, Finland	3rd	S	Aberdeen, WA			Traveled with Mr. Johan W. Salonen.
Niklasson, Mr. Samuel	28	Orust, Sweden	3rd	S	unknown			Traveled with Karl J. Johansson and Oscar Olsson.
Nile, Edith								see Mrs. Benjamin Peacock.
Nilsson, Mr. August Ferdinand	21	Sweden	3rd	S	St. Paul, MN			Traveled with Mr. Olof Vendel.
Nilsson, Miss Berta Olivia	18	Ransbysäter, Sweden	3rd	S	Missoula, MT	D		Traveled with fiancé Edvard Larsson-Rondberg.
Nilsson, Miss Helmina Josefina	26	Ramkvilla, Sweden	3rd	S	Joliet, IL	13		
Nirva, Mr. Lisakki A.	41	Finland	3rd	S	Sudbury, Ontario, Canada			Traveled with Nikolai Kallio, Matti Maenpaa and Matti Rintamaki.
Niskänen, Mr. Johan	39	Vermont	3rd	S	Boston, MA	9		Died by suicide in 1927.
Norman, Mr. Robert D.	28	Glasgow, Scotland	2nd	S	unknown		# 287, buried in Fairview Cemetery, Halifax	

Name *(Maiden Name)[Other Name]* *Names in italic indicate survivors*	Age	Residence	Class	E	Destination	L/B	Body # Recovered / Where Buried	Notes
Norton, Margaret								see Mrs. William Rice
Nosworthy, Mr. Richard Cater	21	Newton Abbot, England	3rd	S	Buffalo, NY			
Nourney, Alfred (Baron Alfred von Drachstedt)	20	Cologne, Germany	1st	C	New York City, NY	7		

Alfred Nourney was quite a man-about-town. Deciding to travel to America, he took the name Baron Alfred von Drachstedt, a name he had seen in the newspapers. He booked a Second Class room, then upgraded to First Class after *Titanic* left Cherbourg. When *Titanic* hit the iceberg, he and his two card-playing companions William Greenfield and Henry Blank got onto the first lifeboat launched.

Novel, Mr. Mansour		Sherbrooke, Quebec, Canada	3rd	C	Sherbrooke, Quebec, Canada			
Nye, Mrs. Ernest Edward (Elizabeth Ramell)	29	New York City, NY	2nd	S	New York City, NY	11		
Nysten, Miss Anna S.	22	Sweden	3rd	S	Passaic, NJ	13		Traveled with Ernst Danbom and Anders Andersson.
Nysveen, Mr. Johan H.	61	Grand Forks, ND	3rd	S	Grand Forks, ND			

O

O'Brien, Mr. Denis [Timothy]	21	County Cork, Ireland	3rd	Q	New York City, NY			
O'Brien, Mr. Thomas	27	County Limerick, Ireland	3rd	Q	New York City, NY			Traveled with wife Hannah.
O'Brien, Mrs. Thomas (Hannah Godfrey)	26	County Limerick, Ireland	3rd	Q	New York City, NY	?		Traveled with husband Thomas.
O'Connell, Mr. Patrick Denis	17	County Cork, Ireland	3rd	Q	unknown			see Irish Contingent Group Notes
O'Conner, Mr. Patrick	17	County Cork, Ireland	3rd	Q	unknown			see Irish Contingent Group Notes
O'Connor, Mr. Maurice	21	County Cork, Ireland	3rd	Q	New York City, NY			
Ödahl, Mr. Nils Martin	23	Sweden	3rd	S	Peoria, IL			
O'Driscoll, Miss Bridget	24	County Cork, Ireland	3rd	Q	New York City, NY	D		Often listed as "Driscoll".
O'Dwyer, Miss Ellen [Nellie]	23	County Limerick, Ireland	3rd	Q	New York City, NY	?		
Ogden, Marion								see Mrs. Marion Meanwell
Öhman, Miss Velin	22	Sweden	3rd	S	Chicago, IL	C		
Ojala, Maria Emilia								see Mrs. John Panula
O'Keefe, Mr. Patrick	22	County Waterford, Ireland	3rd	Q	New York City, NY	B		
O'Leary, Eileen								see Mrs. Neal McNamee
O'Leary, Miss Hanora [Nora]	16	County Cork, Ireland	3rd	Q	New York City, NY	13		see Irish Contingent Group Notes
Oliva y Ocana, Miss Doña Fermina	39	Madrid, Spain	1st	C		8		Maid to Mrs. Victor Penasco y Castellana.
Olsen, Mr. Henry Margido	28	Bergan, Norway	3rd	S	New York City, NY		#173, buried at sea	Traveled with Albert K. Andersen and Johan Holthen.

Olsen, Mr. Karl and Son								
Olsen, Mr. Karl Siegwart Andreas	42	Brooklyn, NY	3rd	S	Brooklyn, NY			
Olsen, Master Arthur Carl	9	Trondheim, Norway	3rd	S	Brooklyn, NY	13		

Mr. **Karl Olsen** was traveling with his son Arthur who had been living in Norway with his grandmother. Karl Olsen died, but he managed to get his son into a lifeboat. Family members in New York did not know that Karl and the boy were on *Titanic,* or that young Arthur had survived. He had been placed in a children's home when he arrived in New York. It was several days before the error was corrected and the boy was able to go live with his family in Brooklyn.

Olsen, Mr. Ole M.	27	Skjarsvik, Norway	3rd	S	Longford, ND			
Olsson, Miss Elina	31	Sweden	3rd	S	St. Paul, MN			Traveled with fiancé Thure E. Lundstrom.
Olsson [Goransson], Mr. Nils Johan	28	Sweden	3rd	S	unknown			Last name may also be Goransson.
Olsson [Johansson], Mr. Oscar W.	32	Chicago, IL	3rd	S	Chicago, IL	A		Traveled with Karl J. Johansson and Samuel Niklasson.
Olsvigan, Mr. Thor Andersen	20	Vikersund, Norway	3rd	S	Cameron, WI		#89, buried at sea	Sometimes referred to Mr. Thor Andersen.
Omont, Mr. Alfred Fernand	29	Havre, France	1st	C	New York City, NY	7		

Name *(Maiden Name)[Other Name]* *Names in italic indicate survivors*	Age	Residence	Class	E	Destination	L/B	Body # Recovered / Where Buried	Notes
Oreskovic Family								
Oreskovic, Miss Jelka	23	Croatia	3rd	S	Chicago, IL			
Oreskovic, Mr. Luka	20	Croatia	3rd	S	Chicago, IL			
Oreskovic, Miss Marija	20	Croatia	3rd	S	Chicago, IL			
Jelka, Luka and Marija Oreskovic were all relatives emigrating to America. All were lost.								
Osén, Mr. Olof Elon	16	Sweden	3rd	S	Mitchell, SD			
Osman, Miss Maria [Mara]	31	Croatia	3rd	S	Steubenville, OH	?		
Østby, Mr. Engelhart Cornelius	65	Providence, RI	1st	C	Providence, RI		#234, buried in Providence, RI	
Østby, Miss Helen Ragnhild	22	Providence, RI	1st	C	Providence, RI	5		
Mr. **Engelhart Østby** was the owner of the company that was the world's largest producer of gold rings. He was traveling back from Europe with his daughter Helen, who often accompanied him on his trips. Also traveling with him were Frank and Anna Warren, whom Østby had met in Egypt. The two women survived, the men did not.								
O'Sullivan, Miss Bridget	22	County Cork, Ireland	3rd	Q	unknown			
Otter, Mr. Richard	39	Middleburg Heights, OH	2nd	S	Middleburg Heights, OH			Returning from vacation in England.
Ovies y Rodriguez, Mr. Servando J.F.	36	Havana, Cuba	1st	C	Havana, Cuba		#189, buried in Mt. Olivet Cemetery, Halifax	
Oxenham, Mr. Percy Thomas	22	Pondersend, England	2nd	S	New Durham, NJ	13		

P

Padron y Manent, Mr. Julian	26	Havana, Cuba	2nd	C	Havana, Cuba	?		
Julian Padron y Manent traveled with Mr. Emilio Pallas y Castell, Miss Asuncion Duran and Miss Florentina Duran. He later married survivor Florentina Duran y More.								
Pain, Dr. Alfred	23	London, England	2nd	S	Toronto, Ontario, Canada			
Pallas y Castello, Mr. Emilio	29	unknown	2nd	C	Havana, Cuba	9		
Emilio Pallas y Castello traveled with Julian Padron y Manent, Miss Asuncion Duran and Miss Florentina Duran.								
Palsson Family								
Pålsson, Master Gösta Leonard	2	Bjuv, Sweden	3rd	S	Chicago, IL		#4, buried in Fairview Cemetery, Halifax	
Pålsson, Mrs. Nils (Alma Cornelia Berglund)	29	Bjuv, Sweden	3rd	S	Chicago, IL		#206, buried in Fairview Cemetery, Halifax	
Pålsson, Master Paul Folke	6	Bjov, Sweden	3rd	S	Chicago, IL			
Pålsson, Miss Stina Viola	3	Bjuv, Sweden	3rd	S	Chicago, IL			
Pålsson, Miss Torborg Danira	8	Bjuv, Sweden	3rd	S	Chicago, IL			
Mr. **Nils Pålsson** had worked in the U.S. for several years, saving money to bring his family to Chicago. His wife and three children were emigrating, and all were lost. Mrs. Pålsson's body was recovered and buried in Halifax. Buried near her was the body of an unknown young child. Early forensic tests indicate that the body buried near her might be her son Gosta, however recent tests prove otherwise, now confirmed to be Uhro Panula. For many years known as the "unknown child of *Titanic*", the crewmembers of the recovery ship *MacKay Bennett* paid for burial and a monument to the child.								
Panula Family								
Panula, Mr. Ernesti Arvid	16	Coal Center, PA	3rd	S	Coal Center, PA			
Panula, Master Jaako Arnold	14	Coal Center, PA	3rd	S	Coal Center, PA			
Panula, Mrs. John (Maria Emilia Ojala)	41	Coal Center, PA	3rd	S	Coal Center, PA			
Panula, Master Juhn Niilo	7	Coal Center, PA	3rd	S	Coal Center, PA			
Panula, Master Urho Abraham	2	Coal Center, PA	3rd	S	Coal Center, PA			
Panula, Master William	1	Coal Center, PA	3rd	S	Coal Center, PA			
Mrs. John Panula had been living in Coal Center, Pennsylvania with her husband and family, but had taken her five children back to Finland in order to sell the family farm. Returning with her and the children was Sanni Riihivuori, a family friend. All seven were lost. Recent forensic tests show that Urho Panula is the former 'unknown' child buried in Halifax.								
Parker, Mr. Clifford R.	28	Guernsey, England	2nd	S	unknown			

Name *(Maiden Name)[Other Name]* *Names in italic indicate survivors*	Age	Residence	Class	E	Destination	L/B	Body # Recovered / Where Buried	Notes
Parkes, Mr. Francis	25	Belfast, Ireland	2nd	B	New York City, NY			Plumber Apprentice. See H&W Guarantee Group Notes.
Parr, Mr. William Henry Marsh		Belfast, Ireland	1st	B	New York City, NY			Asst. Manager, Electrical Dept. See H&W Guarantee Group Notes.
Parrish, Mrs. Samuel Edward (Lutie Davis Temple)	60	Versailles, KY	2nd	S	Versailles, KY	12		Traveled with daughter Mrs. William Shelley.
Parsons, Gertrude								see Mrs. Edwin N. Kimball Jr.
Partner, Mr. Austin	40	Surrey, England	1st	S	Winnipeg, Manitoba, Canada		#166, buried in Surrey, England	
Pasic, Mr. Jakob	21	Slovenia	3rd	S	Aurora, MN			
Patchett (Potchett), Mr. George	19	Northamptonshire, England	3rd	S	Canada			Traveled with Mr. John Garfirth.
Paulner, Mr. Uscher			3rd	S				
Pavlovic, Mr. Stefo	32	Croatia	3rd	S	Harrisburg, PA			
Payne, Mr. Vivian Ponsonby	22	Montreal, Quebec, Canada	1st	S	Montreal, Quebec, Canada			Personal secretary to Mr. Charles M. Hays.
Peacock Family								
Peacock, Master Alfred E.	9 mo	Southampton, England	3rd	S	Elizabeth, NJ			
Peacock, Mrs. Benjamin (Edith Nile)	26	Southampton, England	3rd	S	Elizabeth, NJ			
Peacock, Miss Treasteall	3	Southampton, England	3rd	S	Elizabeth, NJ			

Mrs. **Peacock** and her two children were emigrating to America, planning to join Mr. Peacock who was already working there. All were lost.

Pearce, Mr. Ernest	32		3rd	S				
Pears, Mr. Thomas Clinton	29	Isleworth, England	1st	S	New York City, NY			
Pears, Mrs. Thomas C. (Edith Wearne)	23	Isleworth, England	1st	S	New York City, NY	8		
Pecruic								see P okrnic
Pede, Mathilde F.								see Mrs. Leopold Weisz
Pedersen, Mr. Olaf	29	Sandefjord, Norway	3rd	S	Seattle, WA			
Peduzzi, Mr. Joseph	24	London, England	3rd	S	unknown			
Peel, Lily May								see Mrs. Jacques H. Futrelle
Pekoniemi, Mr. Edvard	21		3rd	S	New York City, NY			
Peltomaki, Mr. Nikolai Johannes	25	Finland	3rd	S	New York City, NY			
Peñasco y Castellana, Mr. Victor de Satode	18	Madrid, Spain	1st	C	New York City, NY			
Peñasco y Castellana, Mrs. Victor de Satode (Maria Soto y Vallejo)	17	Madrid, Spain	1st	C	New York City, NY	8		

Mr. and Mrs. **Peñasco y Castellana** had already been married for two years, having spent the entire time on their honeymoon. Wealthy beyond their dreams due to various fortunes left by his father and grandfather, the young couple had traveled Europe and Russia for most of that time, returning to Madrid only occasionally to check on the progress of the mansion they were having built. Due to the law at the time, his mother controlled their money and would send them drafts and they in turn sent her postcards showing where they were. The young couple decided to book a trip on *Titanic* as a lark and not tell his mother. To cover their tracks, Victor's butler remained behind in Paris and mailed the weekly card. This continued on even after *Titanic* sank and Victor had died. By Spanish law, Victor couldn't be declared dead without a body, and Maria could not inherit his money for 20 years without one. So one of the unidentified bodies buried at Halifax was declared to be Victor long enough for Maria to collect the inheritance.

Pengelly, Mr. Frederick W.	19	Gunnislake, England	2nd	S	unknown			Traveled with William J. Ware and friends Harry and Shadrach Gale.
Perkin, Mr. John H.	22	Devon, England	3rd	S	Saskatoon, Saskatchewan, Canada			see Braund–Dennis Group Notes.
Pernot, Mr. Rene		Paris, France	2nd	C	New York City, NY			Chauffer to Benjamin Guggenheim.
Perreault, Miss Mary Anne	30	Montreal, Quebec, Canada	1st	S	Montreal, Quebec, Canada	3		Maid to Mrs. Charles M. Hays.
Persson, Elna M.								see Mrs. Wilhelm Strom
Persson, Mr. Ernsk Ulrik	25	Stockholm, Sweden	3rd	S	Indian Harbor, IN	B		Traveled with sister Elna Strom and niece Selma Strom.
Peruschitz, Rev. Joseph M.	41	Scheyern, Germany	2nd	S	Minnesota			

Name *(Maiden Name)[Other Name]* *Names in italic indicate survivors*	Age	Residence	Class	E	Destination	L/B	Body # Recovered / Where Buried	Notes
Peter, Miss Anna [Mary]								see Miss Anna Joseph
Peter, Mrs. Joseph (Catherine Rizk)								see Mrs. Peter Joseph
Peter, Master Michael J.								see Master Michael Joseph
Peters, Miss Katie	26	County Tipperary, Ireland	3rd	Q	New York City, NY			
Peterson [Pedeerson], Mr. Marius	24	Denmark	3rd	S	unknown			
Petranec, Mrs. Matilda	28	Croatia	3rd	S	Harrisburg, PA			Mrs. Petranec was a widow. She traveled with Ignjac Hendekovic.
Petroff, Mr. Nedeca	19	Bulgaria	3rd	S	Chicago, IL			see Gumostnik, Bulgaria Group Notes
Petroff, Mr. Pentcho	29	Bulgaria	3rd	S	Chicago, IL			see Gumostnik, Bulgaria Group Notes
Petterson, Mr. Johan Emil	25	Sodermanland, Sweden	3rd	S	Chicago, IL			Traveled with sister Mrs. Johan Ahlin.
Pettersson, Miss Ellen Natalia	18	Stockholm, Sweden	3rd	S	Iron Mountain, MI			

Ellen Pettersson was emigrating with her friend Jenny Henriksson and the Skoog family. None of the group survived.

Peuchen, Major Arthur Godfrey	52	Toronto, Ontario, Canada	1st	S	Toronto, Ontario, Canada	6		

Canadian Army Major **Arthur Godfrey Peuchen** owned a chemical plant and several large tracks of forest land in Canada. He was also Vice-Commodore of the Royal Canadian Yacht Club and an officer in the Canadian Army. Because there was a shortage of trained seamen on *Titanic*, Peuchen was ordered by Second Officer Lightoller to get into and take command of Lifeboat 6. He left behind over $200,000 in cash in his room. Because he was a First Class passenger and he survived, he was called a coward in the Canadian newspapers and lost his business. Later, in World War I, he survived combat in the trenches, but was never promoted. After the war, he was again called a coward for surviving the war!

Phillips, Miss Alice Francis Louise	12	Devon, England	2nd	S	New Brighton, PA	12		Traveled with father Robert Phillips.
Phillips, Mr. Robert	43	Devon, England	2nd	S	New Brighton, PA			A widower, he traveled with his 12-year old daughter Alice.
Phillips, Miss Kate Florence	19	Worcester, England	2nd	S	Los Angeles, CA	11		

Miss **Kate Florence Phillips** was eloping with Mr. Henry Morley, and she was traveling under the name Kate Phillips Marshall. Kate became pregnant either shortly before leaving Southampton or while on *Titanic*. It wasn't until she was returning to England after a short stay in New York City that she discovered she was pregnant. Kate Marshall had a baby girl, born in January, 1913.

Pickard [Trembisky], Mr. Berk	32	London, England	3rd	S	unknown	9		He changed his name from Trembisky when he bought his ticket.
Pinsky, Miss Rosa	32	Brooklyn, NY	2nd	S	Brooklyn, NY	9		Returning home from visiting relatives in Warsaw, Poland.
Plotcharsky, Mr. Vasil			3rd	S				
Pokrnic [Pecruic], Mr. Mate	17	Croatia	3rd	S	Chicago, IL			
Pokrnic [Pecruic], Mr. Tome	24	Croatia	3rd	S	Chicago, IL			
Polk, Lucile								see Mrs. William E. Carter
Ponesell, Mr. Martin	34	Denmark	2nd	S	New York City, NY			
Portaluppi, Mr. Emilio Ilario G.	31	Milford, NH	2nd	C	Milford, NH	14		

Mr. **Emilio Portaluppi** was one of the very few survivors picked up by a lifeboat that went back for that purpose. By the time he was picked up, he had been in the water over two hours, yet managed to survive the intense cold.

Porter, Mr. Walter Chamberlain	46	Worcester, MA	1st	S	Worcester, MA		#207, buried in Worcester, MA	Traveled with Mr. George Clifford and Mr. John Maguire.
Posse, Sigrid								see Mrs. Carl J. Lindström
Potchett, Mr. George								see Mr. George Patchett
Potter, Olive								see Mrs. Boulton Earnshaw
Potter, Mrs. Thomas Jr. (Lily A. Wilson)	56	Philadelphia, PA	1st	C	Philadelphia, PA	7		Traveled with daughter Mrs. Boulton Earnshaw.
Pulbaum, Mr. Franz	27	New York City, NY	2nd	C	New York City, NY			

Name *(Maiden Name)[Other Name]* *Names in italic indicate survivors*	Age	Residence	Class	E	Destination	L/B	Body # Recovered / Where Buried	Notes
Q								
Quick Family								
Quick, Mrs. Frederick Charles (Jane Richards)	33	Detroit, MI	2nd	S	Detroit, MI	11		
Quick, Miss Phyllis May	2	Detroit, MI	2nd	S	Detroit, MI	11		Died by suicide in 1954.
Quick, Miss Winifred Vera	8	Detroit, MI	2nd	S	Detroit, MI	11		Winifred Quick died on July 4, 2002 at the age of 98.
Qurban, Latifa								see Mrs. Solomon Baclini
R								
Radeff, Mr. Alexander	27	Bulgaria	3rd	S	Chicago, IL			
Raihed [Raibid], Mr. Razi			3rd	C				Also listed as last name Raibid or Razi.
Ramell, Elizabeth								see Mrs. Ernest E. Nye
Rasmussen, Mrs. Rasmus (Lena Jakobson Solvang)	63	Norway	3rd	S	South Dakota			Often listed as Lena Solvang.
Razi, Anna (or Hannah)								see Mrs. Darwin Touma
Reed, Mr. James G.	19	Cardiff, So. Wales	3rd	S	unknown			
Reeves, Mr. David	36	Brighton, England	2nd	S	unknown			
Rekic, Mr. Tido	38	Bosnia	3rd	S	unknown			
Renouf, Mr. Peter Henry	34	Guernsey, England	2nd	S	Elizabeth, NJ			
Renouf, Mrs. Peter H. (Lillian Jefferys)	30	Guernsey, England	2nd	S	Elizabeth, NJ	12		

Mr. and Mrs. **Peter Renouf** were traveling with her brothers Clifford and Ernest Jefferys and family friend Herbert Denbury. They were all traveling together to Elizabeth, New Jersey. Everyone except Lillian Renouf were lost when *Titanic* sank.

Name	Age	Residence	Class	E	Destination	L/B	Body # Recovered / Where Buried	Notes
Reuchlin, Mr. John George	38	Rotterdam, Netherlands	1st	C	New York City, NY			

Mr. **John Reuchlin** was a director of the Holland America Line (HAL), a steamship company owned by the International Mercantile Marine, a corporation which also owned the White Star Line, owners of *Titanic.* The HAL had ordered two ships similar in size to *Titanic,* and Reuchlin was traveling on *Titanic* to see how it operated so he could recommend changes to the ships HAL was building.

Name	Age	Residence	Class	E	Destination	L/B	Body # Recovered / Where Buried	Notes
Reynaldo, Mrs. Encarnacion	28	Spain	2nd	S	New York City, NY	9		
Reynolds, Mr. Harold J.	21	London, England	3rd	S	Toronto, Ontario, Canada		#327, buried in Fairview Cemetery in Halifax.	
Rheims, Mr. George A.L.		Paris, France	1st	C	New York City, NY	A		Traveled with brother-in-law Mr. Joseph Loring.
Rice Family								
Rice, Master Albert	10	County Athlone, Ireland	3rd	Q	Spokane, WA			
Rice, Master Arthur	4	County Athlone, Ireland	3rd	Q	Spokane, WA			
Rice, Master Eric	7	County Athlone, Ireland	3rd	Q	Spokane, WA			
Rice, Master Eugene	2	County Athlone, Ireland	3rd	Q	Spokane, WA			
Rice, Master George Hugh	8	County Athlone, Ireland	3rd	Q	Spokane, WA			
Rice, Mrs. William (Margaret Norton)	39	County Athlone, Ireland	3rd	Q	Spokane, WA		#12, buried in Mt. Olivet Cemetery, Halifax	

Mrs. **Rice** was a widow; her husband was killed in a train wreck. She had traveled home to Ireland with her family, and was now traveling back to Spokane, Washington where she had lived for several years. None of the family survived.

Name	Age	Residence	Class	E	Destination	L/B	Body # Recovered / Where Buried	Notes
Richard, Mr. Emile	23	Paris, France	2nd	C	Montreal, Quebec, Canada			Traveled with the Mallet family.
Richards, Jane								see Mrs. Frederick C. Quick

Key: **Names** are in alphabetical order except where family members are grouped together. Names listed in italic were survivors. Names in parenthesis (name) are the maiden (or birth) name of the person. Names in brackets [name] are other names the passenger used. **Age** is the person's age at the time of the sinking. **Residence** is where the person's home was located. **Class** indicates the class the person was traveling. "**E**" indicates where the person embarked Titanic (**B** is for Belfast, Ireland; **C** is for Cherbourg, France; **S** is for Southampton, England and **Q** is for Queenstown (now Cobh) Ireland. **Destination** is where the passenger was traveling. **L/B** indicates which Lifeboat the person escaped on, if known. **Body Recovered / Where Buried** indicates in what sequence the body was recovered and where it was buried. **Family** groups are kept together and have dark shade fore easy reference and if there are any family notes they are listed after the last family name. Individuals with notes have the note after the name. Listings in light shade are designed only to assist the reader in following the text across the page.

Name *(Maiden Name)[Other Name]* *Names in italic indicate survivors*	Age	Residence	Class	E	Destination	L/B	Body # Recovered / Where Buried	Notes
Richards Family								
Richards, Master Sibley George	10 mo	Cornwall, England	2nd	S	Akron, OH	4		see Hocking-Richards Group Notes
Richards, Mrs. Sidney (Emily Hocking)	24	Cornwall, England	2nd	S	Akron, OH	4		see Hocking-Richards Group Notes
Richards, Master William Rowe	3	Cornwall, England	2nd	S	Akron, OH	4		see Hocking-Richards Group Notes
Ridsdale, Miss Lucy	50	London, England	2nd	S	Milwaukee, WI	13		
Riihiivuori, Miss Sanni [Susanna]	23	Finland	3rd	S	Coal Center, PA			Traveled with Maria Panula.
Ringhin i, Mr. Sante	22	New York City, NY	1st	C	New York City, NY		#232, buried in New York City, NY	Manservant to Mrs. John Stuart White.
Rintamaki, Mr. Matti	35	Finland	3rd	S	Sudbury, Ontario, Canada			Traveled with Matti Maenpaa, Lisakki Nivra and Nikolai Kallio.
Riordan, Miss Hannah	20	County Cork, Ireland	3rd	Q	New York City, NY	13		see Irish Contingent Group Notes
Risien, Mr. Samuel B.	70	Groesbeck, TX	3rd	S	Groesbeck, TX			
Risien, Mrs. Samuel B. (Emma Lellyet)	58	Groesbeck, TX	3rd	S	Groesbeck, TX			

Mr. **Samuel B. Risien** was wealthy as Mrs. Risien's family owned several diamond mines in Africa. Apparently Mr. Risien was carrying a large amount of diamonds on him and in their luggage. They were going back to Texas, traveling 3rd Class in order to avoid suspicion. If there were any diamonds on board, they are still at the bottom of the Atlantic Ocean.

Rizk, Catherine								see Mrs. Peter Joseph
Robbins, Mr. Victor		New York City, NY	1st	C	New York City, NY			Manservant to Mr. John Jacob Astor.
Robert, Mrs. Edward Scott (Elisabeth Walton McMillan)	43	St. Louis, MO	1st	S	St. Louis, MO	2		

Mrs. **Edward Scott Robert** was twice widowed, and was returning from a trip to Europe after the loss of her second husband. She was traveling with her daughter Georgette Madill, niece Elisabeth Allen and her maid Emilie Kreuchen, all of whom survived the trip.

Robins, Mr. Alexander A.	50	Yonkers, NY	3rd	S	Yonkers, NY		#119, buried in Yonkers, NY	Traveled with wife and nephew William Nancarrow.
Robins, Mrs. Alexander A. (Grace Charity Laury)	47	Yonkers, NY	3rd	S	Yonkers, NY		#7, buried in Yonkers, NY	Traveled with husband and nephew William Nancarrow.
Roebling, Mr. Washington Augustus II	31	Trenton, NJ	1st	S	Trenton, NJ			

Mr. **Washington A. Roebling** was a nephew of Colonel Washington A. Roebling, who was the builder of the Brooklyn Bridge in New York City. His grandfather was John A. Roebling, who actually designed the bridge, and helped build it until his death, when his son took over. Washington Roebling was the President of the Roebling Wire Company. He had been on vacation in Europe, having gone there with a friend, Stephen W. Blackwell. While in Europe, they met the George Wick family and Miss Caroline Bonnell. Roebling helped load several women and children into lifeboats, and was last seen talking to Mr. John Jacob Astor.

Rogers, Mr. Reginald Harry	19	Devon, England	2nd	S	Wilkes-Barre, PA			
Rogers, Mr. William J.	29	Wales	3rd	S	unknown			
Rogers, Selena								see Mrs. Arthur Cook
Romaine, Mr. Charles Hallace	45	London, England	1st	S	New York City, NY	9		

A professional gambler, **Charles Romaine** traveled under the name Harry Romain (without the "e".) He died in 1922 after being struck by a taxi in New York City (New York City cab drivers were a hazard even then!)

Rommetvedt, Mr. Karl K.K.	49	Norway	3rd	S	New York City, NY			
Rood, Mr. Hugh R.	39	Seattle, WA	1st	S	New York City, NY			

Mr. **Hugh R. Rood** was vacationing in Europe with his wife, and was making a short business trip back to New York City. His wife remained in Europe and was not with him.

Rosblom Family								
Rosblom, Miss Salli Helena	2	Finland	3rd	S	Astoria, OR			
Rosblom, Mr. Viktor R.	18	Finland	3rd	S	Astoria, OR			
Rosblom, Mrs. Viktor (Helena W.)	41	Finland	3rd	S	Astoria, OR			

The **Rosblom** family was emigrating to Oregon. Another child, a 10-year old boy, refused to go on a ship *"to drown"* and remained in Finland with family members.

Rosen, Leah								see Mrs. Samual Aks
Rosenbaum [Russell], Miss Edith L.	33	Paris, France	1st	C	New York City, NY	11		

Edith Rosenbaum was a famous fashion correspondent. During World War I, she was the first female war correspondent, spending time with the troops in the trenches.

Name *(Maiden Name)[Other Name]* *Names in italic indicate survivors*	Age	Residence	Class	E	Destination	L/B	Body # Recovered / Where Buried	Notes
Rosenshine [Thorne], Mr. George	46	New York City, NY	1st	C	New York City, NY		#16, buried in Brooklyn, NY	

George Rosenshine was on vacation in Europe and he traveled under the name George Thorne because he was traveling with his mistress Gertrude Thorne.

Ross, Mr. John Hugo	36	Winnipeg, Manitoba, Canada	1st	C	Winnipeg, Manitoba, Canada			

Mr. **John Hugo Ross** was returning home from an extended Asian and African tour. He traveled with Thomson Beattie and Thomas McCaffry. He was so ill with dysentery he had to be carried aboard *Titanic* on a stretcher. None of the survivors recalled seeing him after *Titanic* left Cherbourg.

Roth, Miss Sarah A.	26	London, England	3rd	S	New York City, NY	C		

Sarah Roth was emigrating to America to get married. One week after *Carpathia* arrived in New York, Sarah Roth was married and her bridesmaid was fellow passenger Emily Badman.

Rothes, the Countess of								see Dyer-Edwards, Mrs. Noël Lucy Martha
Rothschild, Mr. Martin	47	New York City, NY	1st	C	New York City, NY			Returning from vacation with his wife.
Rothschild, Mrs. Martin (Elizabeth L. Barrett)	53	New York City, NY	1st	C	New York City, NY	6		

Although her husband went down with the ship, **Mrs. Rothschild** managed to save her Pomeranian dog. She was a devout Catholic, her husband was Jewish. In later years she was very active in the Archdiocese of New York, and was awarded the Papal Distinguished Merit Cross.

Rouse, Mr. Richard H.	50	Kent, England	3rd	S	Cleveland, OH			
Rowe, Mr. Alfred G.	59	Middlesex, England	1st	S	Donley County (McLean), TX.		#109, buried in Liverpool, England	

Mr. **Alfred Rowe** and his brothers owned almost 100 sections (100 square miles) of Texas ranch land. He was making one of his several annual trips to Texas to check on his holdings.

Rowley, Annie Louise								see Mrs. Thomas Meek
Rugg, Miss Emily	21	Guernsey, England	2nd	S	Wilmington, DE	12		
Rush, Mr. Alfred George J.	16	Kent, England	3rd	S	Detroit, MI			Traveled with the Frank Goldsmith family. He celebrated his 16th birthday on the ship.
Russell, Edith								see Edith L. Rosenbaum
Ryan, Mr. Edward	23	County Tipperary, Ireland	3rd	Q	New York City, NY	14		

Because he had a towel over his head to keep warm, many surviving passengers thought **Edward Ryan** was a woman, or a guy dressed as a woman in order to get into a lifeboat, a myth that lives on to this day.

Ryan, Mr. Patrick		County Limerick, Ireland	3rd	Q	Bronx, NY			

Ryerson Family

Ryerson, Mr. Alfred Larned	61	Haverford, PA	1st	C	Cooperstown, NY			
Ryerson, Mrs. Arthur Larned (Emily Maria Borie)	48	Haverford, PA	1st	C	Cooperstown, NY	4		
Ryerson, Miss Emily Borie	18	Haverford, PA	1st	C	Cooperstown, NY	4		
Ryerson, Master John Borie	13	Haverford, PA	1st	C	Cooperstown, NY	4		
Ryerson, Miss Suzette Parker	21	Haverford, PA	1st	C	Cooperstown, NY	4		

Mr. **Alfred Ryerson** was a wealthy businessman. His family had been on vacation in Europe when they got news that their eldest son, Yale University student Arthur Ryerson Jr. had been killed in an automobile accident. The family was in mourning, and caught the first ship going to New York, which happened to be *Titanic*. As Lifeboat 4, the lifeboat that carried many wives and children of wealthy passengers was being loaded, Ryerson tried to get 13-year old John into the lifeboat. Second Officer Lightoller refused, but Ryerson said he should go because he was only 13 and should remain with his mother. Lightoller relented, but made the comment *"no more boys"*.

S

Saad, Mr. Amin			3rd	C				
Saalfeld, Mr. Adolphe	47	Manchester, England	1st	S	New York City, NY	3		
Sadlier, Mr. Matthew	20	County Leitrim, Ireland	3rd	C	Lakewood, NJ			

Name *(Maiden Name)[Other Name]* *Names in italic indicate survivors*	Age	Residence	Class	E	Destination	L/B	Body # Recovered / Where Buried	Notes
Sadowitz, Mr. Harry	17	London, England	3rd	S	Providence, RI			
Sæther [Sæter, Sather], Mr. Simon S.	43	Johannesburg, So uth Africa	3rd	S	unknown		#32, buried in Fairview Cemetery, Halifax	
Sage Family								
Sage, Miss Ada	9	Peterborough, England	3rd	S	Jacksonville, FL			
Sage, Miss Constance G.	7	Peterborough, England	3rd	S	Jacksonville, FL			
Sage, Miss Dorothy	13	Peterborough, England	3rd	S	Jacksonville, FL			
Sage, Mr. Douglas B.	18	Peterborough, England	3rd	S	Jacksonville, FL			
Sage, Mr. Frederick	16	Peterborough, England	3rd	S	Jacksonville, FL			
Sage, Mr. George John	19	Peterborough, England	3rd	S	Jackso nville, FL			
Sage, Mr. John George	44	Peterborough, England	3rd	S	Jacksonville, FL			
Sage, Mrs. John G. (Annie Elizabeth Cazaly)	44	Peterborough, England	3rd	S	Jacksonville, FL			
Sage, Miss Stella Anne	20	Peterborough, England	3rd	S	Jacksonville, FL			
Sage, Master Thomas H.	4	Peterborough, England	3rd	S	Jacksonville, FL			
Sage, Master William	11	Peterborough, England	3rd	S	Jacksonville, FL		#67, buried at sea	

Mr. **John Sage** and his son George had worked in Canada and Florida, where they bought land. They then returned to England to sell their business and move the family. All eleven members of the Sage family boarded *Titanic*, and none of them survived. The Sage family is the largest family group lost. Only the body of William Sage was ever recovered.

Sägesser, Miss Emma	24	Paris, France	1st	C	New York City, NY	9		Maid to Madame Leontine Aubart. see Mrs. Edgar J. Meyer
Saks, Leila								
Salander, Mr. Karl J.	24	Tjarby, Sweden	3rd	S	Red Wing, MN			
Salkjelsvik, Miss Anna	21	Alesund, Norway	3rd	S	Proctor, MN	?		

Anna Salkjelsvik traveled with Karen Abelseth, Olaus Abelseth, Adolf Humblen, Sigrid Moen and Peter A.L.A.Soholt.

Salonen, Mr. Johan W.	39		3rd	S	Aberdeen, WA			
Samaan Family (father, two sons)								
Samaan, Mr. Elias	18	Syria	3rd	C	Wilkes Barre, PA			
Samaan, Mr. Hanna	40	Syria	3rd	C	Wilkes Barre, PA			
Samaan, Mr. Youssef	16	Syria	3rd	S	Wilkes Barre, PA			

Mr. **Hanna Samaan** and his two sons Elias and Youssef were emigrating to America. All three were lost.

Sandstrom Family								
Sandstrom, Miss Beatrice Irene	1	San Francisco, CA	3rd	S	San Francisco, CA	13		
Sandstrom, Mrs. Hjalmar (Agnes C. Bengtsson)	24	San Francisco, CA	3rd	S	San Francisco, CA	13		
Sandstrom, Miss Marguerite Rut	4	San Francisco, CA	3rd	S	San Francisco, CA	13		

Mrs. Hjalmar Sandstrom and her daughters Marguerite and Beatrice had been visiting family in Sweden. They were traveling with friends Elan and Selma Strom. The Sandstrom's survived, the Strom's did not.

Sap [Sop], Mr. Jules	25	Belgium	3rd	S	Detroit, MI	11?		Traveled with Mr. Jean Scheerlinckx and Theodore de Mulder.
Saundercock, Mr. William H.	19	Cornwall, England	3rd	S	unknown			Traveled with Mr.Ernest Cann.
Sawyer, Mr. Frederick C.	51	Hampshire, England	3rd	S	Halley, MI		#284, buried in Fairview Cemetery, Halifax	
Scanlan, Mr. James	22	County Limerick, Ireland	3rd	Q	New York City, NY			
Schabert, Mrs. Paul (Emma Mock)	35	New York City, NY	1st	C	New York City, NY	11		Returning home from vacation with her brother Philipp E. Mock.
Scheerlinckx, Mr. Jean	29	Belgium	3rd	S	Detroit, MI	11		Traveled with Jules Sap and Theodore de Mulder.
Sdycoff, Mr. Todor	42	Bulgaria	3rd	S	Chicago, IL			
Sedgwick, Mr. Charles Frederick W.	25	Liverpool, England	2nd	S	Mexico			

Charles F.W. Sedgwick had only been married for a week. He left his wife at home and was traveling to Mexico on business.

Name *(Maiden Name)[Other Name]* *Names in italic indicate survivors*	Age	Residence	Class	E	Destination	L/B	Body # Recovered / Where Buried	Notes
Serreplan, Miss Auguste	30	Bryn Mawr, PA	1st	C	Bryn Mawr, PA	4		Maid to Mrs. William E. Carter.
Seward, Mr. Frederic Kimber	34	New York City, NY	1st	S	New York City, NY	7		

Frederic Seward was a corporate lawyer. After Seward and 704 additional people had been rescued by Captain Arthur Rostron and the crew of *Carpathia*, Seward organized a group of *Titanic* survivors and set out to honor their rescuers. They collected money to buy Rostron a silver Loving Cup and medals for all 328 of *Carpathia's* crew. The remaining money was donated to the crew, each of whom received an equivalent of two months salary. Except for the Duff-Gordon's, there was no attempt made to reward the surviving *Titanic* crew for helping save the survivors.

Name	Age	Residence	Class	E	Destination	L/B	Body	Notes
Sharp, Mr. Percival J.	27	Hornsey, England	2nd	S	New York City, NY			Traveled with Henry J. Beauchamp.
Shaughnesay, Mr. Patrick		Ireland	3rd	Q	New York City, NY			
Shawah, Mr. Youssef Ibrahim	30	Syria	3rd	C	New York City, NY			
Shellard, Mr. Frederick B.	55	Troy, NY	3rd	S	Troy, NY			

Frederick Shellard was returning from a vacation in England where he had spent several months visiting relatives. Traveling with him was his friend Thomas Everett. Neither survived the trip.

Name	Age	Residence	Class	E	Destination	L/B	Body	Notes
Shelley, Mrs. William (Imanita Parrish Hall)	25	Deer Lodge, MT	2nd	S	Deer Lodge, MT	12		Traveled with her mother Lutie Parrish.
Shine, Miss Ellen	20	County Cork, Ireland	3rd	Q	New York City, NY	?		Died in 1993, aged 101.
Shorney, Mr. Charles J.	22	Brighton, England	3rd	S	New York City, NY			
Shutes, Miss Elizabeth W.	40	Greenwich, CT	1st	S	Greenwich, CT	3		Governess to Miss Margaret Graham. see Mrs. Tyrell William Cavendish
Siegel, Julia Florence								
Silvén, Miss Lyyli K.	18	Finland	2nd	S	Minneapolis, MN	16		Traveled with Rev. and Mrs. William Lahtinen.
Silverthorne, Mr. Spencer Victor	35	St. Louis, MO	1st	S	St. Louis, MO	5		
Silvey, Mr. William Baird	50	Duluth, MN	1st	S	Duluth, MN			
Silvey, Mrs. William Baird (Alice Munger)	39	Duluth, MN	1st	S	Duluth, MN	11		
Simmons, Mr. John	39	unknown	3rd	S	unknown			
Simonius-Blumer, Col. Alfons	56	Basel, Switzerland	1st	S	New York City, NY	3		Traveled to New York on business with Dr. Max Staehelin -Maeglin.
Sincock, Miss Maude	20	Cornwall, England	2nd	S	Hancock, MI	11		Traveled with friend Mrs. Agnes Davies and her son John Davies.
Sirayanian, Mr. Arsun	22	Turkey	3rd	C	Brantford, Ontario, Canada			
Sirota [Serota], Mr. Maurice	20	London, England	3rd	S	New York City, NY			
Siukonnen [Siukkonen, Sinkkonen], Miss Anna	30	Finland	2nd	S	Brighton, MA	10		Traveled with Lylli Silven
Sivic, Mr. Husein	40	Bosnia	3rd	S	Harrisburg, PA			
Sivola, Mr. Antti W.	21	unknown	3rd	S	Mountain Home, ID			
Sjöblom, Miss Anna Sofia	18	Finland	3rd	S	Olympia, WA	16		Traveled with Karl and Jakob Wiklund.
Sjöstedt, Mr. Ernst A.	59	Sault St. Marie, Ontario, Canada	2nd	S	Sault St. Marie, Ontario, Canada			
Skoog Family								
Skoog, Master Harald	4	Iron Mountain, MI	3rd	S	Iron Mountain, MI			
Skoog, Master Karl	10	Iron Mountain, MI	3rd	S	Iron Mountain, MI			
Skoog, Miss Mabel	9	Iron Mountain, MI	3rd	S	Iron Mountain, MI			
Skoog, Miss Margit	2	Iron Mountain, MI	3rd	S	Iron Mountain, MI			
Skoog, Mr. William	40	Iron Mountain, MI	3rd	S	Iron Mountain, MI			
Skoog, Mrs. William (Anna B. Karlsson)	43	Iron Mountain, MI	3rd	S	Iron Mountain, MI			

Mr. **William Skoog**, his wife, four children and two friends Jenny Henriksson and Ellen Pettersson were all traveling together. None of the eight survived.

Name	Age	Residence	Class	E	Destination	L/B	Body	Notes
Slabenoff, Mr. Petco	42	Bulgaria	3rd	S	unknown			
Slater, Miss Hilda Mary	30	Halifax, Nova Scotia, Canada	2nd	Q	Halifax, Nova Scotia, Canada	13		
Sleman, Mr. Richard J.	35	Cornwall, England	2nd	S	Nashua, NH			
Slocovski, Mr. Selman	31	Poland	3rd	S	unknown			

Name *(Maiden Name)[Other Name]* *Names in italic indicate survivors*	Age	Residence	Class	E	Destination	L/B	Body # Recovered / Where Buried	Notes
Sloper, Mr. William Thompson	28	New Britain, CT	1st	S	New Britain, CT	7		

Mr. **William Sloper** was a wealthy stockbroker, returning from a vacation in Europe. He helped several women get into lifeboats, and Dorothy Gibson insisted he join her in Lifeboat 7. First Officer Murdoch was in charge, and since there weren't any additional women or children around, he allowed Sloper to get in. He found a towel and placed it over his head to keep the cold out. When *Carpathia* picked up Lifeboat 7, Sloper still had the towel over his head, and the rumor got started that he had dressed as a woman to get into a lifeboat, (the same problem Mr. Edward Ryan had.). This was published in several newspapers, and Sloper spent years trying to convince people that he hadn't done so. Sloper also had a dog with him, but it did not survive.

Slow, Alice Adelaide								see Mrs. Charles A. Louch
Smart, Mr. John Montgomery	56	New York City, NY	1st	S	New York City, NY			
Smiljanovic, Mr. Mile	37	Austria	3rd	S	New York City, NY			
Smith [Schmidt], Mr. Augustus	26	London, England	2nd	S	Newark, NJ			
Smith, Mr. James Clinch	56	Long Island, NY	1st	C	Long Island, NY			

James Clinch Smith was the brother-in-law of the world-famous architect Stanford White. White kept a mistress, an aspiring young actress named Evelyn Nesbit. In 1906 Harry Thaw, the estranged husband of Evelyn Nesbit, murdered White on the roof of Madison Square Garden. Smith witnessed the murder and was part of the sensational "trial of the century" that followed. Smith was traveling with his good friend Archibald Gracie.

Smith, Mr. Lucian Philip	24	Huntington, WV	1st	S	Huntington, WV			
Smith, Mrs. Lucian Philip (Mary Eloise Hughes)	18	Huntington, WV	1st	S	Huntington, WV	6		

Mr. **Lucian Smith** and his wife Mary were returning from their honeymoon in Europe, accompanied by their pet dog. He and the dog did not survive. Later, Mary Smith would marry *Titanic* survivor Robert Daniel.

Smith, Miss Marion	40	London, England	2nd	S	Washington, DC	9		
Smith, Mr. Richard William		Surrey, England	1st	S	unknown			
Smyth, Miss Julia	20	County Covan, Ireland	3rd	Q	New York City, NY	13		
Snyder, Mr. John Pillsbury	24	Minneapolis, MN	1st	S	Minneapolis, MN	7		Traveling on honeymoon.
Snyder, Mrs. John Pillsbury (Nelle Stevenson)	23	Minneapolis, MN	1st	S	Minneapolis, MN	7		Traveling on honeymoon.
Sobey, Mr. Samuel J. Hayden	25	Houghton, MI	2nd	S	Houghton, MI			Traveled with Fred Banfield and Joseph Fillbrook.
Søholt, Mr. Peter A.L.A.	19	Alesund, Norway	3rd	S	Minneapolis, MN			

Peter Soholt traveled with cousin Olaus Abelseth and friends Sigrid Moen, Karen Abelseth, Anna Salkjelsvik and Adolf Humblen.

Solomon, Mr. Abraham L.	43	New York City, NY	1st	S	New York City, NY	1		
Solvang, Lena Jacobson								see Mrs. Rasmus Rasmussen
Somerton, Mr. Francis William	30	Cheltenham, England	3rd	S	New York City, NY			
Soto y Vallejo, Miss Maria								see Mrs. Victor de Penasco y Castellana
Spector, Mr. Woolf	23	London, England	3rd	S	unknown			
Spedden Family								
Spedden, Mr. Frederick Oakley	45	Tuxedo Park, NY	1st	C	Tuxedo Park, NY	3		
Spedden, Mrs. Frederick Oakley (Margaretta Corning Stone)	40	Tuxedo Park, NY	1st	C	Tuxedo Park, NY	3		
Spedden, Master Robert Douglas	6	Tuxedo Park, NY	1st	C	Tuxedo Park, NY	3		

The **Spedden Family** was returning from vacation in Europe. They traveled with maid Helen A. Wilson and the son's nurse Elizabeth M. Burns. One of the most famous existing photos taken on *Titanic* before it left Queenstown is of young Robert spinning a top on the boat deck while his father looks on. Three years later, nine-year old Robert was struck and killed by a car near his family summer home. It was the first recorded automobile verses pedestrian fatality in the state of Maine.

Spencer, Mr. William Augustus	57	Paris, France	1st	C	Brooklyn, NY			
Spencer, Mrs. William A. (Marie Eugenie)		Paris, France	1st	C	Brooklyn, NY	6		Traveled with husband William and maid Elise Lurette.
Spinner [Skinner], Mr. Henry J.	32	Worcester, England	3rd	S	Gloversville, MA			

Name *(Maiden Name)[Other Name]* *Names in italic indicate survivors*	Age	Residence	Class	E	Destination	L/B	Body # Recovered / Where Buried	Notes
Stählin-Maeglin, Dr. Max	32	Basel, Switzerland	1st	S	New York City, NY	3		
Staneff, Mr. Ivan	23	Bulgaria	3rd	S	Chicago, IL			
Stankovic, Mr. Jovan	33	Croatia	3rd	C	New York City, NY			
Stanley, Miss Amy Elsie	24	Oxford, England	3rd	S	New Haven, CT	C		
Stanley, Mr. Edward R.	21	Bristol, England	3rd	S	Cleveland, OH			Traveled with Ernest Crease
Stanlick, Cordelia								see Mrs. William A. Lobb
Stanton, Mr. Samuel Ward	41	New York City, NY	2nd	S	New York City, NY			
Stauffer, Marion								see Mrs. Frederick R. Kenyon
Stead, Mr. William Thomas	62	Middlesex, England	1st	S	New York City, NY			

William Stead was a world famous author and journalist, traveling to New York to at the request of President William Howard Taft to address a peace congress at Carnegie Hall. In 1886 Stead wrote a fictional article entitled *"How the Mail Steamer Went Down in Mid-Atlantic, by a Survivor"* in which a steam ship collides with another ship and there is a large loss of life because of a shortage of lifeboats. Then in 1892 he wrote another piece of fiction entitled *"From the Old World to the New"* about an accident involving a ship that collided with an iceberg. The night *Titanic* sank, he was at a large dinner gathering and was telling stories, one which was about an Egyptian mummy that had a curse, and everyone who came into contact with it died. One of the survivors of the sinking told the story to a newspaper reporter, and it soon made the rounds that there was an Egyptian mummy on *Titanic* and it's curse is what caused it to sink. Stead died much like his fictional characters. The "urban legend" mummy story still makes the rounds on the Internet.

Name	Age	Residence	Class	E	Destination	L/B	Body #	Notes
Stehli, Margaretha								see Mrs. Maxmilian Frolicher-Stehli
Stengel, Mr. Charles Emil Henry	54	Newark, NJ	1st	C	Newark, NJ	1		
Stengel, Mrs. Charles Emil Henry (Annie May Morris)	43	Newark, NJ	1st	C	Newark, NJ	5		

Mrs. Charles Stengel was placed into a lifeboat but her husband couldn't join her. He later got into another lifeboat and they met up on *Carpathia*. Mrs. Stengel suffered several broken ribs when Dr. Henry Frauenthal jumped into the lifeboat and landed on top of her.

Name	Age	Residence	Class	E	Destination	L/B	Body #	Notes
Stephenson, Mrs. Walter B. (Martha Eustis)	52	Haverford, PA	1st	C	Haverford, PA	4		

Talk about bad timing. In April 1906 **Mrs. Stephenson** was staying at the St. Francis Hotel in downtown San Francisco when the great San Francisco earthquake struck, dumping her out of her bed and forcing her to flee San Francisco on foot. On another April night six years later, Mrs. Stephenson found herself in the center of another tragedy, climbing into a lifeboat in time to watch the great *Titanic* sink.

Name	Age	Residence	Class	E	Destination	L/B	Body #	Notes
Sternin, Miriam								see Mrs. Sinai Kantor
Stevenson, Nelle								see Mrs. John Pillsbury Snyder
Stewart, Mr. Albert A.	54	Cincinnati, OH	1st	C	Cincinnati, OH			
Stokes, Mr. Philip J.	25	Kent, England	2nd	S	Detroit, MI		#81, buried at sea	
Stone, Margaretta Corning								see Mrs. Frederick Oakley Spedden
Stone, Mrs. George N. (Martha Evelyn)	62	New York City, NY	1st	S	New York City, NY	6		

Mrs. George Stone, a widow, was returning from a vacation in Europe and was accompanied by her maid Amelie Icard. When Lifeboat 6 was lowered into the water, the drain plug wasn't in place and the lifeboat started to fill with water. Once located, the plug couldn't be inserted into the hole so that it would stay, so Mrs. Stone spent the entire seven hours she was in the lifeboat standing on the plug to keep it from coming loose and flooding the lifeboat.

Name	Age	Residence	Class	E	Destination	L/B	Body #	Notes
Storey, Mr. Thomas	51	Liverpool, England	3rd	S			#261, buried in Fairview Cemetery, Halifax	see American Lines Group Notes
Stoyehoff, Mr. Ilia	19	Bulgaria	3rd	S	Chicago, IL			see Gumostnik, Bulgaria Group Notes
Strandberg, Miss Ida S.	22	Abo, Finland	3rd	S	New York City, NY			
Strandén, Mr. Juho	31	Finland	3rd	S	Duluth, MN	9		
Straus, Mr. Isidor	67	New York City, NY	1st	S	New York City, NY		#96, buried in Bronx, NY	
Straus, Mrs. Isidor (Ida Blun)	63	New York City, NY	1st	S	New York City, NY			

Mr. and Mrs. **Isador Straus** were returning from a vacation in Europe. Mrs. Straus' maid Ellen Bird and his manservant John Farthing accompanied them. Straus was the owner of R.H. Macy's Department Store, and during the American Civil War had been a blockade-runner for the Confederacy. As the lifeboats were being loaded, Mrs. Straus was offered a seat in one, and when she found out Mr. Straus could not join her, she refused to get it, telling her husband *"We have lived together many years. I will not be separated from my husband. As we have lived, so will we die. Together."* When it was suggested that, because of his advanced age it would be ok for Mr. Straus to join his wife, he replied *"No. I do not wish any distinction in my favor which is not granted others."* The Strauses ordered their maid Ellen Bird into the lifeboat, and then they sat down on chairs on "A" deck to watch events around them. They were last seen heading to their cabin, which is probably where they died. Mrs. Straus was one of the four First Class women to die.

Name (Maiden Name)[Other Name] *Names in italic indicate survivors*	Age	Residence	Class	E	Destination	L/B	Body # Recovered / Where Buried	Notes
Strilic, Mr. Ivan	27	Croatia	3rd	S	Chicago, IL			
Ström, Miss Selma M.	2	Indiana Harbor, IN	3rd	S	Indiana Harbor, IN			Traveled with mother Elna and uncle Ernst Persson.
Ström, Mrs. Wilhelm (Elna M. Persson)	29	Indiana Harbor, IN	3rd	S	Indiana Harbor, IN			Traveled with daughter Selma and brother Ernst Persson.
Strouse, Blanche								see Mrs. Leo D. Greenfield
Sunderland, Mr. Victor F.	19	London, England	3rd	S	Cleveland, OH	B		
Sundman, Mr. Johan J.	44	Munsala, Finland	3rd	S	Cheyenne, WY	15		
Sutehall, Mr. Henry Jr.	26	Buffalo, NY	3rd	S	Buffalo, NY			Returning home from a two-year world tour.
Sutherland, Lucy Christina Wallace								see Lady Cosmo Duff-Gordon
Sutton, Mr. Frederick	61	Haddonfield, NJ	1st	S	Haddenfield, NJ		#46, buried at sea	
Svensson, Mr. Johan	74	Reftele, Sweden	3rd	S	Effington Rut, SD			

Mr. **Johan Svensson** had no living relatives in Sweden, so his son Johan Ekstrom had gone to Sweden to bring him back to South Dakota to live with him. Neither survived the voyage.

Svensson, Mr. Johan C.	14	Sweden	3rd	S	Beresford, SD	13		
Svensson, Mr. Olof	24	Osby, Sweden	3rd	S	unknown			
Swane, Mr. George	26	Montreal, Quebec, Canada	2nd	S	Montreal, Quebec, Canada		#294, buried in Fairview Cemetery, Halifax	Chauffeur to Mr. Hudson Allison.
Sweet, Mr. George	14	Somerset, England	2nd	S	Barnardsville, NJ			Traveled with parents Samuel and Jane Herman and two sisters.
Swift, Mrs. Frederick J. (Margaret Welles Barron)	46	Brooklyn, NY	1st	S	Brooklyn, NY	8		

Mrs. Frederick J. Swift traveled with friends Dr. Alice Leader, Frederick R. Kenyon and Marion Kenyon.

Sylfven, Anna								see Mrs. William Lahtinen

T

Tate, Charlotte								see Mrs. Harvey Collyer
Taussig Family								
Taussig, Mr. Emil	52	New York City, NY	1st	S	New York City, NY			
Taussig, Mrs. Emil (Tillie Mandelbaum)	39	New York City, NY	1st	S	New York City, NY	8		
Taussig, Miss Ruth	18	New York City, NY	1st	S	New York City, NY	8		
Taylor, Mr. Elmer Zebley	48	London, England	1st	S	East Orange, NJ	5		Traveled with wife Juliet and business partner Fletcher Williams.
Taylor, Mrs. Elmer Z. (Juliet Cummins Wright)		London, England	1st	S	East Orange, NJ	5		Traveled with husband Elmer.
Taylor, Mr. Percy Cornelius	32	London, England	2nd	S	unknown			see Musician's Group Notes
Temple, Lutie Davis								see Mrs. Samuel E. Parrish
Tenglin, Mr. Gunnar Isidor	25	Stockholm, Sweden	3rd	S	Burlington, IA	A		
Thayer, Florence Briggs								see Mrs. John B. Cummings
Thayer Family								
Thayer, Mr. John [Jack] Borland, Jr.	17	Haverford, PA	1st	C	Haverford, PA	B,12		
Thayer, Mr. John Borland	49	Haverford, PA	1st	C	Haverford, PA			
Thayer, Mrs. John B. (Marion Longstreth Morris)	39	Haverford, PA	1st	C	Haverford, PA	4		

Mr. **John B. Thayer**, his wife Marion and son John Jr. (Jack) were returning to Pennsylvania after an extended vacation in Europe. Thayer was a Vice-President of the Pennsylvania Railroad. Mrs. Thayer was placed into Lifeboat 4, but Mr. Thayer and her son weren't allowed to get in. Her last sight of them was as they stood with John Jacob Astor watching the lifeboat being rowed away. As *Titanic* was sinking, young Jack ended up in the water, and somehow managed to get onto overturned Collapsible Lifeboat B, and survived. He met up with his mother on *Carpathia*. Mr. John Thayer did not survive. When Mrs. Thayer and Jack arrived in New York, the Pennsylvania Railroad sent a private train to pick them up and take them home. Jack killed himself in 1945 after learning his son had died in combat in World War II.

Name *(Maiden Name)[Other Name]* *Names in italic indicate survivors*	Age	Residence	Class	E	Destination	L/B	Body # Recovered / Where Buried	Notes
Theobald, Mr. Thomas L.	34	Kent, England	3rd	S	Detroit, MI		#176, buried at sea	

Mr. **Thomas Theobald** was emigrating to America, and traveled with friends Frank and Emily Goldsmith. As *Titanic* was sinking, he gave his wedding ring to Emily to give onto his wife, which she did.

Thomas Family								
Thomas, Mrs. Alexander [Thelma]	16	Lebanon	3rd	C	Wilkes-Barre, PA	14		
Thomas, Master Assad A.	5 mo	Lebanon	3rd	C	Wilkes-Barre, PA	16		
Thomas, Mr. Charles		Lebanon	3rd	C	Wilkes-Barre, PA			

Mrs. Alexander Thomas was traveling with her brother Charles Thomas and her infant son Assad. As *Titanic* was sinking, Thelma and Charles were split up, and Charles had little Assad with him. Charles gave the baby to Winnie Troutt to take care of because he couldn't find his sister. Thelma was reunited with her son on *Carpathia*. Charles was lost.

Thomas, Mr. John Jr.	15	unknown	3rd	C	unknown			
Thomas, Mr. Tannous		Syria	3rd	C	Youngstown, OH			
Thomson, Mr. Alexander M.	36	Scotland	3rd	S	unknown			
Thorne, Mr. George								Assumed name. See Mr. George Rosenshine.
Thorne, Miss Gertrude Maybelle		New York City, NY	1st	C	New York City, NY	D		

George Thorne was in reality George Rosenshine. He was traveling back from a European vacation with his mistress **Gertrude Thorne,** so in order not to arouse suspicion, he was traveling under the name George Thorne.

Thorneycroft, Mr. Percival	36	London, England	3rd	S	Clinton, NY			
Thorneycroft, Mrs. Percival (Florence Kate White)	32	London, England	3rd	S	Clinton, NY	12		Traveled with husband and a famliy friend Robert Guest.
Thorpe, Lillian E.								see Mrs. William E. Minahan
Thuillard, Marie M.								see Mrs. Amin S. Jerwan
Tikkanen, Mr. Juho	32	Finland	3rd	S	New York City, NY			
Tobin, Margaret								see Brown, Mrs. James J."Molly"
Tobin, Mr. Roger		County Tipperary, Ireland	3rd	Q	New York City, NY			
Todoroff, Mr. Lalio	23	Bulgaria	3rd	S	Chicago, IL			
Toerber, Mr. Ernest W.	44	London, England	3rd	S	unknown			
Tomlin, Mr. Ernest Portage	22	Middlesex, England	3rd	S	unknown		#50, buried at sea	
Toogood, Carrie Constance								see Mrs. Herbert F. Chaffee
Toomey, Miss Ellen	50	Indianapolis, IN	2nd	S	Indianapolis, IN	9		
Torfa, Mr. Assad	20	Syria	3rd	C	unknown			
Törnquist, Mr. William Henry	25	Boston, MA	3rd	S	New York City, NY	A,15		see American Lines Group Notes
Toufik, Mr. Nahil	17	Syria	3rd	C	unknown			
Touma Family								
Touma, Mrs. Darwis (Hannah [Anna] Youssef Razi)	29	Syria	3rd	C	Dowagiac, MI	C		Emigrating to America with children, to join husband in Michigan.
Touma, Master Georges [George Thomas]	7	Syria	3rd	C	Dowagiac, MI	C		
Touma, Miss Maria Youssef [Mary Thomas]	9	Syria	3rd	C	Dowagiac, MI	C		
Towner, Mary Aline								see Mrs. Alexander O. Holverson
Trainer, Winnie [Minnie]								see Mrs. William Coutts
Trembisky, Mr. Berk								see Mr. Berk Pickard
Trevaskis, Addie								see Mrs. Arthur H. Wells
Troupiansky, Mr. Moses A.	23	London, England	2nd	S	unknown			
Trout, Mrs. William H.	28	Columbus, OH	2nd	S	Columbus, OH	9		

Name *(Maiden Name)[Other Name]* *Names in italic indicate survivors*	Age	Residence	Class	E	Destination	L/B	Body # Recovered / Where Buried	Notes
Troutt, Miss Edwina [Winnie] Celia	27	Bath, England	2nd	S	Auburndale, MA	16?		

Winnie Troutt was traveling to America to be with her sister who was having a baby. As *Titanic* was sinking, she took responsibility for baby Assad Thomas when it was determined the child's uncle Charles Thomas would not be getting into a lifeboat. In later years Winnie was very popular at the various *Titanic* survivors meetings and shows. She appeared in many of the movies and videos made in the 70's and 80's. She made her last Atlantic crossing at the age of 99, and died in 1984, 100 years old.

Name	Age	Residence	Class	E	Destination	L/B	Body #	Notes
Tucker, Mr. Gilbert M. Jr.	31	Albany, NY	1st	C	Albany, NY	7		
Turcin, Mr. Stefan	36	Croatia	3rd	S	Youngstown, OH			
Turja, Miss Anna Sofia	18	Finland	3rd	S	Ashtabula, OH	15		
Turkula, Mrs. Isaac (Hedvig Holma)	63	Finland	3rd	S	Hibbing, MN	15		
Turpin, Mr. William John	29	Plymouth, England	2nd	S	Salt Lake City, UT			
Turpin, Mrs. William J. (Dorothy Ann Wonnacott)	27	Plymouth, England	2nd	S	Salt Lake City, UT			Traveled with husband.
Tyler, Augusta								see Mrs. Frederick Goodwin

U

Name	Age	Residence	Class	E	Destination	L/B	Body #	Notes
Uruchurtu, Mr. Manuel E.	40	Mexico City, Mexico	1st	C	Mexico City, Mexico			

Manuel Uruchurtu, a Mexican national, had so much money the Mexican government exiled him to France because he was "too rich". He was returning to Mexico with the government's approval in order to arrange for his wife to join him in Paris, originally planning to travel on a different ship but transferred to *Titanic* at the last minute.

Name	Age	Residence	Class	E	Destination	L/B	Body #	Notes
Uzelas, Mr. Jovo								see Mr. Jovo Calic

V

Van Billiard Family

Name	Age	Residence	Class	E	Destination	L/B	Body # Recovered / Where Buried	Notes
Van Billiard, Master James William	10	Cape Town, South Africa	3rd	S	North Wales, PA			
Van Billiard, Master Walter John	9	Cape Town, South Africa	3rd	S	North Wales, PA		#1, buried in Flourtown, PA	
Van Billiard, Mr. Austin Blyler	35	Cape Town, South Africa	3rd	S	North Wales, PA		#255, buried in Flourtown, PA	

Mr. **Austin Van Billiard** was a diamond merchant traveling to Pennsylvania with his two sons to visit relatives and for business. When his body was recovered, twelve uncut diamonds were found on it.

Name	Age	Residence	Class	E	Destination	L/B	Body #	Notes
Van de Velde, Mr. Johannes [John] Joseph	36	Belgium	3rd	S	Gladstone, MI			
Van de Walle [Vandewalle], Mr. Nestor	28	Belgium	3rd	S	unknown			
Van den Steen, Mr. Leo Peter	28	Belgium	3rd	S	unknown			

Mr. **Leo Van den Steen** was emigrating to America. His brother was supposed to go with him, but was refused passage on *Titanic* due to illness. So Leo made the trip with friends Alphonse de Pelsmaeker and Rene Lievens. His brother was supposed to follow later. None of the three friends survived.

Name	Age	Residence	Class	E	Destination	L/B	Body #	Notes
Vandercruyssen [Van der Cruyssen], Mr. Victor	47	Zwevezele, Belgium	3rd	S	Fremont, OH			Sometimes referred to as Victor Vereruysse.

Vanderplancke Family

Name	Age	Residence	Class	E	Destination	L/B	Body #	Notes
Vanderplancke [Plancke, Van der Planke], Jules	31	Fremont, OH	3rd	S	Fremont, OH			
Vanderplancke [Plancke, Van der Planke], Miss Augusta Maria	18	Zwevezele, Belgium	3rd	S	Fremont, OH			
Vanderplancke [Plancke, Van der Planke], Mr. Leo E.	15	Zwevezele, Belgium	3rd	S	Fremont, OH			
Vanderplancke [Plancke, Van der Planke], Mrs. Jules (Emilie M. Vandemoortele)	31	Zwevezele, Belgium	3rd	S	Fremont, OH			

Jules and **Emile Vanderplancke** were newly wed, and they were returning to his home in Ohio. Traveling with them were Jules' brother Leo and sister Augusta. None of them survived.

Name *(Maiden Name)[Other Name]* *Names in italic indicate survivors*	Age	Residence	Class	E	Destination	L/B	Body # Recovered / Where Buried	Notes
Van Derhoef, Mr. Wyckoff	61	Brooklyn, NY	1st	B	Brooklyn, NY		#245, buried in Brooklyn, NY	

Mr. **Wyckoff Van Derhoef** actually boarded *Titanic* in Belfast as its only paying passenger for the ships shakedown cruise and voyage to Southampton.

Name	Age	Residence	Class	E	Destination	L/B	Body # Recovered / Where Buried	Notes
Van Impe Family								
Van Impe, Miss Catharine	10	Kerksken, Belgium	3rd	S	unknown			
Van Impe, Mr. Jean Baptiste	36	Kerksken, Belgium	3rd	S	unknown			
Van Impe, Mrs. Jean Baptiste (Rosalie Govaert)	30	Kerksken, Belgium	3rd	S	unknown			
Van Melkebeke, Mr. Philemon	23	Belgium	3rd	S	unknown			
Vandemoortele, Emilie								see Mrs. Jules Van der Planke
Vartanian [Vartunian], Mr. David	22	Turkey	3rd	C	Hamilton, Ontario, Canada	A/15		
Vassilios, Mr. Catavelas								see Mr. Vassilios Katavelas
Veale, Mr. James	41	Barre, VT	2nd	S	Barre, VT			
Vendel, Mr. Olof Edvin	29	Sweden	3rd	S	unknown			Traveled with August Nilsson.
Vereruysse, Mr. Victor								see Mr. Victor Vandercruyssen
Veström, Miss Hulda Amanda A.	14	Salmunds, Sweden	3rd	S	Los Angeles, CA			She traveled with her aunt Hulda Klasen.
Vidaver, Ruth								see Mrs. Washington Dodge
von Drachstedt, Baron Alfred								see Alfred Nourney
Vonk [Vovk], Mr. Jenko	22	Austria	3rd	S	St. Joseph, MN			

W

Name	Age	Residence	Class	E	Destination	L/B	Body # Recovered / Where Buried	Notes
Waelens, Mr. Achille	22	Belgium	3rd	S	Stanton, OH		#140, buried in Fairview Cemetery, Halifax	
Walcroft, Miss Ellen [Nellie]	35	Berkshire, England	2nd	S	Mamaroneck, NY	14		
Walker, Mr. William Anderson	47	East Orange, NJ	1st	S	East Orange, NJ			
Wallach, Irene								see Mrs. Henry B. Harris
Walton, Helen								see Mrs. Dickinson Bishop
Ward, Emma Eliza								see Mrs. William R. Bucknell
Ward, Miss Anna	35	Chestnut Hill, PA	1st	C	Chestnut Hill, PA	3		Maid to Mrs. James W. Cardeza.
Ware, Mr. Frederick W.	34	London, England	3rd	S	unknown			
Ware, Mr. John James	30	Bristol, England	2nd	S	New Britain, CT			Traveled with wife Florence.
Ware, Mrs. John J. (Florence L. Long)	28	Bristol, England	2nd	S	New Britain, CT	10		
Ware, Mr. William J.	23	Cornwall, England	2nd	S	Butte, MT			
Warne, Edith								see Mrs. Thomas C. Pears
Warren, Mr. Charles W.	30	Hampshire, England	3rd	S	unknown			
Warren, Mr. Frank M.	63	Portland, OR	1st	C	Portland, OR			Traveled with wife Anna.
Warren, Mrs. Frank M. (Anna S. Atkinson)	60	Portland, OR	1st	C	Portland, OR	5		Traveled with husband Frank.
Watson, Eliza								see Mrs. Andrew E. Johnson
Watson, Margaret Ann								see Mrs. Arthur Ford
Watson, Mr. Ennis H.		Belfast, Ireland	2nd	B	New York City, NY			Electrician Apprentice. See H&G Guarantee Group.
Watt, Miss Bertha	12	Aberdeen, Scotland	2nd	S	Portland, OR	9		Traveled with mother Mrs. James Watt.
Watt, Mrs. James (Bessie I. Milne)	40	Aberdeen, Scotland	2nd	S	Portland, OR	9		Traveled with daughter Bertha.
Wazli, Mr. Yousif	25	Lebanon	3rd	C	unknown			

Name *(Maiden Name)[Other Name]* *Names in italic indicate survivors*	Age	Residence	Class	E	Destination	L/B	Body # Recovered / Where Buried	Notes
Webber, Miss Susan	36	Cornwall, England	2nd	S	Hartford, CT	12		see Braund-Dennis Group Notes
Webber, Mr. James	66	San Francisco, CA	3rd	S	unknown			
Weir, Colonel John	60	Salt Lake City, UT	1st	S	Salt Lake City, UT			
Weisz, Mr. Leopold	28	Montreal, Quebec, Canada	2nd	S	Montreal, Quebec, Canada		#293, buried in Montreal	
Weisz, Mrs. Leopold (Mathilde F. Pede)	29	Bromsgrove, England	2nd	S	Montreal, Quebec, Canada	?		

Leopold and **Mathilde Weisz** were emigrating to America. Before leaving England, Mr. Weisz had his wife sew $15,000 in gold into the lining of his jacket, and when his body was recovered, the gold was still there. It was returned to Mrs. Weisz. Without the money, she would have been deported back to England.

Wells Family								
Wells, Master Ralph Lester	2	Cornwall, England	2nd	S	Akron, OH	14		
Wells, Miss Joan	4	Cornwall, England	2nd	S	Akron, OH	14		
Wells, Mrs. Arthur H. (Addie Trevaskis)	29	Cornwall, England	2nd	S	Akron, OH	14		
Wennerström [Andersson], Mr. August Edvard	27	Malmo, Sweden	3rd	S	unknown	A		

Mr. **August Andersson** was a very vocal and radical socialist at a time where that got him into a lot of trouble. So he decided to flee Sweden and go to America, and to do so he changed his name to August Wennerstrom. Otherwise he would have been arrested before he left Sweden.

West Family								
West, Miss Barbara J.	1	Bournemouth, England	2nd	S	Florida	10		
West, Miss Constance M.	5	Bournemouth, England	2nd	S	Florida	10		
West, Mr. Edwy Arthur	36	Bournemouth, England	2nd	S	Florida			
West, Mrs. Edwy A. (Ada M. Worth)	33	Bournemouth, England	2nd	S	Florida	10		

Barbara West died in October, 2007. She shunned publicity all her life, and did not want her passing announced until after her burial. She was one of the last two survivors.

Whabee, Mrs. George								see George, Mrs. Shawneene
Wheadon, Mr. Edward	66	Guernsey, England	2nd	S	unknown			
Wheeler, Mr. Edwin [Frederick] C.	25	Asheville, NC	2nd	S	Asheville, NC			

Edwin Wheeler was the personal valet to Mr. George Washington Vanderbilt, one of the wealthiest men in the world. Mr. and Mrs. Vanderbilt were supposed to sail on *Titanic,* but changed their minds at the last minute. Because their considerable amount of luggage had already been loaded on *Titanic,* they sent Wheeler along with the luggage to retrieve it upon arrival in New York City.

White, Elizabeth Agnes Mary								see Mrs. John M. Davies
White, Florence Kate								see Mrs. Percival Thorneycroft
White, Mr. Percival Wayland	54	Brunswick, ME	1st	S	Brunswick, ME			Traveled with son Richard White.
White, Mr. Richard Frasar	21	Brunswick, ME	1st	S	Brunswick, ME		#169, buried in Massachusetts	Traveled with his father Percival White.
White, Mrs. John Stuart (Ella Holmes)	55	New York City, NY	1st	C	New York City, NY	8		Traveled with maid Amelia Bissette and manservant Sante Ringhini.
Wick Family								
Wick, Miss Mary Natalie	31	Youngstown, OH	1st	S	Youngstown, OH	8		
Wick, Mr. George Dennick	57	Youngstown, OH	1st	S	Youngstown, OH			
Wick, Mrs. George D. (Mary Hitchcock)	45	Youngstown, OH	1st	S	Youngstown, OH	8		
Widegren, Mr. Charles Peter	51	Long Island, NY	3rd	S	Long Island, NY			
Widener Family								
Widener, Mr. George Dunton	50	Elkins Park, PA	1st	C	Elkins Park, PA			
Widener, Mr. Harry Elkins	27	Elkins Park, PA	1st	C	Elkins Park, PA			
Widener, Mrs. George D. (Eleanor Elkins)	50	Elkins Park, PA	1st	C	Elkins Park, PA	4		

Mr. **George Widener** was the son of Mr. P.A.B. Widener who was a member of the board of the bank that owned the International Mercantile Marine, owners of the White Star Line. George Widener was probably the richest man in Philadelphia. Mr. and Mrs. Widener and their son Harry were returning from vacation in Europe. The night *Titanic* sank, the Widener's hosted a dinner for *Titanic's* captain Edward J. Smith, and most of the rich-and-famous passengers attended. Most of the men were still in the Smoking Lounge when *Titanic* struck the iceberg. They all helped load passengers into the lifeboats, and were last seen standing together, smoking and talking, as the ship sank. To honor her son Harry Widener, Mrs. Widener donated the money, designed and had built the Harry Elkins Widener Memorial Library at Harvard University, which today is the focal point for the huge Harvard Library complex.

Name *(Maiden Name)[Other Name]* *Names in italic indicate survivors*	Age	Residence	Class	E	Destination	L/B	Body # Recovered / Where Buried	Notes
Wiggins, Nellie								see Mrs. Samuel L. Goldenberg
Wiklund, Mr. Jacob A.	18	Finland	3rd	S	Montreal, Quebec, Canada			Traveled with brother Karl and friend Anna Sjoblom.
Wiklund, Mr. Karl Johan	21	Finland	3rd	S	Montreal, Quebec, Canada			Traveled with brother Jacob and friend Anna Sjoblom.
Wilhelms, Mr. Charles	31	London, England	2nd	S	New York City, NY	9		
Wilkes, Mrs. James (Ellen Needs)	45	Cornwall, England	3rd	S	Akron, OH	16		Traveled with sister Mrs. Eliza Hocking.
Wilkinson, Miss Elizabeth Anne	29	Liverpool, England	2nd	S	Philadelphia, PA	16		Mistress to Mr. Harry Faunthorpe.
Mrs. **Harry Faunthorpe** was the name Elizabeth Wilkinson was traveling under. She appears to be the mistress of Harry Faunthorpe.								
Willard, Miss Constance	21	Duluth, MN	1st	S	Duluth, MN	8/10		
Willer, Mr. Aaron	37	Paris, France	3rd	C	Chicago, IL			
Willey, Mr. Edward	18	Drayton, England	3rd	S	Schenectady, NY			
Williams, Mr. Charles D.	51	Geneva, Switzerland	1st	C	Radnor, PA			Traveled with son Richard N. Williams.
Williams, Mr. Richard Norris II	21	Geneva, Switzerland	1st	C	Radnor, PA	8/14		
Richard Williams traveled with his father Charles D. Williams. Richard saw his father killed when the forward funnel fell on him. He managed to get into Collapsible Lifeboat A, and had to stand in waist deep water for several hours in the half submerged lifeboat. Doctors wanted to amputate both of his legs due to the cold, but he wouldn't let them. In later years, Richard Williams became an Olympic Gold Medal Tennis Champion.								
Williams, Mr. Charles Eugene	21	Harrow, England	2nd	S	New York City, NY	14		
A famous squash racquets player, **Charles Williams** was traveling to New York to defend his title.								
Williams, Mr. Fletcher Lambert		London, England	1st	S	New York City, NY			Traveled on business with Mr. Elmer Z. Taylor.
Williams, Mr. Howard Hugh	28	Gurnsey, England	3rd	S	unknown			
Williams, Mr. Leslie		Tonypandy, Wales	3rd	S	unknown		#14, buried at sea	
Wilson, Lily Alexenia								see Mrs. Thomas Porter Jr.
Wilson, Miss Helen Alice	35	London, England	1st	C	Tuxedo Park, NY	3		Maid to Mrs. Frederick Spedden.
Windeløv, Mr. Einar	21	Denmark	3rd	S	unknown			
Winfield, Ada Maria								see Mrs. Charles V. Clarke
Wirz, Mr. Albert	27	Zurich, Switzerland	3rd	S	Beloit, WI		#131, buried in Beloit, WI	
Wiseman, Mr. Phillippe	54	London, England	3rd	S	Quebec, Canada			
Wittevrongel [Wittenrongel], Mr. Camilius	36	Belgium	3rd	S	Detroit, MI			
Wizoski, Hannah								see Mrs. Samuel Abelson
Wonnacott, Dorothy Ann								see Mrs. William J. Turpin
Woodward, Mr. John Wesley	32	Oxford, England	2nd	S				see Musician's Group Notes
Woolner, Mr. Hugh	45	London, England	1st	S	New York City, NY	D		
Worth, Ada Mary								see Mrs. Edwy A. West
Wright, Juliet Cummins								see Mrs. Elmer Z. Taylor
Wright, Miss Marion	26	Yeovill, England	2nd	S	Cottage Grove, OR	9		
Wright, Mr. George	62	Halifax, Nova Scotia	1st	S	Halifax, Nova Scotia			

Y

Yazbeck, Mr. Antoni	27	Lebanon	3rd	C	Wilkes-Barre, PA			Traveling on honeymoon.
Yazbeck, Mrs. Antoni (Celiney [Selini] Alexander)	15	Lebanon	3rd	C	Wilkes-Barre, PA	C		Newly-wed and a widow at age 15. Traveling on honeymoon.
Young, Miss Marie Grice	36	New York City, NY	1st	C	Washington, DC	8		

Key: **Names** are in alphabetical order except where family members are grouped together. Names listed in italic were survivors. Names in parenthesis (name) are the maiden (or birth) name of the person. Names in brackets [name] are other names the passenger used. **Age** is the person's age at the time of the sinking. **Residence** is where the person's home was located. **Class** indicates the class the person was traveling. "**E**" indicates where the person embarked Titanic (**B** is for Belfast, Ireland; **C** is for Cherbourg, France; **S** is for Southampton, England and **Q** is for Queenstown (now Cobh) Ireland. **Destination** is where the passenger was traveling. **L/B** indicates which Lifeboat the person escaped on, if known. **Body Recovered / Where Buried** indicates in what sequence the body was recovered and where it was buried. **Family** groups are kept together and have dark shade fore easy reference and if there are any family notes they are listed after the last family name. Individuals with notes have the note after the name. Listings in light shade are designed only to assist the reader in following the text across the page.

Name *(Maiden Name)[Other Name]* *Names in italic indicate survivors*	Age	Residence	Class	E	Destination	L/B	Body # Recovered / **Where Buried**	Notes
Yousef, Anna								see Mrs. Dawsis Touma
Yousef, Master Georges								see Master Georges Touma
Yousef, Miss Maria								see Miss Marie Touma
Yousif, Mr. Wazli								see Mr. Yousif Wazli
Youssiff, Mr. Gerios	26	Lebanon	3rd	C	Youngstown, OH			
Yrois, Miss Henriette	24	Paris, France	2nd	S	New York City, NY			Mistress to Mr. William H. Harbeck.

Z

Zabour, Miss Hileni		unknown	3rd	C	unknown		#328, buried in Mt. Olivet Cemetery, Halifax	
Zabour, Miss Tamini		unknown	3rd	C	unknown			Traveled with Hileni Zabour.
Zakarian, Mr. Artun	27	Armenia	3rd	C	Canada			
Zakarian, Mr. Mapreider		Armenia	3rd	C	Canada		#304, buried in Fairview Cemetery, Halifax	
Zenni, Mr. Fahim [Philip]	25	Syria	3rd	C	Dayton, OH	6		see Mr. Fahim Leeni.
Zievens, Mr. René								see Mr. Rene Lievens.
Zimmerman, Mr. Leo	29	Germany	3rd	S	Saskatoon, Canada			

GROUP NOTES

American Lines Group Notes: Six employees of the American Line were traveling on a free ticket, deadheading back to New York because their assigned ship was docked due to the coal strike. The six employees were Alfred Carver, Alfred Johnson, William Johnson Jr., Lionel Leonard, Thomas Storey and William H. Tornquist. Of the six, only Tornquist survived. Of the remaining five, only Thomas Storey's body was recovered.

Backstrom-Gustafsson Group Notes: Maria M. Gustafsson had visited the United States, but had returned home to Finland to marry Karl Backstrom. She was seven months pregnant when Maria, Karl and Maria's brothers Johan Gustafsson and Anders Gustafsson decided to emigrate to America. They traveled Third Class, and all but Maria perished that night. Maria, after a short stay in New York, returned home to Finland in time to give birth to a daughter.

Braund-Dennis Group Notes: Lewis and Owen Braund were brothers living in England. Another brother had emigrated to Canada. The brother in Canada had convinced Lewis and Owen to emigrate too. So Lewis and Owen Braund, their cousins Samuel Dennis, William Dennis, John Lovell and John Perkin and family friend Susan Webber all decided to travel together. They traveled Third Class, and everyone except Susan Webber died that night.

Donaldson Line Group Notes: Several survivors on Lifeboats 13, 14 and Collapsible Lifeboat C reported the presence of "Chinamen" in their lifeboats. None of the survivors seemed to have anything positive to say about them, feeling they were all stowaways. In fact, they were Third Class passengers who had paid tickets for the trip: Lee Bing, Chang Chip, Choong Foo, Ling Hee, Ali Lam, Len Lam, Fong Lang and Lee Ling. They were all employed by the Donaldson Line, a steamship company which had a vessel hung up in England because of the coal strike. The Donaldson Line was sending the employees (deadheading) back to New York to help crew another one of their ships. Since they were all quartered together near the bow of the ship, had a common language and had some experience at sea, they probably took the first opportunity to get into any available lifeboat. All except Len Lam and Lee Ling survived.

Ford-Johnston-Harknett Group Notes: Mrs. Edward Ford, whose husband had left her with five children, was emigrating to America with four of those children: Dollina, Edward, William and Robina. The fifth and oldest child Francis was already living in America. Mrs. Ford's sister Eliza Johnston, her husband Andrew and their children William and Catherine also decided to make the trip. Finally, Alice Harknett, a friend of Francis Ford, also decided to go. In all, ten people from three families. None of them survived.

Gusmostnik, Bulgaria, Group Notes: Eight young men, most of whom were potters from the small village of Gusmostnik, Bulgaria, boarded *Titanic* with plans to emigrate to America. All eight (Peju Colcheff, Lailio Junkoff, Marin Markoff, Lazer Minkoff, Penko Naidenoff; Nadialco Petroff and Ilia Stoytcheff) were lost. One can imagine the effect this large of loss would have on the small village.

Harland and Wolff Group Notes: Harland and Wolff, builders of the RMS *Titanic,* always sent a group of employees on all maiden voyages to make checks, help train the crew and generally be available for assistance during the voyage. This group was called the Harland and Wolff Guarantee Group, and there were nine members of the group on *Titanic,* three traveling First Class (Thomas Andrews, Managing Director; Roderick R.C. Chisholm, Chief Ships Draftsman and William H.M. Parr, Assistant Manager, Electrical Department.) The remaining six members (William Campbell, Alfred Cunningham, Anthony Frost, Robert Knight, Francis Parkes and Ennis Watson) all traveled Second Class. None of the group survived the voyage.

Hickman Group Notes: Leonard Hickman was a successful farmer in Canada, and had returned to England to persuade his family to emigrate. All eleven members decided to emigrate, but only three of them, brothers Leonard, Lewis and Stanley actually made the trip. They were accompanied by four friends, Charles Davies, Percy Deacon, William Dibden and Ambrose Hood. None of the seven survived, and only Lewis Hickman's body was found.

Hocking-Richards Group Notes: Mrs. William R. (Eliza) Hocking had two sons, Richard and Sidney, who lived in Akron, Ohio. Eliza decided to join them there, so Richard traveled back to England to escort his mother to Ohio. Accompanying them on the trip were Eliza's sister Ellen Wilkes, Eliza's daughters Nellie Hocking and Emily Richards and Emily's sons (Eliza's grandsons) George Richards and William Richards. Richard Hocking managed to get his mother, aunt and cousins into Lifeboat 4, and they all survived. Richard did not. Upon arriving in New York, Sidney Hocking met his family and took them on to Ohio.

Irish Contingent Group Notes: Third Class passenger Daniel Buckley of County Cork, Ireland was the group leader for several Irish passengers who were emigrating to America. The group included Bridget Bradley, Michael Linehan, Patrick O'Connell, Patrick O'Connor, Nora O'Leary and Hannah Riordan. Of the group, Buckley and the three women survived, the remainder of the men did not.

Lundstrom Group Notes: Mr. Thure E. Lundstrom was traveling with his fiancé Elida Olsson, friend Agnes Sandstrom, Hulda Klasen and over a dozen other people who were making the trip to New York City. Lundstrom and Agnes Snadstrom survived, none of the others did.

Musicians Group Notes: The eight musicians were employed by the C.W. and F.N. Black Company of Liverpool, under contract to the White Star Line. Consequently, the same musicians usually worked together, but they weren't assigned to a specific ship. The musicians were divided into two groups: a trio composed of a violinist (George Krins), a cellist (Roger Bricoux) and a pianist (Theodore R. Brailey). The second group was a quintet, led by Wallace Hartley (violin), John F.P. Clark (Bass) John L. Hume (violin), Percy C. Taylor (piano) and John W. Woodward (cello). Normally, the trio played in the Café Parisian and the à la carte restaurant while the quintet played in the First Class Lounge and First Class Reception Room. Shortly after the ship struck the iceberg, both orchestras were playing, but at some point, they joined together, less the two piano players, on the port side of the Boat deck. There they played until the very end, eventually having to brace themselves to prevent slipping off the deck. None of the musicians survived.

Crew Listing

Name *(Maiden Name)* Survivors names in italic	Age	Title/Function	Department	Residence	E	L/B	Body # Recovered / Where Buried	Notes
A								
Abbott, Ernest W.	21	Lounge Pantry Steward (First Class)	Victualling	Southampton	S			
Abrams, William	33	Fireman	Engineering	Southampton	S			
Acavino, Candido	42	à la Carte Carver	Vendor	London, England	S			see à la Carte Group Notes
Adams, Robert	26	Fireman	Engineering	Southampton	S			
Ahier, Percy S.	20	First Class Saloon Steward	Victualling	Southampton	S			
Akerman, Joseph F.	35	Assistant Pantryman Steward (First Class)	Victualling	Southampton	S		#205, buried in Fairview Cemetery, Halifax	Served with brother Albert Akerman.
Akermann, Albert	28	Third Class Steward	Victualling	Southampton	S			Served with brother Joseph Akerman.
Allan, Robert S.	36	First Class Bedroom Steward	Victualling	Southampton	S			
Allaria, Battista A.	22	à la Carte Assistant Waiter	Vendor	Southampton	S		#221, buried in Fairview Cemetery, Halifax	see à la Carte Group Notes
Allen, Ernest F.	24	Trimmer	Engineering	Southampton	S	B		Brother of Frederick Allen.
Allen, Frederick	17	Lift (Elevator) Steward (First Class)	Victualling	Southampton	S			Brother of Ernest Allen.
Allen, George	26	Scullion	Victualling	Southampton	S			
Allen, Henry	32	Fireman	Engineering	Southampton	S		#145, buried in Fairview Cemetery, Halifax	
Allsop, Frank R.	43	First Class Saloon Steward	Victualling	Southampton	S			Served with sister Mrs. Henry McLaren.
Allsop, Katherine			Victualling					see Mrs. Henry McLaren
Allsop, Mr. Alfred S.	34	2nd Electrician	Engineering	Southampton	B			
Anderson, James	40	Able Bodied Seaman	Deck	Southampton	S	3		
Anderson, Walter J.	48	First Class Bedroom Steward	Victualling	Southampton	S		#146, buried at sea	
Andrews, Charles E.	19	Second Class Saloon Steward	Victualling	Southampton	S	16		
Archer, Ernest E.	36	Able Bodied Seaman	Deck	Southampton	S	16		
Ashcroft, Austin A.	26	Ships Clerk	Victualling	Seacombe, England	S			
Ashe, Henry W.	32	Glory-Hole Steward	Victualling	Liverpool, England	S		#34, buried in Fairview Cemetery, Halifax	
Asperlach, Georges	27	à la Carte Assistant Plateman	Vendor	London, England	S			see à la Carte Group Notes
Avery, James F.	22	Trimmer	Engineering	Southampton	S	15		
Ayling, George E.	23	Assistant Vegetable Cook	Victualling	Southampton	S			
B								
Back, Charles F.	32	Assistant Lounge Steward (First Class)	Victualling	Southampton	B			
Baggott, Allen M.	28	First Class Saloon Steward	Victualling	Southampton	S	9		
Bagley, Edward E.	31	First Class Saloon Steward	Victualling	Southampton	S			
Bailey, George F.	36	Second Class Saloon Steward	Victualling	Southampton	B		#161, buried in Fairview Cemetery, Halifax	
Bailey, George W.		Fireman	Engineering	Southampton	S			
Bailey, Joseph H.	43	Master at Arms	Deck	Southampton	S	16		

Joseph Bailey commanded Lifeboat 16. Because it was already in the water, he entered the lifeboat by climbing down the falls (ropes).

Name	Age	Title/Function	Department	Residence	E	L/B	Body	Notes
Baines, Richard		Greaser	Engineering	Southampton	S			

Key: **Names** are in alphabetical order. **"E"** indicates where embarked (**B** is for Belfast, **S** is for Southampton). **L/B** indicates which lifeboat they escaped on, if known. **Body # Recovered / Where Buried** indicates in what sequence the body was recovered, and where it was buried. For descriptions of job functions, see **Glossary**.

Name *(Maiden Name)* *Survivors names in italic*	Age	Title/Function	Department	Residence	E	L/B	Body # Recovered / Where Buried	Notes
Ball, Percy	19	Plates Steward (First Class)	Victualling	Southampton	S	13		
Ball, W. (William?)		Fireman	Engineering	Southampton	S			For some reason, he signed on as James Carter.
Bamfi, Ugo	24	à la Carte Waiter	Vendor	London, England	S			see à la Carte Group Notes
Bannon, John		Greaser	Engineering	Southampton	S			
Barker, Albert	18	Assistant Baker	Victualling	Winchester, England	S			
Barker, Ernest T.	37	First Class Saloon Steward	Victualling	London, England	S		#159, buried at sea	
Barker, Reginald L.	40	Asst. Purser	Victualling	Hampshire	B			
Reginald Barker was last seen with Dr. William O'Loughlin, Dr. John Simpson, Hugh McElroy and Second Officer Lightoller, shaking hands and saying goodbye. Only Lightoller survived.								
Barlow, Charles		Fireman	Engineering	Southampton	S			
Barlow, George	36	Second Class Bedroom Steward	Victualling	Southampton	S			
Barnes, Charles		Fireman	Engineering	Southampton	S			
Barnes, Frederick		Fireman	Engineering	Southampton	S			
Barnes, Frederick	37	Assistant Baker	Victualling	Southampton	S			
Barrett, A.	15	Bell Boy (First Class)	Victualling	Southampton	S			
Barrett, Frederick W.	24	Fireman	Engineering	Southampton	S			
Barrett, Fredrick W.	28	Leading Fireman	Engineering	Liverpool	S	13		Commanded Lifeboat 13.
There were two men named **Frederick W. Barrett** on *Titanic*. They probably were not related.								
Barringer, Arthur W.	33	First Class Saloon Steward	Victualling	Southampton	S			
Barrow, Charles	35	Assistant Butcher	Victualling	Southampton	S			
Barrows, William	32	First Class Saloon Steward	Victualling	London, England	S			
Barton, Sidney J.	25	Third Class Steward	Victualling	Southampton	S			
Basilico, Giovanni	27	à la Carte Waiter	Vendor	London, England	S			see à la Carte Group Notes
Bassant, E.	31	Baggage Steward (First Class)	Victualling	Southampton	S			
Baxter, Harry R.	51	Third Class Steward	Victualling	Southampton	S			
Baxter, Thomas F.	48	Linen Steward	Victualling	Southampton	S		#235, buried in Fairview Cemetery, Halifax	
Bazzi, Narciso	23	à la Carte Waiter	Vendor	London, England	S			see à la Carte Group Notes
Beattie, Joseph	34	Greaser	Engineering	Belfast, Ireland	B			
Beauchamp, George W.	22	Fireman	Engineering	Southampton	S	13		
Beedem, George A.	34	Second Class Bedroom Steward	Victualling	London, England	S			
Beere, William	19	Kitchen Porter	Victualling	Hampshire, England	S			
Bell, Joseph	51	Chief Engineer	Engineering	Liverpool, England	B			
Bendell, Frederick		Fireman	Engineering	Southampton	S			
Benham, Frederick	29	Second Class Saloon Steward	Victualling	Southampton	S			
Bennett, George A.	31	Fireman	Engineering	Southampton	S			
Bennett, Mrs. Mabel		First Class Stewardess	Victualling	Southampton	S	5		
Benville, E.		Fireman	Engineering	Southampton	S			
Bernardi, Battista	22	à la Carte Assistant Waiter	Vendor	London, England	S		#215, buried in Mount Olivet Cemetery, Halifax	see à la Carte Group Notes
Bertoldo, Fioravante G.	23	à la Carte Assistant Scullery	Vendor	Southampton	S			see à la Carte Group Notes
Bessant, William E.		Fireman	Engineering	Southampton	S			
Best, Alfred E.	38	First Class Saloon Steward	Victualling	Southampton	S			
Beux, David	26	à la Carte Assistant Waiter	Vendor	London, England	S			see à la Carte Group Notes
Bevis, James H.		Trimmer	Engineering	Southampton	S			
Biddlecombe, Charles		Fireman	Engineering	Southampton	S			
Bietrix, George B.	28	à la Carte Sauce Cook	Vendor	London, England	S			see à la Carte Group Notes
Biggs, Edward C.	21	Fireman	Engineering	Southampton	S			
Billows, J.		Trimmer	Engineering	Southampton	S			

Name (Maiden Name) Survivors names in italic	Age	Title/Function	Department	Residence	E	L/B	Body # Recovered / Where Buried	Notes
Binstead, Walter	19	Trimmer	Engineering	Southampton	S	3		
Bishop, Walter	34	First Class Bedroom Steward	Victualling	Southampton	B			
Black, Alexander		Fireman	Engineering	Southampton	S			
Black, Daniel	41	Fireman	Engineering	Southampton	S			see Substitutes Group Notes
Blackman, Henry	32	Fireman	Engineering	Southampton	S			
Blake, Percival A.		Trimmer	Engineering	Southampton	S	15		
Blake, Seaton		Mess Steward (Crew)	Engineering	Southampton	S			
Blake, Thomas	36	Fireman	Engineering	Southampton	S			
Blaney, James		Fireman	Engineering	Southampton	S			
Blann, Eustace H.		Fireman	Engineering	Southampton	S			
Bliss, Mrs. Ernest J. (Emma Junod)	46	First Class Stewardess	Victualling	Southgate, England	S	15		
Blumet, Jean B.	26	à la Carte Plateman	Vendor	Southampton	S			see à la Carte Group Notes
Bochatay, Joseph A.	30	Assistant Chef	Victualling	Southampton	S			
Bochet, Pietro G.	43	à la Carte Second Head Waiter	Vendor	London, England	S			see à la Carte Group Notes
Bogie, Leslie N.	46	Second Class Bedroom Steward	Victualling	Hampshire, England	S		#274, buried in Fairview Cemetery, Halifax	
Bolhuis, Hendrik	30	à la Carte Larder Cook	Vendor	Southampton	S			see à la Carte Group Notes
Bond, William J.	40	First Class Bedroom Steward	Victualling	Southampton	B			
Boothby, W.	37	Second Class Bedroom Steward	Victualling	Southampton	S		#107, buried at sea	
Boston, William J.	30	Assistant Deck Steward (First Class)	Victualling	Southampton	B			
Bott, W.	44	Greaser	Engineering	Southampton	S			
Bourhton, B.	24	First Class Saloon Steward	Victualling	Southampton	S			
Bowker, Miss Ruth	27	à la Carte Cashier	Vendor	Cheshire, England	S	6		see à la Carte Group Notes
Boxhall, Mr. Joseph G.	30	Fourth Officer	Deck	Hull, England	B	2		

Fourth Officer **Joseph G. Boxhall** had been at sea since he was 17 years old, and had worked for White Star Line for five years. Like most of the ships' officers, he took part in the shakedown cruise from Belfast to Southampton. He was scheduled to go on watch at midnight April 14-15 to relieve First Officer Murdoch, and was near the bridge when *Titanic* struck the iceberg. Sent below by Captain Smith to look for damage, Boxhall found none, however he hadn't gone below "E" deck. As crewmembers from the boiler room began reporting leaks to the bridge, Smith ordered Boxhall to fix the ships exact position so the Marconi operators could send out the distress call. Later placed in charge of Lifeboat 2, Boxhall testified at both the U.S. and British hearings. Boxhall died in 1967, and his ashes were scattered over the site where *Titanic* sank.

Boyd, John	35	First Class Saloon Steward	Victualling	Southampton	S			
Boyes, John H.	31	First Class Saloon Steward	Victualling	Southampton	S			
Bradford, William B.	31	Assistant Roast Cook	Victualling	Hampshire, England	S			
Bradley, F.		Able Bodied Seaman	Deck	Southampton	S			
Bradley, Patrick		Fireman	Engineering	Southampton	S			
Bradshaw, J.A.	43	Plates Steward (First Class)	Victualling	Southampton	S			
Brewer, Henry		Trimmer	Engineering	Southampton	S			
Brewster, G.H.	48	First Class Bedroom Steward	Victualling	Southampton	B			
Brice, Walter T.	42	Able Bodied Seaman	Deck	Southampton	S	11		

Walter T. Brice commanded Lifeboat 11. Because it was already in the water, he entered the lifeboat by climbing down the falls (ropes).

Bride, Harold S.	22	Assistant Marconi Telegrapher	Victualling	Southampton	B	B		

Harold S. Bride was the Second Marconi Operator, and was employed by the Marconi Company. After *Titanic* struck the iceberg, Phillips, who was on duty and Bride, who was getting ready to go on duty, remained at the wireless set, continuously sending out CQD and SOS signals. At some point shortly before the ship sank, Bride had to fight off a sailor who was trying to steal a lifejacket from Phillips. Bride remained with Phillips until the power went out and water was rushing in the door of the wireless room. Bride went into the water and somehow ended up under the overturned Collapsible Lifeboat B. In the dark, he managed to swim out from under the lifeboat, and climbed onto the top of it along with several other people. Someone sat on his feet during the night and crushed them between the wooden slats. When he was rescued, he had to be treated for frostbite and two crushed feet. As *Carpathia* returned to New York, Bride, with his bandaged feet and legs, stayed awake for almost three days, helping *Carpathia's* Marconi operator send messages from the survivors to their families. Bride was the last person to leave *Carpathia,* having to be carried off because of his feet.

Bright, Arthur J.	40	Quartermaster	Deck	Southampton	S	14		
Bristow, Harry	39	First Class Saloon Steward	Victualling	Kent, England	S			

Name *(Maiden Name)* *Survivors names in italic*	Age	Title/Function	Department	Residence	E	L/B	Body # Recovered / Where Buried	Notes
Bristow, Robert C.	31	Third Class Steward	Victualling	Southampton	S		#290, buried in Fairview Cemetery, Halifax	
Brookman, John	27	Third Class Steward	Victualling	Southampton	S			Married three days prior to the voyage.
Brooks, J.		Trimmer	Engineering	Southampton	S			
Broom, H.	33	Bath Steward (First Class)	Victualling	Southampton	B			
Broome, Athol F.	30	Verandah Steward (First Class)	Victualling	Southampton	S			
Brown, Edward	24	First Class Saloon Steward	Victualling	Southampton	B	A		
Brown, John	35	Fireman	Engineering	Southampton	S		# 267, buried in Fairview Cemetery, Halifax	
Brown, Joseph J.	30	Fireman	Engineering	Eastleigh, England	S			see Substitutes Group Notes
Brown, Walter J.	28	First Class Saloon Steward	Victualling	Southampton	B			
Buckley, H.E.	34	Assistant Vegetable Cook	Victualling	Southampton	S			
Buley, Edward J.	27	Able Bodied Seaman	Deck	Southampton	S	10		
Bull, W.	30	Scullion	Victualling	Southampton	S			
Bulley, H.A.	22	Second Class Boots Steward	Victualling	Southampton	S			
Bunnell, W.	20	Plates Steward (First Class)	Victualling	Southampton	B			
Burgess, Charles R.	19	Extra Third Baker	Victualling	Southampton	S	15		
Burke, Richard E.	30	Lounge Steward (First Class)	Victualling	Southampton	B			
Burke, William	30	Second Saloon Steward (First Class)	Victualling	Southampton	S	10		
Burr, Eward S.	29	First Class Saloon Steward	Victualling	Southampton	S			
Burrage, Alfred	20	Plates Steward (Second Class)	Victualling	Southampton	S	13		
Burroughs, Arthur		Fireman	Engineering	Southampton	S			
Burton, Edward J.		Fireman	Engineering	Southampton	S			
Butt, Robert	22	First Class Saloon Steward	Victualling	Southampton	S		#10, buried in Fairview Cemetery, Halifax	
Butt, William	30	Fireman	Engineering	Southampton	S		#77, buried at sea	
Butterworth, J.	23	First Class Saloon Steward	Victualling	Southampton	S		#116, buried at sea	
Byrne, J.E.	31	Second Class Bedroom Steward	Victualling	Ilford, England	S			

C

Name *(Maiden Name)* *Survivors names in italic*	Age	Title/Function	Department	Residence	E	L/B	Body # Recovered / Where Buried	Notes
Calderwood, Hugh		Trimmer	Engineering	Southampton	S			
Camner, James		Fireman	Engineering	Southampton	S			
Campbell, Donald S.	28	Ships Clerk	Victualling	Melbourne, Australia	S			
Carney, William	31	Lift (Elevator) Steward (First Class)	Victualling	Liverpool	B		#251, buried in Fairview Cemetery, Halifax	
Carr, Richard S.		Trimmer	Engineering	Southampton	S			
Carter, James			Engineering					see W. (William) Ball
Cartwright, James E.	32	First Class Saloon Steward	Victualling	Southampton	B		#320, buried in Fairview Cemetery, Halifax	
Casali, Giulio	32	à la Carte Waiter	Vendor	London, England	S			see à la Carte Group Notes
Casey, T.		Trimmer	Engineering	Southampton	S			
Casswill, Charles	32	First Class Saloon Steward	Victualling	Southampton	S			
Castleman, Edward		Greaser	Engineering	Southampton	S			
Caton, Miss Annie	50	Turkish Bath Stewardess	Victualling	London, England	S	11		
Caunt, W.	27	Grill Cook	Victualling	Southampton	S			
Cave, Herbert		First Class Saloon Steward	Victualling	Corydon, England	S		#218, buried in Fairview Cemetery, Halifax	The only existing copy of the First Class passenger accommodation list was found on his body.

Name (Maiden Name) *Survivors names in italic*	Age	Title/Function	Department	Residence	E	L/B	Body # Recovered / Where Buried	Notes
Cavell, George H.		Trimmer	Engineering	Southampton	S	15		
Cecil, Charles	20	Third Class Steward	Victualling	Southampton	S			
Chapman, Joseph C.	22	Second Class Boots Steward	Victualling	Southampton	S	9		
Charboisson, Adrien F.	25	à la Carte Roast Cook	Vendor	London, England	S			see à la Carte Group Notes
Charman, John	25	Second Class Saloon Steward	Victualling	Southampton	S			
Cherrett, William V.		Fireman	Engineering	Southampton	S			
Cheverton, W.F.	27	First Class Saloon Steward	Victualling	South Wales	S		#334, buried at sea	

Cheverton's body was found in the water in June 1912, having floated several hundred miles from where *Titanic* sank. His was the last body recovered.

Chisnall, George A.	35	Senior Boilermaker	Engineering	Southampton	B		#111, buried at sea	
Chitty, Archibald G.	28	Third Class Steward	Victualling	Southampton	S			
Chitty, G.	44	Assistant Baker	Victualling	Southampton	S			
Chorley, John	25	Fireman	Engineering	Southampton	S			
Christmas, H.	33	Second Class Saloon Steward	Victualling	Southampton	S			
Clark, T.	37	First Class Bedroom Steward	Victualling	Southampton	S			
Clark, William	39	Fireman	Engineering	Southampton	S	15		
Clench, Frederick	31	Able Bodied Seaman	Deck	Southampton	S	12		
Clench, George		Able Bodied Seaman	Deck	Southampton	S			
Coe, Harry		Trimmer	Engineering	Southampton	S			
Coleman, Albert E.	28	First Class Saloon Steward	Victualling	Southampton	S			
Coleman, John		Mess Steward (Crew)	Engineering	Southampton	S			
Colgan, Joseph	33	Scullion	Victualling	Southampton	S	13		
Collins, John	17	Scullion	Victualling	Belfast	B	B		
Collins, Samuel	35	Fireman	Engineering	Southampton	S	1		
Combes, George		Fireman	Engineering	Southampton	S	3		
Conway, P.W.	25	Second Class Saloon Steward	Victualling	London, England	B			
Cook, George	42	First Class Saloon Steward	Victualling	Southampton	S			
Coombs, C.	38	Assistant Cook	Victualling	Southampton	S			
Cooper, Harry		Fireman	Engineering	Southampton	S			
Cooper, James		Trimmer	Engineering	Southampton	S			
Copperthwaite, B.	22	Fireman	Engineering	Southampton	S			
Corben, Ernest T.	27	Assistant Printer Steward	Victualling	Southampton	S			
Corcoran, Dennis		Fireman	Engineering	Southampton	S			
Cornaire, Marcel R.A.	19	à la Carte Assistant Roast Cook	Vendor	London, England	S			see à la Carte Group Notes
Cotton, A.		Trimmer	Engineering	Southampton	S			see Substitutes Group Notes
Couch, Frank	28	Able Bodied Seaman	Deck		S		#253, buried in Fairview Cemetery, Halifax	
Couch, John H.		Greaser	Engineering	Southampton	S			
Couper, Robert	20	Fireman	Engineering	Southampton	S	3		
Coutin, Auguste L.	28	à la Carte Entree Cook	Vendor	Southampton	S			

Auguste Coutin was not listed on the original crew list, but was listed on the hearing lists. His is one of the "mystery names" that often doesn't get counted. See à la Carte Group Notes.

Cox, William D.	29	Third Class Steward	Victualling	Southampton	S		#300, buried in Fairview Cemetery, Halifax	see Cox, Hart and Pearcy Group Notes
Coy, Francis E.G.	26	Junior Assistant Third Engineer	Engineering	Southampton	B			
Crabb, H.		Trimmer	Engineering	Southampton	S			
Crafter, Frederick	27	First Class Saloon Steward	Victualling	Southampton	S	15		
Crawford, Alfred	36	First Class Bedroom Steward	Victualling	Southampton	S	8		
Creese, Henry P.	44	Deck Engineer	Engineering	Southampton	B			
Crimmins, James		Fireman	Engineering	Southampton	S	13		
Crisp, Albert H.	35	First Class Saloon Steward	Victualling	Southampton	S			

Name *(Maiden Name)* *Survivors names in italic*	Age	Title/Function	Department	Residence	E	L/B	Body # Recovered / Where Buried	Notes
Crispin, William	34	Glory-Hole Steward	Victualling	Hampshire, England	S			
Crosbie, J.B.	42	Turkish Bath Steward		Southampton	S			
Cross, William		Fireman	Engineering	Southampton	S			
Crovella, Luigi	17	à la Carte Assistant Waiter	Vendor	Southampton	S			see à la Carte Group Notes
Crowe, George F.	30	First Class Saloon Steward	Victualling	Southampton	S	14		
Crumplin, Charles	35	First Class Bedroom Steward	Victualling	Southampton	B			
Cullan, Charles	35	First Class Bedroom Steward	Victualling	Southampton	S	11		
Cunningham, Andrew	38	First Class Bedroom Steward	Victualling	Southampton	S	4		He was picked up from the water.
Cunningham, B.	30	Fireman	Engineering	Southampton	S			
Curtis, Arthur		Fireman	Engineering	Southampton	S			

D

Name *(Maiden Name)*	Age	Title/Function	Department	Residence	E	L/B	Body # Recovered / Where Buried	Notes
Daniels, Sidney E.	18	Third Class Steward	Victualling	Southampton	S	B		
Dashwood, William G.	18	Second Class Saloon Steward	Victualling	Southampton	S		#83, buried in Fairview Cemetery, Halifax	
Davies, Gordon R.	33	First Class Bedroom Steward	Victualling	Southampton	S			
Davies, John J.	28	Extra Second Baker	Victualling	Southampton	B		#200, buried at sea	
Davies, Robert J.	26	Second Class Saloon Steward	Victualling	Southampton	S		#191, buried in Fairview Cemetery, Halifax	
Davies, Thomas	33	Leading Fireman	Engineering	Southampton	S			
Davis, Stephen J.	39	Able Bodied Seaman	Deck	Hampshire	S			
Dawson, Joseph	23	Trimmer	Engineering	Dublin, Ireland	S		#227, buried in Fairview Cemetery, Halifax	
de Marsico, Gianni	20	à la Carte Assistant Waiter	Vendor	London, England	S			see à la Carte Group Notes
Dean, George H.	19	Second Class Saloon Steward	Victualling	Southampton	S		#252, buried in Fairview Cemetery, Halifax	
Debreucq, Maurice E.V.	17	à la Carte Assistant Waiter	Vendor	London, England	S		#244, buried in Mount Olivet Cemetery, Halifax	see à la Carte Group Notes
Deeble, Alfred A.	29	First Class Saloon Steward	Victualling	Southampton	S		#270, buried in Fairview Cemetery, Halifax	
Derrett, A.	26	First Class Saloon Steward	Victualling	Southampton	S			
Deslands, Percival S.	30	First Class Saloon Steward	Victualling	Southampton	S		#212, buried in Fairview Cemetery, Halifax	
Desvernine, Louis G.	20	à la Carte Assistant Pastry Cook	Vendor	London, England	S			see à la Carte Group Notes
Diaper, James		Fireman	Engineering	Southampton	S	?		
Dickson, William	36	Trimmer	Engineering	Southampton	S			see Substitutes Group Notes
Dilley, John		Fireman	Engineering	Southampton	S	?		
Dillon, Thomas P.	34	Trimmer	Engineering	Southampton	S	4		Pulled from the water along with two others who died.
Dinage, James R.	46	First Class Saloon Steward	Victualling	Southampton	S			
Dodd, Edward C.	38	Junior Third Engineer	Engineering	Southampton	B			
Dodd, George C.	44	Chief Second Steward (First Class)	Victualling	Southampton	B			
Dodds, Henry W.	27	Junior Assistant Fourth Engineer	Engineering	Southampton	S			see Substitutes Group Notes
Doel, Frederick		Fireman	Engineering	Southampton	S	C		
Dolby, Joseph	36	Reception Room Steward (First Class)	Victualling	Southampton	B			
Donati, Italo F.	17	à la Carte Assistant Waiter	Vendor	London, England	S		#311, buried in Fairview Cemetery, Halifax	see à la Carte Group Notes
Donoghue, T.	35	First Class Bedroom Steward	Victualling	Southampton	B			

Name (Maiden Name) *Survivors names in italic*	Age	Title/Function	Department	Residence	E	L/B	Body # Recovered / Where Buried	Notes
Dore, Albert	22	Trimmer	Engineering	Southampton	S	?		
Dornier, Louis A.	21	à la Carte Assistant Fish Cook	Vendor	Southampton	S			see à la Carte Group Notes
Doughty, N.	22	Second Class Saloon Steward	Victualling	Southampton	S			
Doyle, Lawrence		Fireman	Engineering	Southampton	S			
Duffy, William	29	Chief Engineer's Clerk	Engineering	Dublin, Ireland	B			
Dunford, William	41	Third Class Hospital Steward	Victualling	Southampton	S		#71, buried at sea	
Dyer, Henry R.	24	Senior Assistant Fourth Engineer	Engineering	Southampton	B			
Dyer, William	30	First Class Saloon Steward	Victualling	Southampton	S			
Dymond, Frank		Fireman	Engineering	Southampton	S	15		Commanded Lifeboat 15.

E

Eagle, A.J.		Trimmer	Engineering	Southampton	S			
Eastman, Charles		Greaser	Engineering	Southampton	S			
Edbroke, F.	24	Third Class Steward	Victualling	Portsmouth, England	S			
Ede, George B.	22	Third Class Steward	Victualling	Southampton	S			
Edge, J.W.	37	Second Class Deck Steward	Victualling	Southampton	S			
Edwards, C.	38	Assistant Pantryman Steward (First Class)	Victualling	Southampton	S			
Egg, W.H.	24	Third Class Steward	Victualling	Southampton	S			
Elliott, Everett E.		Trimmer	Engineering	London, England	S		#317, buried in Fairview Cemetery, Halifax	
Ellis, John B.	30	Assistant Vegetable Cook	Victualling	Southampton	S	2		
Ennis, Walter	35	Turkish Bath Steward	Victualling	Southport, England	S			
Ervine, Albert G.	19	Assistant Electrician	Engineering	Belfast, Ireland	B			
Etches, Henry S.	41	First Class Bedroom Steward	Victualling	Southampton	S	5		
Evans, Alfred F.	24	Lookout	Deck	Southampton	S	15		
Evans, Frank O.	27	Able Bodied Seaman	Deck	Southampton	S	10		

Frank Evans commanded Lifeboat 10. He was transferred to Lifeboat 14 by Fifth Officer Lowe to look for survivors. He pulled four people from the water and later rescued survivors on Collapsible Lifeboats A and B.

Evans, George	32	First Class Saloon Steward	Victualling	Southampton	B			
Evans, George	33	Third Class Steward	Victualling	Southampton	S			
Evans, William	32	Trimmer	Engineering	Southampton	S		#31, buried at sea	

F

Fairall, H.	38	First Class Saloon Steward	Victualling	Southampton	S			
Farendon, E.	32	Confectioner	Victualling	Hampshire, England	S			
Farquharson, William E.	39	Senior Second Engineer	Engineering	Southampton	B			
Faulkner, William S.		First Class Bedroom Steward	Victualling	Southampton	S	11		
Fay, Thomas	30	Greaser	Engineering	Southampton	S			
Fei, Carlo	19	à la Carte Scullery	Vendor	London, England	S			see à la Carte Group Notes
Fellows, Alfred J.	29	Assistant Boots Steward (First Class)	Victualling	Southampton	S		#138, buried in Fairview Cemetery, Halifax	
Feltham. G.	36	Vienna Baker	Victualling	Southampton	S			
Ferray, Anton		Trimmer	Engineering	Southampton	S			
Ferris, William	38	Leading Fireman	Engineering	Southampton	S			
Finch, Harry	18	Third Class Steward	Victualling	Southampton	S			
Fitzpatrick, Charles W.N.		Mess Steward (Crew)	Engineering	Southampton	S	B/12		
Fitzpatrick, Hugh J.	27	Junior Boilermaker	Engineering	Belfast	B			

Name *(Maiden Name)* *Survivors names in italic*	Age	Title/Function	Department	Residence	E	L/B	Body # Recovered / Where Buried	Notes
Flarty, Edward		Fireman	Engineering	Southampton	S	?		
Fleet, Frederick	24	Lookout	Deck	Southampton	S	6		

Frederick Fleet was stationed in the crow's nest with Reginald Lee. It was Fleet who first saw the iceberg, and he then rang the crows nest bell three times to alert the bridge while picking up the phone and passing the word on to Sixth Officer Moody.

Name *(Maiden Name)*	Age	Title/Function	Department	Residence	E	L/B	Body # Recovered / Where Buried	Notes
Fletcher, P.W.	29	Bugler (First Class)	Victualling	Southampton	S			
Foley, John	44	Storekeeper	Deck	Southampton	B	4		
Foley, William C.	26	Third Class Steward	Victualling	Southampton	S	13		
Ford, Ernest	31	Third Class Steward	Victualling	Southampton	S			
Ford, F.	37	Second Class Bedroom Steward	Victualling	Southampton	S.			
Ford, H.		Trimmer	Engineering	Southampton	S			
Ford, Thomas	30	Leading Fireman	Engineering	Southampton	S			
Forward, James	27	Able Bodied Seaman	Deck	Southampton	S	16		
Foster, A.	37	Storekeeper (Engineering)	Engineering	Southampton	S			
Fox, William T.	28	Third Class Steward	Victualling	Hampshire, England	S			
Franklin, Alan V.	29	Second Class Saloon Steward	Victualling	Southampton	S		#262, buried in Fairview Cemetery, Halifax	
Fraser, James	29	Junior Assistant Third Engineer	Engineering	Southampton	B			
Fraser, James		Fireman	Engineering	Southampton	S			
Fredricks, W.		Trimmer	Engineering	Southampton	S	15		
Freeman, Ernest E.S.	43	Secretary to J. Bruce Ismay	Victualling	Southampton	S		#229, buried in Fairview Cemetery, Halifax	
Fryer, Albert E.	26	Trimmer	Engineering	Southampton	S	13		

G

Name *(Maiden Name)*	Age	Title/Function	Department	Residence	E	L/B	Body # Recovered / Where Buried	Notes
Gardner, F.		Greaser	Engineering	Southampton	S			
Gatti, Gaspare A.P. "Luigi"	36	à la Carte Manager	Vendor	Southampton	S		#313, buried in Fairview Cemetery, Halifax	see à la Carte Group Notes
Geddes, Richard C.	31	First Class Bedroom Steward	Victualling	Southampton	S			
Geer, Alfred E.	24	Fireman	Engineering	Southampton	S			see Substitutes Group Notes
Gibbons, Jacob W.	37	Second Class Saloon Steward	Victualling	Dorset, England	S	11		
Gilardino, Vincenzo P.	32	à la Carte Waiter	Vendor	Southampton	S			see à la Carte Group Notes
Giles, John R.	30	Second Baker	Victualling	Southampton	S			
Gill, Joseph S.	31	First Class Bedroom Steward	Victualling	Southampton	B		#49, buried at sea	
Gill, P.	38	Ship's Cook	Victualling	Southampton	S			
Godley, George		Fireman	Engineering	Southampton	S	?		
Godwin, Frederick W.	34	Greaser	Engineering	Hampshire	S			
Gold, Mrs. Katherine	40	First Class Stewardess	Victualling		S	11		Survived the grounding of the White Star Line ship *Suevic* in 1907.
Golder, Martin W.		Fireman	Engineering	Southampton	S			
Gollop, F.	29	Assistant Passenger Cook	Victualling	Southampton	S			
Gordon, J.	29	Trimmer	Engineering	Southampton	S			see Substitutes Group Notes
Goree, Frank	28	Greaser	Engineering	Southampton	S		#222, buried in Fairview Cemetery, Halifax	
Goshawk, Arthur J.	31	First Class Saloon Steward	Victualling	Southampton	S			
Gosling, Bertram J.		Trimmer	Engineering	Southampton	S			
Gosling, S.		Trimmer	Engineering	Southampton	S			
Graham, Thomas G.		Fireman	Engineering	Belfast, Ireland	B	?		

Name *(Maiden Name)* *Survivors names in italic*	Age	Title/Function	Department	Residence	E	L/B	Body # Recovered / Where Buried	Notes
Graves, Stanley			Engineering					

Stanley Graves is listed on some of the ship's registers, but he never boarded *Titanic*. His place was taken by a friend, Sidney Rutter, who died that night.

Name	Age	Title/Function	Department	Residence	E	L/B	Body # Recovered / Where Buried	Notes
Green, George		Trimmer	Engineering	Southampton	S			
Gregory, David		Greaser	Engineering	Southampton	S			
Gregson, Miss Mary	40	First Class Stewardess	Victualling	Southampton	S	16		
Grodidge, Ernest E.	32	Fireman	Engineering	Southampton	S		#276, buried in Fairview Cemetery, Halifax	
Grosclaude, Gerald	24	à la Carte Assistant Coffee Maker	Vendor	London, England	S			see à la Carte Group Notes
Gumery, George	24	Mess Steward (Crew)	Engineering	Birmingham, England	S			
Gunn, J.T.	28	Second Class Saloon Steward	Victualling	Southampton	S			
Guy, Edward J.	28	Assistant Boots Steward (First Class)	Victualling	Southampton	S	5		
Gwinn, William L.	37	Postal Clerk	Postal	Asbury Park, NJ	S			see Postal Clerk Group Notes

H

Name	Age	Title/Function	Department	Residence	E	L/B	Body # Recovered / Where Buried	Notes
Hagan, John	30	Fireman	Engineering	Southampton	B	3		
Haines, Albert M.	31	Boatswain's Mate	Deck	Southampton	B	9		Commanded of Lifeboat 9.
Halford, Richard	22	Third Class Steward	Victualling	Southampton	S	15		
Hall, F.A.J.	38	Scullion	Victualling	Southampton	S			
Hall, Joseph		Fireman	Engineering	Southampton	S			
Hallett, Mr. George		Fireman	Engineering	Southampton	S			
Hamblyn, Ernest W.	41	Second Class Bedroom Steward	Victualling	Southampton	S			
Hamilton, E.	25	Assistant Smoking Room Steward (First Class)	Victualling	Southampton	B			
Hands, B.		Fireman	Engineering	Southampton	S			
Hannam, George		Fireman	Engineering	Southampton	S			
Harder, William	39	Window Washer	Deck	Southampton	S	14		
Harding, A.	20	Asst Pantry Steward (Second Class)	Victualling	Southampton	S			
Hardwick, Reginald	21	Kitchen Porter	Victualling	Southampton	S	13		
Hardy, John T.	36	Chief Second Class Steward	Victualling	Southampton	B	D		

John Hardy was already in the water when Collapsible Lifeboat D floated by him. He managed to climb into the lifeboat and survived.

Name	Age	Title/Function	Department	Residence	E	L/B	Body # Recovered / Where Buried	Notes
Harris, C.H.	16	Bell Boy (First Class)	Victualling	Southampton	S			
Harris, C.W.	18	Second Class Saloon Steward	Victualling	Southampton	S			
Harris, E.	18	Assistant Pantryman Steward (First Class)	Victualling	Winchester, England	S			
Harris, Edward		Fireman	Engineering	Southampton	S			
Harris, Frederick	34	Fireman	Engineering	Southampton	S	14		
Harris, Frederick		Trimmer	Engineering	Southampton	S			
Harrison, Aragon D.	40	First Class Saloon Steward	Victualling	Southampton	S	9		
Harrison, Norman	39	Assistant Second Engineer	Engineering	Southampton	B			
Hart, John E.	31	Third Class Steward	Victualling	Southampton	S	15		

One of the true heroes of the *Titanic* disaster, **John E. Hart** was responsible for saving 58 Third Class women and children. Leading them in two groups through the maze of decks, ladders and compartments up to the boat deck, he helped place them into lifeboats 8 and 15. See Cox-Hart-Pearcey Group Notes.

> Key: **Names** are in alphabetical order. **"E"** indicates where embarked (**B** is for Belfast, **S** is for Southampton). **L/B** indicates which lifeboat they escaped on, if known. **Body # Recovered / Where Buried** indicates in what sequence the body was recovered, and where it was buried. For descriptions of job functions, see **Glossary**.

Name	Age	Title/Function	Department	Residence	E	L/B	Body # Recovered / Where Buried	Notes
Hart, Thomas	49	Fireman	Engineering	Southampton	S			

Thomas Hart never actually got on the ship. His Discharge Book (i.e. identification) was stolen when he was mugged at a bar, and someone unknown used it to board *Titanic* as a fireman. That unknown person died. Hart, apparently embarrassed that he had gone on a drinking binge and lost his Discharge Book, didn't tell his family and left town for a few weeks. Hart's family was notified he was lost, however three weeks after the sinking, without warning he walked into his house, causing his mother to pass out and almost causing her to have a heart attack.

Name (Maiden Name) Survivors names in italic	Age	Title/Function	Department	Residence	E	L/B	Body # Recovered / Where Buried	Notes
Hartnell, Frederick	20	First Class Saloon Steward	Victualling	Southampton	S	11		
Harvey, Herbert G.	34	Junior Assistant Second Engineer	Engineering	Southampton	B			
Haslin, James		Trimmer	Engineering	Southampton	S			
Hatch, H.	22	Scullion	Victualling	Southampton	S			
Hawkesworth, John	38	Second Class Saloon Steward	Victualling	Southampton	S			
Hawksworth, William W.	38	Assistant Deck Steward (First Class)	Victualling	Southampton	S			
Hayter, Arthur	44	First Class Bedroom Steward	Victualling	Southampton	B		#25, buried at sea	
Head, Albert		Fireman	Engineering	Southampton	S			
Hebb, A.		Trimmer	Engineering	Southampton	S	B		
Heinen, Joseph	30	Second Class Saloon Steward	Victualling	London, England	S			
Hemming, Samuel E.	40	Lamp Trimmer	Deck	Southampton	S	4		He was picked up from the water.
Hendrickson, Charles G.	29	Leading Fireman	Engineering	Southampton	S	1		
Hendy, Edward M.	38	First Class Saloon Steward	Victualling	Southampton	B			
Hensford, H.G.	29	Assistant Butcher	Victualling	Southampton	S			
Hesketh, John H.	33	Assistant Second Engineer	Engineering	Southampton	B			
Hewett, T.	37	First Class Bedroom Steward	Victualling	Liverpool, England	B		#168, buried at sea	
Hichens, (Hitchens) Robert	30	Quartermaster	Deck	Southampton	S	6		

Robert Hichens was the quartermaster who was at the wheel when *Titanic* struck the iceberg. Later he was assigned to command Lifeboat 6, a lifeboat that contained among others, Margaret "Molly" Brown. Before the ship sank, Margaret Brown wanted to go back to pick up survivors, and Hichens refused. Later, Molly and some of the other women wanted to help row in order to keep warm, and again Hichens refused, and made some nasty comments about Margaret and women in general. Not suffering fools lightly, Margaret Brown then threatened to toss Hichens overboard, which she could easily have done. Hichens, deciding to give up the fight, crawled under a canvas sail and remained there, out of sight and out of mind, until rescued by *Carpathia*. The passengers of Lifeboat 6 never had anything good to say about Hichens.

Name (Maiden Name) Survivors names in italic	Age	Title/Function	Department	Residence	E	L/B	Body # Recovered / Where Buried	Notes
Hill, H.P.	36	Third Class Steward	Victualling	Southampton	S			
Hill, J		Trimmer	Engineering	Southampton	S			
Hill, James C.	31	First Class Bedroom Steward	Victualling	Southampton	B		#152, buried at sea	
Hinckley, G.	35	Second Class Bath Steward	Victualling	Southampton	S		#66, buried at sea	
Hine, William E.	36	Third Baker	Victualling	Southampton	S			
Hinton, William S.		Trimmer	Engineering	Southampton	S		#85, buried at sea	
Hiscock, S.	22	Plates Steward (First Class)	Victualling	Southampton	S			
Hoare, Leonad J.	21	First Class Saloon Steward	Victualling	Southampton	B			
Hodge, Charles	29	Senior Assistant Third Engineer	Engineering	Southampton	B			
Hodges, W.		Fireman	Engineering	Southampton	S			
Hodgkinson, Leonard	46	Senior Fourth Engineer	Engineering	Southampton	B			
Hogg, Charles W.	37	First Class Bedroom Steward	Victualling	Liverpool, England	B			
Hogg, George A.	29	Lookout	Deck	Southampton	S	7		
Hogue, Edward	22	Plates Steward (First Class)	Victualling	Hampshire	S			
Holland, Thomas	28	Reception Room Steward (First Class)	Victualling	Liverpool, England	B			
Holloway, Sidney	20	Assistant Clothes Presser Steward (First Class)	Victualling	Southampton	S		#273, buried in Fairview Cemetery, Halifax	
Holman, Harry	27	Able Bodied Seaman	Deck	Southampton	S			
Hopkins, F.	16	Plates Steward (First Class)	Victualling	Southampton	S			
Hopkins, Robert J.		Able Bodied Seaman	Deck	Belfast	B	15		
Horswell, Albert E.J.	33	Able Bodied Seaman	Deck	Southampton	S	1		
Hosgood, Richard	22	Fireman	Engineering	Euston, England	S		#242, buried in Fairview Cemetery, Halifax	see Substitutes Group Notes
Hosking, George F.	36	Senior Third Engineer	Engineering	Southampton	B			
House, William	38	First Class Saloon Steward	Victualling	Southampton	B			

Name *(Maiden Name)* *Survivors names in italic*	Age	Title/Function	Department	Residence	E	L/B	Body # Recovered / Where Buried	Notes
Howell, Arthur A.	31	First Class Saloon Steward	Victualling	Southampton	B		#319, buried in Fairview Cemetery, Halifax	
Hughes, W.T.	33	Asst. Second Steward (First Class0	Victualling	Southampton	S			
Humby, F.	16	Plates Steward (Second Class)	Victualling	Southampton	S			
Humphreys, Sidney J.	48	Quartermaster	Deck	Southampton	S	11		Commanded Lifeboat 11.
Humphreys, Toms H.	28	Second Class Saloon Steward	Victualling	Southampton	S			
Hunt, Albert	22	Trimmer	Engineering	Southampton	S	C		
Hunt, T.	28	Fireman	Engineering	Southampton	S			
Hurst, Charles J.		Fireman	Engineering	Southampton	S			
Hurst, Walter	27	Fireman	Engineering	Southampton	S	B		

Walter Hurst and his father-in-law William Mintram served together. The night of the sinking, Mintram had a life jacket and Hurst did not. Mintram gave Hurst his life jacket, and Hurst survived but his father-in-law did not.

Hutchinson, J.	29	Vegetable Cook	Victualling	Southampton	S		#250, buried in Fairview Cemetery, Halifax	
Hutchinson, Mr. John H.	28	Joiner	Deck	Southampton	S			
Hyland, James L.	19	Third Class Steward	Victualling	Southampton	S	11		

I

Ide, Harry J.	32	First Class Bedroom Steward	Victualling	Southampton	S			
Ingram, Charles		Trimmer	Engineering	Southampton	S		#204, buried in Fairview Cemetery, Halifax	
Ingrouille, Henry	21	Third Class Steward	Victualling	Southampton	S			
Ings, W.	20	Scullion	Victualling	Southampton	S			
Instance, T.		Fireman	Engineering	Southampton	S			

J

Jackson, C.	29	Assistant Boots Steward (First Class)	Victualling	Southampton	S			
Jacobson, John		Fireman	Engineering	Southampton	S			
Jago, J.		Greaser	Engineering	Southampton	S			
Jaillet, Henri M.	38	à la Carte Pastry Cook	Vendor	London, England	S		#277, buried in Mount Olivet Cemetery, Halifax	see à la Carte Group Notes
James, Thomas		Fireman	Engineering	Southampton	S			
Janaway, William F.	35	First Class Bedroom Steward	Victualling	Southampton	B			
Janin, Claude M.	30	à la Carte Soup Cook	Vendor	London, England	S			see à la Carte Group Notes
Jarvis, William	37	Fireman	Engineering	Southampton	S			
Jeffery, William A.	24	à la Carte Controller	Vendor	Southampton	S			see à la Carte Group Notes
Jenner, Harry	41	Second Class Saloon Steward	Victualling	Southampton				
Jensen, Charles V.	25	Second Class Saloon Steward	Victualling	Southampton	S			
Jessop, Miss Violet C.	24	First Class Stewardess	Victualling	London, England	S	16		

Miss **Violet C. Jessop** was a Stewardess for the First Class passengers. *Titanic* was her second ship as she had served earlier on RMS *Olympic*. She was on *Olympic* when it was struck broadside by a British warship, HMS *Hawke*. Jessop then transferred to *Titanic,* and although she was a member of the crew and offered to remain behind, she was ordered into a lifeboat because she was a woman. Jessop survived, and then later became a nurse for the British Red Cross during World War I. She then later transferred to the new RMS *Britannic, Titanic's* sister ship. She was on *Britannic* when it struck an underwater mine off the Greek islands, and sank in 1915. So young Violet Jessop had the dubious honor of serving on all three of the Olympic-Class ships, and was involved in either an accident or sinking of them all.

Jewell, Archibald	24	Lookout	Deck	Southampton	S	7		
Joas, N.		Fireman	Engineering	Southampton	S			
Johnson, H	36	Assistant Ship's Cook	Victualling	Southampton	S			

Name *(Maiden Name)* *Survivors names in italic*	Age	Title/Function	Department	Residence	E	L/B	Body # Recovered / Where Buried	Notes
Johnson, James		First Class Saloon Steward	Victualling	Southampton	S	2		
Jones, Albert	17	Second Class Saloon Steward	Victualling	Southampton	S			
Jones, Arthur E.	38	Plates Steward (Second Class)	Victualling	Southampton	S			
Jones, H.	29	Roast Cook	Victualling	Southampton	S			
Jones, Reginald V.	20	First Class Saloon Steward	Victualling	Southampton	S			
Jones, Thomas W.		Able Bodied Seaman	Deck	Wales	S	8		Commanded Lifeboat 8.
Jouannault, Georges J.	20	à la Carte' Assistant Sauce Cook	Vendor	Southampton	S			see à la Carte Group Notes
Joughin, Charles J.	33	Chief Baker	Victualling	Southampton	B	B		

Charles Joughin was the Chief Baker, and was on duty when *Titanic* struck the iceberg. As the lifeboats were being loaded, he carried loaves of bread out to the passengers, which as it turns out was the only food on the lifeboats. Later, having found access to the liquor stock, Joughin proceeded to consume an entire bottle of scotch. He wasn't feeling either pain nor the cold when he stood on top the stern railing and held onto the flagstaff (just like in the James Cameron movie), and rode the ship into the water like, as he put it, *"riding on an elevator"*. He didn't even get his hair wet. Joughin floated in the water for well over an hour before enough of the survivors standing on top of the overturned Collapsible Lifeboat B died and fell off. He finally managed to get onto the lifeboat, and was rescued there. Even after that much exposure to the water, Joughin survived with little after affects, always claiming that the alcohol he consumed kept him from freezing.

Name	Age	Title/Function	Department	Residence	E	L/B	Body #	Notes
Judd, Charles E.	32	Fireman	Engineering	Southampton	S	B		
Jukes, James	35	Greaser	Engineering	Southampton	S			
Junod, Emma			Victualling					see Mrs. Ernest J. Bliss
Jupe, Herbert	31	Assistant Electrician	Engineering	Southampton	S		#73, buried at sea	

K

Name	Age	Title/Function	Department	Residence	E	L/B	Body #	Notes
Kaspar, Franz V.	40	Fireman	Engineering	Southampton	S	9		
Kearl, Charles H.		Greaser	Engineering	Southampton	S			
Kearl, G.	24	Trimmer	Engineering	Hampshire, England	S			
Keegan, James	38	Leading Fireman	Engineering	Southampton	S			
Keene, Percy E.	28	First Class Saloon Steward	Victualling	Southampton	S	15		
Kelland, T.	21	Second Class Library Steward	Victualling	Hampshire	S			
Kelly, James		Greaser	Engineering	Southampton	S			
Kelly, William	35	Assistant Electrician	Engineering	Dublin, Ireland	B			
Kemish, George		Fireman	Engineering	Southampton	S	9		
Kemp, Thomas H.	43	Assistant Fourth Engineer	Engineering	Southampton	B			
Kenchenten, Frederick		Greaser	Engineering	Southampton	S			
Kennel, Charles	30	Kosher Cook	Victualling	Southampton	S			
Kenzler, Augustus	43	Storekeeper (Engineering)	Engineering	Southampton	S			
			Engineering					
Kerley, W.T.	28	Second Class Saloon Steward	Victualling	Salisbury, England	S			
Kerr, Thomas		Fireman	Engineering	Southampton	S			
Ketchley, Henry	30	First Class Saloon Steward	Victualling	Southampton	B			
Kieran, Michael	31	Storekeeper	Victualling	Southampton	S			
Kiernan, James W.	30	Chief Third Class Steward	Victualling	Southampton	S			
King, Alfred	18	Lift (Elevator) Steward (First Class)	Victualling	Southampton	S		#238, buried in Fairview Cemetery, Halifax	
King, Ernest W.	28	Ships Clerk	Victualling	Clones, Ireland	S		#321, buried in Fairview Cemetery, Halifax	
King, G.	20	Scullion	Victualling	Southampton	S			
King, Thomas W.		Master at Arms	Deck	Yarmouth	S			
Kingscote, William F.	43	First Class Saloon Steward	Victualling	Southampton	S			
Kinsella, Leonard	30	Fireman	Engineering	Southampton	S			see Substitutes Group Notes
Kirkham, J.		Greaser	Engineering	Southampton	S			
Kitching, Arthur A.	30	First Class Saloon Steward	Victualling	Southampton	S			
Klein, Herbert	33	Barber (Second Class)	Vendor	Southampton	S			see Barber's Group Notes

Name *(Maiden Name)* *Survivors names in italic*	Age	Title/Function	Department	Residence	E	L/B	Body # Recovered / Where Buried	Notes
Knight, George	44	First Class Saloon Steward	Victualling	Southampton	S	13		
Knight, Leonard G.	21	Third Class Steward	Victualling	Hampshire, England	S			
Knowles, Thomas	39	Firemen's Messman	Engineering	Lymington, England	S	C		

L

Name	Age	Title/Function	Department	Residence	E	L/B	Body # Recovered / Where Buried	Notes
Lacey, Bert	21	Second Class Saloon Steward	Victualling	Salisbury, England	S			
Lahy, Thomas E.		Fireman	Engineering	London, England	S			
Lake, William	35	First Class Saloon Steward	Victualling	Southampton	B			
Lane, Albert E.	34	First Class Saloon Steward	Victualling	Southampton	S			
Latimer, Andrew	55	Chief Steward (First Class)	Victualling	Liverpool, England	S			
Lavington, Miss Bessie	39	First Class Stewardess	Victualling	Winchester, England	S	11		
Lawrence, Arthur	35	First Class Saloon Steward	Victualling	Southampton	B		#90, buried in Liverpool, England	
Leader, A.	22	Assistant Confectioner	Victualling	Southampton	S			
Leather, Mrs. Elizabeth M.	41	First Class Stewardess	Victualling	Liverpool, England	S	16		
Lee, H.		Trimmer	Engineering	Southampton	S			
Lee, Reginald R.	42	Lookout	Deck	Southampton	S	13		

Reginald R. Lee was one of the two lookouts in the crow's nest (along with Frederick Fleet) and saw the iceberg before *Titanic* struck it.

Name	Age	Title/Function	Department	Residence	E	L/B	Body # Recovered / Where Buried	Notes
Lefebvre, Paul G.	36	First Class Saloon Steward	Victualling	Southampton	S		#211, buried in Fairview Cemetery, Halifax	
Leonard, Matthew	26	Third Class Steward	Victualling	Belfast	B			
Levett, G.	21	Assistant Pantryman Steward (First Class)	Victualling	Southampton	B			
Lewis, Arthur E.R.	27	Third Class Steward	Victualling	Southampton	S			
Light, C.	23	Plates Steward (First Class)	Victualling	Hampshire	S			
Light, Charles		Fireman	Engineering	Southampton	S			
Light, W.		Fireman	Engineering	Southampton	S			
Lightoller, Mr. Charles H.	38	Second Officer	Deck	Southampton	B	B		

By the time **Charles H. Lightoller** was 21, he had been at sea eight years, had survived a cyclone, a fire at sea, several de-mastings, a bout with malaria and a shipwreck where he was stranded on a deserted island. He joined the White Star Line in 1900 and worked his way up through postings and ever-larger ships until he was assigned as the First Officer on *Olympic* and then *Titanic*. The day before *Titanic* left Southampton, WSL assigned Henry T. Wilde to be Chief Officer, which bumped Lightoller down to Second Officer behind Murdoch. Lightoller was asleep when the ship struck the iceberg. Captain Smith later ordered him to prepare the port side lifeboats for launching and when the order came down to launch the lifeboats, Lightoller began to fill them with women and children and enough crewmembers to operate the oars and tiller. No other males, passengers or crew, were allowed into the lifeboats on the port side. As *Titanic* made it's final plunge, Lightoller ended up in the water next to the overturned Collapsible Lifeboat B. He and about 30 other men managed to get onto the lifeboat, where they spent the rest of the night standing on the bottom of the lifeboat. Several of the men died during the night, including John Phillips, the Marconi operator. During World War I Lightoller was awarded several medals for his service in the Royal Navy, ending the war a full Commander. At the beginning of World War II, Lightoller and his son helped evacuate the British Army from Dunkirk. He lost both of his sons during the war, and Lightoller died in 1952.

Name	Age	Title/Function	Department	Residence	E	L/B	Body # Recovered / Where Buried	Notes
Lindsay, William C.		Fireman	Engineering	Southampton	S	B		
Littlejohn, Alexander J.	35	First Class Saloon Steward	Victualling	Southampton	B	13		
Lloyd, Humphrey	32	First Class Saloon Steward	Victualling	Southampton	B		#57, buried at sea	
Lloyd, W.	29	Fireman	Engineering	Southampton	S			see Substitutes Group Notes
Locke, A.	32	Scullion	Victualling	Southampton	S			see Substitutes Group Notes
Long, Frank	28	Trimmer	Engineering	Southampton	S			
Long, W.		Trimmer	Engineering	Southampton	S			
Longmuir, John D.	19	Assistant Pantry Steward (Second Class)	Victualling	Southampton	S			
Lovell, J.	32	Grill Cook	Victualling	Southampton	S			

Name *(Maiden Name)* *Survivors names in italic*	Age	Title/Function	Department	Residence	E	L/B	Body # Recovered / Where Buried	Notes
Lowe, Mr. Harold G.	30	Fifth Officer	Deck	Wales	B	14		

Fifth Officer **Harold Lowe** went to sea when he was 14 years old. He had been with White Star Line for only about two years before signing on as part of *Titanic's* crew. One of his jobs prior to leaving Southampton was to inventory each lifeboat to make sure everything was present. He signed off on the inventory, stating that all material was available, but this only meant oars, mast and sail, not water or food. Later, he helped with the one lifeboat drill that was made to check the condition of the lifeboats. After *Titanic* struck the iceberg, and while helping load the lifeboats, Lowe is the officer who ordered J. Bruce Ismay to stop trying to help. Lowe was afraid Ismay was going to end up dumping a lifeboat and its passengers into the water. Lowe was ordered into Lifeboat 14 and later when in the water, he rounded up four other lifeboats, moved passengers around to equalize the loads. Lowe then went back to look for survivors in the water and picked up four, one of whom later died from exposure. After *Carpathia* was sighted, Lowe rigged a sail on his lifeboat, took Collapsible Lifeboat"A" in tow, picked up the three survivors off Collapsible Lifeboat"D", and led them all to the rescue ship.

Name *(Maiden Name)*	Age	Title/Function	Department	Residence	E	L/B	Body # Recovered / Where Buried	Notes
Lucas, William	26	Able Bodied Seaman	Deck	Southampton	S	D		
Lucas, William B.	30	First Class Saloon Steward	Victualling	Southampton	B	A		
Lydiatt, Charles	28	First Class Saloon Steward	Victualling	Southampton	S			
Lyons, William H.	26	Able Bodied Seaman	Deck	Southampton	S		buried at sea	

William H. Lyons was one of four crewmen rescued from the water. He lived until placed onto *Carpathia,* but he died that night and was buried at sea.

M

Name *(Maiden Name)*	Age	Title/Function	Department	Residence	E	L/B	Body # Recovered / Where Buried	Notes
Mabey, J.	24	Third Class Steward	Victualling	Southampton	S			
MacKay, Charles D.	30	First Class Saloon Steward	Victualling	Southampton	S	11		
Mackie, G.W.	34	Second Class Bedroom Steward	Victualling	Southampton	S			
Mackie, William D.	32	Junior Fifth Engineer	Engineering	London, England	AB			
Major, Thomas E.	35	Bath Steward (First Class)	Victualling	Southampton	B			
Major, William		Fireman	Engineering	Southampton	S	13		
Mantle, Roland F.	36	Third Class Steward	Victualling	Southampton	S			
March, John S.	48	Postal Clerk	Postal	Newark, NJ	S		#225, buried in Evergreen Cemetery, Hillside, NJ	see Postal Clerk Group Notes
Marks, J.	26	Asst. Pantryman Steward (First Class)	Victualling	Southampton	S			
Marrett, G.		Fireman	Engineering	Southampton	S			
Marriott, J.W.	25	Asst. Pantryman Steward (First Class)	Victualling	Southampton	S		#2, buried in Fairview Cemetery, Halifax	
Marsden, Miss Evelyn	28	First Class Stewardess	Victualling	Southampton	S	16		
Marsh, Frederick C.	28	Fireman	Engineering	Southampton	S		#268, buried in Fairview Cemetery, Halifax	
Martin, F.	29	Scullion	Victualling	Hampshire, England	S	13		
~~*Martin, Miss Margaret E.*~~	~~20~~	~~à la Carte Second Cashier~~	~~Vendor~~	~~London, England~~	~~S~~	~~6~~		~~see à la Carte Group Notes~~
Martin, Mrs. Annie	33	First Class Stewardess	Victualling	Portsmouth, England	S	11		
Maskell, L.A.		Trimmer	Engineering	Southampton	S			
Mason, Frank A.R.	32	Fireman	Engineering	Southampton	S	B		
Mason, James	39	Leading Fireman	Engineering	Southampton	S			
Matherson, David	30	Able Bodied Seaman	Deck	Southampton	S		#192, buried in Fairview Cemetery, Halifax	
Mathias, Montague V.	27	Officers Mess Steward	Deck	Southampton	S			
Mattman, Adolf	30	à la Carte Ice Maker	Vendor	Southampton	S			see à la Carte Group Notes
Mauge, Paul A.M.G.	24	à la Carte Kitchen Cook	Vendor	London, England	S	13		see à la Carte Group Notes
Maxwell, John	31	Carpenter	Deck	Southampton	B			
May, Arthur	23	Fireman	Engineering	Southampton	S			Served with his father Arthur W. May.
May, Arthur W.	60	Fireman's Messman	Engineering	Southampton	S			Served with his son Arthur May.
Maynard, Isaac	32	Entree Cook	Victualling	Southampton	B	B		
Mayo, William P.	27	Leading Fireman	Engineering	Southampton	S		#177, buried at sea	
Maytum, Alfred	49	Chief Butcher	Victualling	Southampton	S		#141, buried in Fairview Cemetery, Halifax	

Name *(Maiden Name)* *Survivors names in italic*	Age	Title/Function	Department	Residence	E	L/B	Body # Recovered / Where Buried	Notes
Mayzes, Thomas	25	Fireman	Engineering	Southampton	S	3		
McAndrew, Thomas		Fireman	Engineering	Southampton	S			
McAndrews, William		Fireman	Engineering	Southampton	S			
McCarthy, Frederick J.	35	First Class Bedroom Steward	Victualling	Southampton	S			
McCarthy, William	47	Able Bodied Seaman	Deck	Cork, Ireland	B	4		
McCastlen, William		Fireman	Engineering	Southampton	S			
McCawley, Thomas W.	36	Gymnasium Steward (First Class)	Victualling	Southampton	S			
McElroy, Hugh W.	37	Purser	Victualling	Southampton	S		#157, buried at sea	

Hugh McElroy was the Purser and in charge of the safe that contained First Class passengers' valuables. All the passengers stopped by and picked up their personal items. Once completed, McElroy went up to the Boat deck to help load passengers into the lifeboats. He was last seen standing with Dr. William O'Loughlin, Dr. John Simpson, Reginald Barker and Second Officer Lightoller, shaking hands and saying goodbye. Only Lightoller survived.

McGann, James		Trimmer	Engineering	Southampton	S	B		
McGarvey, Edward		Fireman	Engineering	Southampton	S			
McGaw, Errol		Fireman	Engineering	Southampton	S			
McGough, George M.		Able Bodied Seaman	Deck	Southampton	S	9		
McGrady, James	27	First Class Saloon Steward	Victualling	Southampton	S		#330, buried in Fairview Cemetery, Halifax	

James McGrady's was the last "official" body recovered by a ship sent out for that purpose. Because numbers 324 and 325 were not used, his was actually the 328th body recovered. Several other bodies were later recovered but not given an official number.

McGregor, J.		Fireman	Engineering	Southampton	S			
McInerney, Thomas		Greaser	Engineering	Southampton	S			
McIntyre, William	22	Trimmer	Engineering	Southampton	S	A		
McLaren, Mrs. Henry (Katherine Allsop)	40	First Class Stewardess	Victualling	Southampton	S	5		Served with her brother Frank Allsop.
McMicken, Arthur	23	First Class Saloon Steward	Victualling	Southampton	S	11		
McMullan, J.	31	First Class Saloon Steward	Victualling	Southampton	B			
McMurray, William E.	43	First Class Bedroom Steward	Victualling	Liverpool, England	B			
McQuillan, William	32	Fireman	Engineering	Belfast	B		#183, buried in Fairview Cemetery, Halifax	
McRae, William A.		Fireman	Engineering	Southampton	S			
McReynolds, William	22	Junior Sixth Engineer	Engineering	Belfast, Ireland	B			
Mellor, Arthur	24	First Class Saloon Steward	Victualling	Southampton	S			
Middleton, Alfred P.	17	Assistant Electrician	Engineering	Belfast, Ireland	B			
Middleton, M.N.	25	Second Class Saloon Steward	Victualling	London, England	S			
Milford, George		Fireman	Engineering	Southampton	S			
Millar, Robert	27	Extra Fifth Engineer	Engineering	Southampton	B			
Millar, Thomas	33	Assistant Deck Engineer	Engineering	Belfast, Ireland	B			
Mills, Charles	52	Assistant Butcher	Victualling	Southampton	S	C		
Mintram, William	46	Fireman	Engineering	Southampton	S			

Walter Hurst and his father-in-law William Mintram served together. The night of the sinking, Mintram had a life jacket and Hurst did not. Mintram gave his son-in-law Hurst his life jacket, and Hurst survived but his father-in-law did not.

Mishellany, A.	52	Printer Steward	Victualling	Southampton	B			
Mitchell, Lawrence		Trimmer	Engineering	Southampton	S			
Monoros, Jean	20	à la Carte Assistant Waiter	Vendor	London, England	S		#27, buried at sea	see à la Carte Group Notes
Monteverdi, Giovanni	23	à la Carte Assistant Entree Cook	Vendor	Southampton	S			see à la Carte Group Notes
Moody, Mr. James P.	24	Sixth Officer	Deck	Lincolnshire, England	B			

Young **James Moody** had only passed his masters examination a year before he was assigned to *Titanic*. On duty when Frederick Fleet spotted the iceberg, it was Moody who took the phone call, and passed the word on to First Officer Murdoch. Moody then helped load several lifeboats, and when ordered to get into one, he refused and remained behind to help launch the two remaining Collapsible Lifeboats. Moody did not survive the sinking.

Name (Maiden Name) *Survivors names in italic*	Age	Title/Function	Department	Residence	E	L/B	Body # Recovered / Where Buried	Notes
Moore, A.E.	37	Second Class Saloon Steward	Victualling	Southampton	S			
Moore, George A.	32	Able Bodied Seaman	Deck	Southampton	S	3		Commanded Lifeboat 3.
Moore, John J.		Fireman	Engineering	Southampton	S	3		
Moore, R.		Trimmer	Engineering	London, England	S			
Moores, Robert H.		Greaser	Engineering	Southampton	S			
Morgan, Arthur H.		Trimmer	Engineering	Southampton	S			
Morgan, C.F.	42	Storekeeper	Victualling	Birkenhead, England	S			
Morgan, Thomas A.	26	Fireman	Engineering	Southampton	S		#302, buried in Mount Olivet Cemetery, Halifax	
Morrell, R.		Trimmer	Engineering	Southampton	S			
Morris, A.		Greaser	Engineering	Southampton	S			
Morris, Frank H.	28	Bath Steward (First Class)	Victualling	Southampton	S	14		
Morris, W.		Trimmer	Engineering	Southampton	S			
Moss, William	34	First Saloon Steward (First Class)	Victualling	Southampton	B			
Moyes, William Y.	23	Senior Sixth Engineer	Engineering	Stirling, Scotland	B			
Muller, L.	36	Interpreter (Third Class)	Victualling	Southampton	S			
Mullin, Thomas A.	20	Third Class Steward	Victualling	Southampton	S		#323, buried in Fairview Cemetery, Halifax	
Murdoch, Mr. W.M.	39	First Officer	Deck					

> **William Murdoch** was initially assigned to be the Chief Officer of *Titanic*, but the day before it left Southampton, the Ships captain, E.J. Smith, brought in Henry Wilde to be Chief Officer, which bumped Murdoch down to First Officer. Murdoch was on the bridge with Sixth Officer Moody when *Titanic* struck the iceberg. After checking for damage, Captain Smith ordered Murdoch to the starboard side to begin loading and launching the lifeboats. Murdoch used the theory of women and children first, then if there is room, let the men into the lifeboats. It is for this reason that most of the male passengers who survived owed their lives to Murdoch. Contrary to the James Cameron movie, Murdoch did not shoot himself. He was last seen in the water by Harold Bride near overturned Collapsible Lifeboat B, but he died in the water. He was engaged to be married when he completed his trip to New York.

Name (Maiden Name) *Survivors names in italic*	Age	Title/Function	Department	Residence	E	L/B	Body # Recovered / Where Buried	Notes
Murdock, William	34	Fireman	Engineering	Belfast	B	?		

N

Name (Maiden Name) *Survivors names in italic*	Age	Title/Function	Department	Residence	E	L/B	Body # Recovered / Where Buried	Notes
Nannini, Francesco L.A.	42	à la Carte Head Waiter	Vendor	London, England	S			see à la Carte Group Notes
Neal, Henry	25	Assistant Baker	Victualling	Southampton	S	13		
Nettleton, George		Fireman	Engineering	Southampton	S			
Newman, Charles T.	32	Storekeeper (Engineering)	Engineering	Southampton	S			
Nicholls, Samuel	39	First Class Saloon Steward	Victualling	Southampton	S			
Nichols, A.D.	34	Third Class Steward	Victualling	Southampton	S			
Nichols, Alfred	42	Boatswain	Deck	Southampton	B			

> **Alfred Nichols** was ordered by Second Officer Lightoller to take six men and open the lower gangway doors. Lifeboats then could be rowed up to the side of the ship and passengers could step into them. They were all trapped and never seen again nor they did not complet e their mission.

Name (Maiden Name) *Survivors names in italic*	Age	Title/Function	Department	Residence	E	L/B	Body # Recovered / Where Buried	Notes
Nichols, Walter H.	36	Second Class Saloon Steward	Victualling	Southampton	S	15		
Noon, John		Fireman	Engineering	Southampton	S			
Norris, James		Fireman	Engineering	Southampton	S			
Noss, Bertram A.	21	Fireman	Engineering	Southampton	S			A relative of Henry Noss.
Noss, Henry	31	Fireman	Engineering	Southampton	S	15		A relative of Bertram Noss.
Nutbean, William	31	Fireman	Engineering	Southampton	S	3		

> **William Nutbean** and five friends were drinking at a local pub and almost missed the sailing. Nutbean and John Podesta jumped onto the ship as it was pulling away from the dock, the other four missed it, and were replaced by four substitutes. Nutbean and Podesta survived; the four substitutes did not.

O

Name (Maiden Name) *Survivors names in italic*	Age	Title/Function	Department	Residence	E	L/B	Body # Recovered / Where Buried	Notes
O'Connor, John	25	Trimmer	Engineering	Southampton	S	B		see Substitutes Group Notes
O'Connor, Thomas P.	35	First Class Bedroom Steward	Victualling	Southampton	B			
Olive, Charles		Greaser	Engineering	Southampton	S			

Key: **Names** are in alphabetical order. **"E"** indicates where embarked (**B** is for Belfast, **S** is for Southampton). **L/B** indicates which lifeboat they escaped on, if known. **Body # Recovered / Where Buried** indicates in what sequence the body was recovered, and where it was buried. For descriptions of job functions, see **Glossary.**

Name *(Maiden Name)* *Survivors names in italic*	Age	Title/Function	Department	Residence	E	L/B	Body # Recovered / Where Buried	Notes
Olive, Ernest R.	28	Clothes Presser Steward (First Class)	Victualling	Southampton	S			
Oliver, H.		Fireman	Engineering	Southampton	S	?		
Olliver, Alfred	28	Quartermaster	Deck	Southampton	S	5		Brother in Law of Walter Perkis.
O'Loughlin, Dr. William F.N.	61	Ships Surgeon	Deck	Southampton	S			
Orpet, Walter H.	21	First Class Saloon Steward	Victualling	Southampton	S			
Orr, J.	40	Assistant Vegetable Cook	Victualling	Southampton	S			
Osborne, William E.	34	First Class Saloon Steward	Victualling	Southampton	S			
Osman, Frank	28	Able Bodied Seaman	Deck	Southampton	S	2		
Othen, Charles		Fireman	Engineering	Southampton	S	?		
Owen, Lewis	43	Second Class Saloon Steward	Victualling	Southampton	S			

P

Name *(Maiden Name)*	Age	Title/Function	Department	Residence	E	L/B	Body # Recovered / Where Buried	Notes
Pacey, Reginald I.	17	Second Class Lift (Elevator) Steward	Victualling	Southampton	S			
Pachera, Jean B.S.	20	à la Carte Assistant Storekeeper	Vendor	Southampton	S			see à la Carte Group Notes
Paice, Richard C.		Fireman	Engineering	Southampton	S			
Painter, Charles	31	Fireman	Engineering	Southampton	S			
Painter, Frank	29	Fireman	Engineering	Southampton	S			
Paintin, James A.	30	Captain's Steward	Victualling	Southampton	S			
Pallas, T.		Greaser	Engineering	Liverpool, England	S			
Parker, T.	32	Assistant Butcher	Victualling	Southampton	S			
Parsons, Edward	35	Chief Storekeeper	Victualling	Southampton	S			
Parsons, Frank A.	27	Senior Fifth Engineer	Engineering	Southampton	B			
Parsons, Richard	18	Second Class Saloon Steward	Victualling	Southampton	S			
Pascoe, Charles H.	46	Able Bodied Seaman	Deck	Southampton	S	8		
Pearce, A.E.	24	Third Class Steward	Victualling	Southampton	S			
Pearcey, Albert V.	32	Third 3rd Class Pantry Steward	Victualling	Southampton	S	C		

Albert Pearcey is one of the three Third Class stewards who led groups of Third Class passenger up to the boat deck, and was responsible for saving many of them. See Cox-Hart-Pearcey Group Notes.

Name *(Maiden Name)*	Age	Title/Function	Department	Residence	E	L/B	Body # Recovered / Where Buried	Notes
Pearse, John		Fireman	Engineering	Southampton	S	15		
Pedrini, Alessandro	21	à la Carte Assistant Waiter	Vendor	Southampton	S			see à la Carte Group Notes
Peerotti, Alfonso	21	à la Carte Assistant Waiter	Vendor	London, England	S			see à la Carte Group Notes
Pelham, George	39	Trimmer	Engineering	Southampton	S	16		
Pennell, Frank H.		Bath Steward (First Class)	Victualling	Southampton	S			
Penny, William C.	30	Second Class Saloon Steward	Victualling	Southampton	S			
Penrose, John P.	49	First Class Bedroom Steward	Victualling	Southampton	S			
Peracchio, Alberto	20	à la Carte Assistant Waiter	Vendor	London, England	S			see à la Carte Group Notes. He was the brother of Sebastiano Peracchio.
Peracchio, Sebastiano	18	à la Carte Assistant Waiter	Vendor	London, England	S			see à la Carte Group Notes. He was the brother of Alberto Peracchio.
Perkins, S.	22	Telephone Steward (First Class)	Victualling	Southampton	S			
Perkis, Walter J.	38	Quartermaster	Deck	Southampton	S	4		

Walter Perkis was in command of Lifeboat 4. His brother-in-law was Alfred Olliver. Lifeboat 4 picked up eight people out of the water, two of whom died from exposure.

Name *(Maiden Name)*	Age	Title/Function	Department	Residence	E	L/B	Body # Recovered / Where Buried	Notes
Perren, W.C.	22	Second Class Boots Steward	Victualling	Southampton	S			
Perriton, Hubert P.	32	First Class Saloon Steward	Victualling	Southampton	S			
Perry, Edgar L.	19	Trimmer	Engineering	Southampton	S	?		
Perry, Henry		Trimmer	Engineering	Southampton	S			
Peters, William C.	26	Able Bodied Seaman	Deck	Southampton	S	9		
Petty, Edwin H.	35	Second Class Bedroom Steward	Victualling	Southampton	S		#82, buried at sea	
Pfropper, Richard	30	Second Class Saloon Steward	Victualling	Southampton	S	9		
Phillimore, Harold C.W.	23	Second Class Saloon Steward	Victualling	Southampton	S	14		

Name *(Maiden Name)* *Survivors names in italic*	Age	Title/Function	Department	Residence	E	L/B	Body # Recovered / Where Buried	Notes
Phillips, G.		Greaser	Engineering	Southampton	S			
Phillips, John G.	27	Lead Marconi Telegrapher	Victualling	Liverpool	B	B		

John "Jack" Phillips was the Senior Marconi Operator and was employed by the Marconi Company. After *Titanic* struck the iceberg, Phillips, who was on duty at the time, was ordered by Captain E.J. Smith to send out the "CQD" (Come Quick Danger) message and to try the new "SOS" which had just been recently developed as a substitute for "CQD". Phillips started transmitting the CQD at 12:10 am, just ten minutes after most of the Marconi systems on nearby ships had shut down for the night. Most of the ships Phillips communicated with were too far away to help, and only *Carpathia* was close enough and had a captain who took emergency actions to get to the site of the tragedy. Phillips stayed at his post behind the pilothouse on the Boat deck until water started to flood the compartment. His last message was at 2:18 a.m., two minutes before *Titanic* sank. Phillips and his assistant Harold Bride both ended up in the water and later on top of overturned Collapsible Lifeboat B, but during the night, Phillips died of exposure to the cold.

Phillips, Walter J.	32	à la Carte Storekeeper	Vendor	Southampton	S			see à la Carte Group Notes
Piatti, Louis	17	à la Carte Assistant Waiter	Vendor	London, England	S			see à la Carte Group Notes
Piazzo, Pompeo	30	à la Carte Waiter	Vendor	London, England	S		#266, buried in Mount Olivet Cemetery, Halifax	see à la Carte Group Notes
Pitfield, William J.		Greaser	Engineering	Southampton	S			
Pitman, Mr. Herbert J.	34	Third Officer	Deck	Somerset, England	B	5		

Third Officer **Herbert J. Pitman** had served at sea for 17 years and with the White Star Line for the past five years. Pitman was off watch and asleep when *Titanic* struck the iceberg. He got up and reported to the bridge, and later to the starboard side Boat deck to help prepare the lifeboats. Since First Officer Murdoch and Second Officer Lightoller were in charge of lowering the lifeboats, Murdoch ordered Pitman into the Lifeboat 5, the second lifeboat launched, in order to take command of the lifeboats as they were lowered into the water. Since it was so dark, Pitman couldn't find many boats, but he helped gather a couple of them together, then had them row to the lower gangway doors that Boatswain Nichols was supposed to open to allow passengers to step into the lifeboats. The doors were never opened, and Pitman had his lifeboats row away from the ship.

Platt, W.	18	Scullion	Victualling	Southampton	S			
Podesta, John	25	Fireman	Engineering	Southampton	S	3		see notes on Nutbean
Poggi, Emilio	26	à la Carte Waiter	Vendor	Southampton	S		#301, buried in Fairview Cemetery, Halifax	see à la Carte Group Notes
Poingdestre, John D.	26	Able Bodied Seaman	Deck	Southampton	S	12		Commanded Lifeboat 12.
Pond, George	32	Fireman	Engineering	Souhampton	S			
Pook, Philip	34	Asst. Pantry Steward (Second Class)	Victualling	Southampton	S			
Port, Frank	23	Third Class Steward	Victualling	Southampton	S	13		
Prangnell, George	31	Greaser	Engineering	Southampton	S	B		
Prentice, Frank G.	22	Storekeeper	Victualling	Southampton	S	4		He was pulled from the water.
Preston, Thomas C.	20	Trimmer	Engineering	Southampton	S			
Price, Ernest	17	à la Carte Barman	Vendor	Southampton	S		#186, buried in Fairview Cemetery, Halifax	see à la Carte Group Notes
Prichard, Mrs. A.	33	First Class Stewardess	Victualling	London, England	S	11		
Prideaux, Jack A.	23	Third Class Steward	Victualling	Southampton	S			
Priest, Arthur J.	23	Fireman	Engineering	Southampton	S	15		

Whereas Violet Jessop had served on all three of the Olympic Class ships, **Arthur J. Priest** also served on them all and survived. He went on to work on *Alcantara* and later *Donegal*, both of which were torpedoed and sunk by German submarines during World War I. After the last one, Priest had to retire because no one would serve on the same ship with him.

Prior, Harold J.	21	Third Class Steward	Victualling	Southampton	S	11		
Proctor, Charles	40	Chef and Kitchen Manager	Victualling	Southampton	B			
Proudfoot, R.		Trimmer	Engineering	Southampton	S			
Pryce, W.	34	First Class Saloon Steward	Victualling	Southampton	S			
Pugh, Alfred	21	Third Class Steward	Victualling	Southampton	S	14		
Pugh, Percy	31	Leading Fireman	Engineering	Hampshire	S			

Cousins **Alfred** and **Percy Pugh** spent too much time in the pub the morning *Titanic* sailed, and they almost missed the ship, which was pulling away from the dock. They had to jump the last couple feet into the open gangway door. Several of their friends missed the departure. Alfred survived, Percy did not.

Pusey, John E.	35	First Class Saloon Steward	Victualling	Itchen, England	S			
Pusey, Robert W.	24	Fireman	Engineering	Southampton	S	1		

Name *(Maiden Name)* *Survivors names in italic*	Age	Title/Function	Department	Residence	E	L/B	Body # Recovered / Where Buried	Notes
R								
Randall, F.H.	27	Second Class Saloon Steward	Victualling	Southampton	S			
Ranger, Thomas G.		Greaser	Engineering	Southampton	S	4		
Ransom, James	33	First Class Saloon Steward	Victualling	Southampton	B			
Rattenbury, William H.	35	Assistant Boots Steward (First Class)	Victualling	Southampton	S			
Ratti, Enrico R.	21	à la Carte Waiter	Vendor	London, England	S			see à la Carte Group Notes
Ray, Frederick D.	33	First Class Saloon Steward	Victualling	Reading, England	S	13		
Read, J.		Trimmer	Engineering	Southampton	S			
Reed, Charles S.	43	Second Class Bedroom Steward	Victualling	Southampton	S			
Reed, Robert		Trimmer	Engineering	Southampton	S			
Reeves, Frederick	30	Fireman	Engineering	Southampton	S		#280, buried in Fairview Cemetery, Halifax	
Revell, William	30	First Class Saloon Steward	Victualling	Southampton	B			
Ricaldone, Rinaldo R.	21	à la Carte Assistant Waiter	Vendor	London, England	S			see à la Carte Group Notes
Rice, Charles	32	Fireman	Engineering	Southampton	S	10		
Rice, John R.		Ships Clerk	Victualling	Liverpool, England	S		#64, buried in Fairview Cemetery, Halifax	
Rice, Percy	19	Third Class Steward	Victualling	Southampton	S			
Richards, Joseph J.		Fireman	Engineering	Southampton	S			
Rickman, G.		Fireman	Engineering	Southampton	S			
Ricks, Cyril G.	21	Storekeeper	Victualling	Southampton	S		#100, buried at sea	
Ridout, W.	29	Second Class Saloon Steward	Victualling	Southampton	S			
Rigozzi, Abele	22	à la Carte Waiter	Vendor	London, England	S		#115, buried at sea	see à la Carte Group Notes
Rimmer, Gilbert	27	First Class Saloon Steward	Victualling	Southampton	S			
Roberts, Fran J.	36	Third Butcher	Victualling	Hampshire, England	B		#231, buried in Fairview Cemetery, Halifax	
Roberts, George		Fireman	Engineering	Southampton	S			
Roberts, Hugh H.	40	First Class Bedroom Steward	Victualling	Southampton	B		#93, buried at sea	
Roberts, Mrs. Mary K.	31	First Class Stewardess	Victualling	Nottingham, England	S	16		
Robertson, George E.	19	Second Class Saloon Steward	Victualling	Southampton	S		#127, buried at sea	
Robinson, James W.	30	First Class Saloon Steward	Victualling	Southampton	S		#151, buried at sea	
Robinson, Mrs. Annie	40	First Class Stewardess	Victualling	Southampton	S	11		
Rogers, Edward J.M.	32	Storekeeper	Victualling	Southampton	S		#282, buried in Fairview Cemetery, Halifax	
Rogers, M.	27	Second Class Saloon Steward	Victualling	Winchester, England	S			
Ross, Horace L.	36	Scullion	Victualling	Woolston, England	S	13		
Rotta, Angelo M.	23	à la Carte Waiter	Vendor	London, England	S			see à la Carte Group Notes
Rous, Arthur J.	26	Plumber	Engineering	Southampton	S			
Rousseau, Pierre	49	à la Carte Chef	Vendor	London, England	S			see à la Carte Group Notes
Rowe, E.M.	30	First Class Saloon Steward	Victualling	Southampton	B			
Rowe, George T.	32	Quartermaster	Deck	Gosport	S	C		

George T. Rowe was on duty on the Docking Bridge, high on the stern of the ship. He didn't know about the collision with the iceberg until he saw a lifeboat rowing around the stern of the ship, almost 45 minutes after the collision. He called the bridge and was told to bring up some signaling rockets. Rowe was the one who fired the eight white rockets that were seen by the crew of *Californian,* almost 22 miles away. Rowe was later placed in command of Collapsible Lifeboat C with Bruce Ismay aboard.

Name	Age	Title/Function	Department	Residence	E	L/B	Body # Recovered / Where Buried	Notes
Rudd, Henry	23	Storekeeper (Engineering)	Engineering	Southampton	S		#86, buried at sea	
Rule, Samuel J.	50	Bath Steward (First Class)	Victualling	Southampton	S	15		

Name *(Maiden Name)* *Survivors names in italic*	Age	Title/Function	Department	Residence	E	L/B	Body # Recovered / Where Buried	Notes
Russell, Richard	34	Second Class Saloon Steward	Victualling	Redbridge, England	S			
Rutter, Sidney		Fireman	Engineering	Southampton	S			
		Sidney Rutter wasn't scheduled to work on *Titanic,* but he traded places, and names, with a friend who was signed up and for whatever reason, didn't want to go. It was a good move for the friend, not a good one for poor Sidney Rutter.						
Ryan, T.	27	Third Class Steward	Victualling	Southampton	S			
Ryerson, William E.	32	Second Class Saloon Steward	Victualling	Ontario, Canada	S	9		Distant cousin of First Class passenger Arthur Ryerson.

S

Name	Age	Title/Function	Department	Residence	E	L/B	Body # Recovered / Where Buried	Notes
Saccaggi, Giovanni G.E.	24	à la Carte Assistant Waiter	Vendor	London, England	S			see à la Carte Group Notes
Salussolia, Giovanni	25	à la Carte Glass Man	Vendor	London, England	S			see à la Carte Group Notes
Samuel, O.W.	41	Second Class Saloon Steward	Victualling	Southampton	S		#217, buried in Fairview Cemetery, Halifax	
Sangster, Charles		Fireman	Engineering	Southampton	S			
Saunders, D.E.	26	First Class Saloon Steward	Victualling	Southampton	S			
Saunders, Thomas		Fireman	Engineering	Southampton	S			
Saunders, W.	30	Fireman	Engineering	Southampton	S		#184, buried at sea	
Saunders, W.		Trimmer	Engineering	Southampton	S			
Savage, Charles J.	22	Third Class Steward	Victualling	Southampton	S	11		
Sawyer, Robert J.	30	Window Washer	Deck	Southampton	S			
Scarrott, Joseph	34	Able Bodied Seaman	Deck	Southampton	S	14		
Scott, Archibald	40	Fireman	Engineering	Southampton	S			
Scott, Frederick		Greaser	Engineering	Southampton	S	4		He was pulled from the water.
Scott, J.	21	Assistant Boots Steward (First Class)	Victualling	Southampton	S			
Scovell, R.	42	Second Class Saloon Steward	Victualling	Southampton	S			
Sedunary, Sidney F.	25	Second 3rd Class Steward	Victualling	Southampton	S		#178, buried at sea	
Self, Alfred H.		Greaser	Engineering	Southampton	S			
Self, Edward	25	Fireman	Engineering	Southampton	S	?		
Senior, Henry	31	Fireman	Engineering	London, England	S	B		
Sesea, Gino	24	à la Carte Waiter	Vendor	London, England	S			see à la Carte Group Notes
Seward, Wilfred D.	25	Chief Pantry Steward (Second Class)	Victualling	Southampton	B	3		
Shaw, Henry	39	Kitchen Porter	Victualling	Liverpool, England	S			
Shea, John	29	First Class Saloon Steward	Victualling	Southampton	S		#11, buried in Fairview Cemetery, Halifax	
Shea, Thomas	32	Fireman	Engineering	Southampton	S			
Sheath, Frederick	20	Trimmer	Engineering	Southampton	S	1		
Shepherd, Jonathan	32	Junior Assistant Second Engineer	Engineering	Southampton	S			
Shiers, Alfred	24	Fireman	Engineering	Southampton	S	5		
Shillaber, Charles	20	Trimmer	Engineering	Southampton	S		#195, buried in Fairview Cemetery, Halifax	
Siebert, Sidney C.		First Class Bedroom Steward	Victualling	Hampshire, England	S		Buried at sea	Picked up by Lifeboat 4, but died later. He was buried at sea on the *Carpathia.*
Simmons, Alfred	32	Scullion	Victualling	Southampton	S	8		
Simmons, F.G.	27	First Class Saloon Steward	Victualling	Southampton	S			
Simmons, W.	32	Passenger Cook	Victualling	Southampton	S			
Simpson, Dr. John E.	37	Asst. Surgeon	Deck	Hornsbury, England	S			
Sivier, William	23	Third Class Steward	Victualling	London, England	S			

Name *(Maiden Name)* *Survivors names in italic*	Age	Title/Function	Department	Residence	E	L/B	Body # Recovered / Where Buried	Notes
Skeats, W.		Trimmer	Engineering	Southampton	S			
Skinner, Edward	33	First Class Saloon Steward	Victualling	Southampton	B			
Slight, H.J.	34	Third Class Steward	Victualling	Southampton	S			
Slight, W.	35	Larder Cook	Victualling	Southampton	B			
Sloan, Mary		First Class Stewardess	Victualling	Southampton	S	16		Tried to remain behind with her friends, but was forcibly placed into the lifeboat.
Sloan, Peter	31	Chief Electrician	Engineering	Southampton	B			
Slocombe, Mrs. Maude	30	Turkish Bath Stewardess	Victualling	London, England	S	11		
Small, William	40	Leading Fireman	Engineering	Southampton	S			
Smillie, J.	29	First Class Saloon Steward	Victualling	Southampton	B		#91, buried at sea	
Smith, Charles	38	Kitchen Porter	Victualling	Southampton	S			
Smith, Charles E.	38	Second Class Bedroom Steward	Victualling	Southampton	S		#329, buried in Fairview Cemetery, Halifax	
Smith, Ernest G.		Trimmer	Engineering	Southampton	S			
Smith, F.	20	Asst. Pantryman Steward (First Class)	Victualling	Southampton	B			
Smith, J.	24	Assistant Baker	Victualling	Southampton	S			
Smith, James M.	35	Junior Fourth Engineer	Engineering	Southampton	B			
Smith, John R.J.	35	Postal Clerk	Postal	Cornwall, England	S			see Postal Clerk Group Notes
Smith, Miss Katherine E.	42	First Class Stewardess	Victualling	Southampton	S	11		
Smith, Mr. Edward J.	62	Captain	Deck	Southampton	B			

Captain **Edward J. Smith** was the Senior Captain of the White Star Line with over 49 years at sea, 26 of those with the WSL. A Royal Naval Reserve officer, any ship he commanded was allowed to fly the blue RNR flag. Smith had a few minor incidents in his career, but that changed for the worse in 1911 when *Olympic* collided with HMS *Hawke*. As Senior Captain, Smith always commanded a new ship on its maiden voyage. This voyage was NOT supposed to be his final voyage, as he was set to command *Gigantic* (later renamed *Britannic*) when it was commissioned in 1914. As *Titanic* departed Southampton, Smith was able to avoid a collision with the passenger liner *New York* which was tied up at a dock but, because of the water displacement created by *Titanic,* severed its mooring ropes and drifted into *Titanic's* path. After a rather uneventful voyage, Smith delayed a major course change by 30 minutes, trying to pass his ship around the south end of the huge ice field. Unfortunately it wasn't enough, and *Titanic* struck an iceberg at 11:40 p.m. on April 14. Smith seems to have gone into catatonic shock for he gave very few orders after giving approval to launch the lifeboats. He was last seen standing with John J. Astor and several other men up on the bridge moments before the forward funnel fell on top of the group.

Name	Age	Title/Function	Department	Residence	E	L/B	Body # Recovered / Where Buried	Notes
Smith, R.G.	30	First Class Saloon Steward	Victualling	Southampton	S			
Smith, William	26	Seaman	Deck	Southampton	S			
Smither, Harry J.		Fireman	Engineering	Southampton	S			
Snape, Mrs. Lucy V.	22	Stewardess (Second Class)	Victualling	Southampton	S			
Snellgrove, G.		Fireman	Engineering	Southampton	S			
Snooks, W.		Trimmer	Engineering	Southampton	S			
Snow, Eustace P.	21	Trimmer	Engineering	Southampton	S	B		
Sparkman, Henry		Fireman	Engineering	Southampton	S	?		
Stafford, M.		Greaser	Engineering	Southampton	S			
Stagg, John H.	34	First Class Saloon Steward	Victualling	Southampton	S			
Stanbrook, Augustus	30	Fireman	Engineering	Southampton	S		#316, buried in Fairview Cemetery, Halifax	
Stap, Miss Sarah A.	45	First Class Stewardess	Victualling	Birkenhead, England	S	11		
Stebbings, S.	34	Chief Boots Steward (First Class)	Victualling	Southampton	S			
Steel, Robert E.		Trimmer	Engineering	Southampton	S			see Substitutes Group Notes
Stewart, John	27	Verandah Steward (First Class)	Victualling	Southampton	B	15		
Stocker, Henry		Trimmer	Engineering	Southampton	S			
Stone, Edmond J.	26	First Class Bedroom Steward	Victualling	Southampton	S		#41, buried at sea	
Stone, Edward T.	28	Second Class Bedroom Steward	Victualling	Southampton	S		#243, buried in Fairview Cemetery, Halifax	

Name (Maiden Name) *Survivors names in italic*	Age	Title/Function	Department	Residence	E	L/B	Body # Recovered / Where Buried	Notes
Street, Thomas A.	25	Fireman	Engineering	Southampton	S	9		
Stroud, Edward A.O.	19	Second Class Saloon Steward	Victualling	Southampton	S			
Stroud, Harry J.	36	First Class Saloon Steward	Victualling	Southampton	S			
Strugnell, John H.	30	First Class Saloon Steward	Victualling	Southampton	B			
Stubbings, Harry R.	29	Second Class Cook	Victualling	Southampton	B			
Stubbs, James H.		Fireman	Engineering	Southampton	S			
Sullivan, S.		Fireman	Engineering	Southampton	S			
Swan, W.	45	First Class Bedroom Steward	Victualling	Southampton	B			
Symonds, J.	30	First Class Saloon Steward	Victualling	Southampton	B			
Symons, George T.M.	24	Lookout	Deck	Southampton	S	1		
T								
Talbot, George F.C.	27	Third Class Steward	Victualling	Southampton	S		#150, buried in Fairview Cemetery, Halifax	
Tamlyn, Frederick	20	Officers Mess Steward	Deck	Southampton	S		#123, buried at sea	
Taylor, C.	21	Third Class Steward	Victualling	Southampton	S			
Taylor, Charles	35	Able Bodied Seaman	Deck	Southampton	S			
Taylor, James	25	Fireman	Engineering	Southampton	S	1		
Taylor, John		Fireman	Engineering	Southampton	S			
Taylor, Leonard	23	Turkish Bath Steward	Victualling	Blackpool, England	S			
Taylor, T.		Fireman	Engineering	Southampton	S			
Taylor, W.	30	First Class Saloon Steward	Victualling	Southampton	S			
Taylor, William H.	28	Fireman	Engineering	Southampton	S	15		
Terrell, Bertram	20	Seaman	Deck	Southampton	S			
Terrell, Frank	27	Second Class Saloon Steward	Victualling	Southampton	S	11		
Testoni, Erocle	23	à la Carte Assistant Glass Man	Vendor	London, England	S			see à la Carte Group Notes
Teuton, Thomas M.	28	Second Class Saloon Steward	Victualling	Hampshire, England	S		#226, buried in Fairview Cemetery, Halifax	
Thaler, Montague D.	17	Third Class Steward	Victualling	London, England	S			
Thessinger, Alfred	39	First Class Bedroom Steward	Victualling	Southampton	S	11		He was picked up from the water.
Thomas, Albert C.	23	First Class Saloon Steward	Victualling	Southampton	S	15		
Thomas, Benjamin J.	32	First Class Saloon Steward	Victualling	Southampton	B	15		
Thomas, James		Fireman	Engineering	Southampton	S			
Thompson, H.H.	25	Asst. Storekeeper	Victualling	Southampton	B			
Thompson, John W.	42	Fireman	Engineering	Liverpool	S	A/14		
Thorley, William	39	Assistant Cook	Victualling	Southampton	S			
Threlfall, Thomas	38	Leading Fireman	Engineering	Liverpool	S	14		
Thresher, George	25	Fireman	Engineering	Southampton	S	?		
Tietz, Carlo	27	à la Carte Kitchen Porter	Vendor	Southampton	S			see à la Carte Group Notes
Tizard, Arthur		Fireman	Engineering	Southampton	S			
Toms, Frederick	31	First Class Saloon Steward	Victualling	Southampton	B	15		
Topp, T.	23	Second Butcher	Victualling	Southampton	S			
Tozer, James		Greaser	Engineering	Southampton	S			
Triggs, Robert		Fireman	Engineering	Southampton	S	3		
Tucker, B.	21	Second Pantryman Steward (First Class)	Victualling	Southampton	B			
Turley, Richard		Fireman	Engineering	Southampton	S			

Name *(Maiden Name)* *Survivors names in italic*	Age	Title/Function	Department	Residence	E	L/B	Body # Recovered / Where Buried	Notes
Turner, George F.	32	Stenographer	Victualling	Chiswick, England	S			
Turner, L.	28	First Class Saloon Steward	Victualling	Southampton	B		#29, buried at sea	
Turvey, Charles	16	à la Carte Page Boy	Vendor	London, England	S			see à la Carte Group Notes
U								
Urbini, Robert	22	à la Carte Waiter	Vendor	London, England	S			see à la Carte Group Notes
V								
Valvassori, Ettore L.	35	à la Carte Waiter	Vendor	London, England	S			see à la Carte Group Notes
van der Brugge, Wessel A.	42	Fireman	Engineering	Southampton	S			
Veal, Arthur		Greaser	Engineering	Southampton	S			
Veal, Thomas H.E.	38	First Class Saloon Steward	Victualling	Southampton	S			
Vear, Henry	32	Fireman	Engineering	Southampton	S			Served with brother W. Vear.
Vear, W.	32	Fireman	Engineering	Southampton	S		#59, buried at sea	Served with brother Henry Vear.
Vicat, Alphonse J.E.	21	à la Carte Fish Cook	Vendor	London, England	S			see à la Carte Group Notes
Vigott, Philip F.	32	Able Bodied Seaman	Deck	Southampton	S	13		
Villvarlange, Pierre L.	18	à la Carte Assistant Soup Cook	Vendor	France	S			see à la Carte Group Notes
Vine, H.	18	à la Carte Assistant Controller	Vendor	London, England	S			see à la Carte Group Notes
Vioni, Robert	18	à la Carte Waiter	Vendor	London, England	S			see à la Carte Group Notes
Vogelin-Dubach, Johannes	35	à la Carte Coffee Maker	Vendor	London, England	S			see à la Carte Group Notes
W								
Wake, T.	32	Assistant Baker	Victualling	Southampton	S			
Wallis, Mrs. Catherine J.	35	Second Class Matron	Victualling	Southampton	S			
Wallis, Mrs. Richard J. (Katherine Moore)	32	First Class Stewardess	Victualling	Southampton	S			She was the only First Class Stewardess to be lost.
Walpole, James	48	Chief Pantryman Steward (First Class)	Victualling	Southampton	B			
Ward, Arthur	24	Junior Assistant Fourth Engineer	Engineering	Romsey, England	B			
Ward, Edward	34	First Class Bedroom Steward	Victualling	Southampton	B			
Ward, Joseph	31	Leading Fireman	Engineering	Southampton	S			
Ward, Percy T.	38	First Class Bedroom Steward	Victualling	Hampshire	B			
Ward, William	36	First Class Saloon Steward	Victualling	Southampton	S	9		
Wardner, Fred		Fireman	Engineering	Southampton	S			
Wareham, Robert A.	36	First Class Bedroom Steward	Victualling	Southampton	S		#246, buried in Fairview Cemetery, Halifax	
Warwick, Thomas	35	First Class Saloon Steward	Victualling	Hampshire	S			
Wateridge, Edward L.		Fireman	Engineering	Southampton	S			
Watson, A.W.	14	Bell Boy (First Class)	Victualling	Southampton	S			
Watson, W.		Fireman	Engineering	Southampton	S		#158, buried at sea	
Weatherston, Thomas H.	24	First Class Saloon Steward	Victualling	Southampton	B			
Webb, Brooke	50	Smoking Room Steward (First Class)	Victualling	Southampton	B			
Webb, S.		Trimmer	Engineering	Southampton	S			
Webber, Francis A.	31	Leading Fireman	Engineering	Southampton	S			
Weikman, August H.	51	Barber (First Class)	Vendor	Southampton	S	A		see Barber's Group Notes

Name (Maiden Name) Survivors names in italic	Age	Title/Function	Department	Residence	E	L/B	Body # Recovered / Where Buried	Notes
Welch, W.H.	23	Assistant Cook	Victualling	Southampton	S			
Weller, William	29	Able Bodied Seaman	Deck	Southampton	S	27		
Wheat, Joseph T.	29	Asst. Second Steward (First Class)	Victualling	Southampton	S	11		
Wheelton, Edward E.	29	First Class Saloon Steward	Victualling	Southampton	S	11		
White, Alfred		Greaser	Engineering	Southampton	S	4		He was pulled from the water.
White, Arthur	37	Barber (Third Class)	Vendor	Portsmouth, England	S		#247, buried in Fairview Cemetery, Halifax	see Barber's Group Notes
White, Frank L.		Trimmer	Engineering	Southampton	S			
White, J.	27	Glory-Hole Steward	Victualling	Southampton	S		#272, buried in Fairview Cemetery, Halifax	
White, L.	32	First Class Saloon Steward	Victualling	Southampton	B			
White, William G.	23	Trimmer	Engineering	Northampton	S	15		
Whiteley, Thomas	18	First Class Saloon Steward	Victualling	London, England	S	B		
Whitford, A.H.	37	Second Class Saloon Steward	Victualling	Southampton	S			
Widgery, James G.	37	Second Class Bath Steward	Victualling	Southampton	S	9		
Wilde, Mr. Henry T.	39	Chief Officer	Deck	Liverpool, England	S			

Henry T. Wilde was second-in-command of *Titanic*. He had been Chief officer on *Olympic*, commanded by Captain E.J. Smith when *Olympic* collided with HMS *Hawke*. Wilde was assigned to *Titanic* the day before it left Southampton. Wilde's wife and two children had died two years prior, leaving him with four children under 10 years to raise. It is thought that Wilde is the officer who shot himself.

Name (Maiden Name) Survivors names in italic	Age	Title/Function	Department	Residence	E	L/B	Body # Recovered / Where Buried	Notes
Wildebank, Alfred E.	39	Assistant Cook	Victualling	Southampton	S	13		see Substitutes Group Notes
Williams, Arthur J.	38	Storekeeper	Victualling	Walton, England	S			
Williams, Samuel S.	26	Fireman	Engineering	Southampton	S			
Williams, Walter J.	28	Second Class Saloon Steward	Victualling	Southampton	S	13		
Williamson, James B.	35	Postal Clerk	Postal	Southampton	S			see Postal Clerk Group Notes
Willis, William	66	Third Class Steward	Victualling	Southampton	S			
Wilson, Bertie	28	Senior Assistant Second Engineer	Engineering	Southampton	B			
Wilton, William		Trimmer	Engineering	Southampton	S			
Wiltshire, W.	33	Assistant Butcher	Victualling	Southampton	S			
Witcher, Albert E.	40	Fireman	Engineering	Lymington	S			
Witt, F.		Trimmer	Engineering	Southampton	S			
Witt, Henry D.	40	Fireman	Engineering	Southampton	S			see Substitutes Group Notes
Witter, James W.C.	31	Second Class Smoking Room Steward	Victualling	Hampshire	S	11		
Wittman, Henry	34	First Class Bedroom Steward	Victualling	Southampton	S		#315, buried in Fairview Cemetery, Halifax	
Wood, J.T.	40	Second Class Saloon Steward	Victualling	London, England	S			
Woodford, Frederick	41	Greaser	Engineering	Southampton	S		#163, buried in Fairview Cemetery, Halifax	
Woods, H.		Trimmer	Engineering	Southampton	S			
Woody, Oscar S.	43	Postal Clerk	Postal	Clifton Springs, VA	S		#167, buried at sea	see Postal Clerk Group Notes
Wormald, Frederick W.	48	First Class Saloon Steward	Victualling	Southampton	S		#144, buried in Baron De Hirsch Cemetery, Halifax	
Wrapson, Frederick B.	19	Assistant Pantryman Steward (First Class)	Victualling	Southampton	B			
Wright, Fredrick	24	Racquet Steward	Victualling	London, England	S			
Wright, William	40	Glory-Hole Steward	Victualling	Southampton	S	13		
Wyeth, James		Fireman	Engineering	Southampton	S			
Wynn, Walter	41	Quartermaster	Deck	Southampton	B	9		

Name *(Maiden Name)* *Survivors names in italic*	Age	Title/Function	Department	Residence	E	L/B	Body # Recovered / Where Buried	Notes
Y								
Yearsley, Harry	38	First Class Saloon Steward	Victualling	Southampton	S	9		
Yoshack, James A.	31	First Class Saloon Steward	Victualling	Southampton	S			
Young, Francis J.	30	Fireman	Engineering	Southampton	S			
Z								
Zanetti, Mario	20	à la Carte Assistant Waiter	Vendor	London, England	S			see à la Carte Group Notes
Zarracchi, L.	26	a la Carte Wine Steward	Vendor	Southampton	S			see à la Carte Group Notes

GROUP NOTES

À la Carte Group Notes: The à la Carte Restaurant was located on B Deck just below the fourth funnel. It was a private concession managed by Mr. Luigi Gatti, who owned two restaurants in London, the Gatti's Adelphi and Gatti's Strand, both Ritz restaurants. Gatti also managed the à la Carte Restaurant on *Olympic,* and had most all of the crossings with *Olympic.* Now with a new ship and a new staff, most of who were employees of his London restaurants and several of whom were family members, Gatti set out on the maiden voyage of *Titanic.* The à la Carte Restaurant was open from 6 AM until 10 PM, and was open only to First Class passengers. Passengers could eat their meals in the less formal setting of the à la Carte restaurant if they didn't want to dine in the formal dining room. Credit for meals not eaten in the dining room could be used in the à la Carte restaurant.

The staff of the à la Carte restaurant was not paid by White Star Line, but by Luigi Gatti. The staff was self-sufficient with its own cooks, waiters, clean up crews and other staff. In fact, there were 67 employees on the staff, including two women. Most of the staff were either Italian or French nationals, and as such, were not highly esteemed by the mostly British crew, who considered them "low life continentals". Several survivors indicated that the restaurant employees were locked into their dormitory rooms to prevent them from rushing the lifeboats. This may or may not be true, but of the entire staff of 67, only one male and the two female employees survived. Gatti's body and that of several of his employees were recovered.

Barber's Group Notes: There were three barbers assigned to *Titanic*: August H. Weikman for First Class, Herbert Klein for Second Class and Arthur White for Third Class. None were employed by White Star Line; they all worked for tips only. White Star Line did provide their quarters and meals. All except Weikman were lost.

Cox-Hart-Pearcy Group Notes: Third Class Stewards William D. Cox, John E. Hart and Albert V. Pearcey took the responsibility to lead some of the Third Class passengers out of the lower decks where they were quartered and up to the boat deck. Hart, in particular, was responsible for saving 58 passengers. Once the order to load the lifeboats was given, he was ordered to gather up any women and children from the areas he was responsible for, which contained all single women or women with children. Hart gathered up a group of about 25 of them and led them on a circuitous route up from E Deck, down long passageways, up ladders, through public rooms and eventually up to the boat deck, where most of them ended up loaded into Lifeboat 8. Hart made another trip and picked up the 30 or so remaining people in his area, and led them up to the Boat Deck, where they ended up in Lifeboat 15. In all, every one of the 58 passengers he was responsible for escaped. Hart was going to make a third trip but had to remain with Lifeboat 15 to help hold back some of the people who were trying to rush it. First Officer Murdoch ordered Hart into Lifeboat 15 to help row. Cox and Pearcy helped Hart and also led smaller groups of people up to the Boat Deck. Pearcey survived, Cox did not.

Postal Service Group Notes: RMS stands for Royal Mail Steamer (or Steamship) and as such RMS *Titanic* was chartered and authorized to carry the mail. By the time *Titanic* left Queenstown, Ireland on April 11, almost 2,500 sacks of mail had been loaded, destined for New York City and beyond. During the normal six-day voyage, the five postal clerks assigned to *Titanic* would open every bag of mail and sort it according to U.S. Postal Service requirements so when *Titanic* docked in New York, the mail sacks could be sent directly to the local post offices. Down on the Orlop Deck near the bottom of the ship was the Mail Room. It was located on the Starboard side between the bow and the Number 6 Boiler Room. This is where mail was stored. The next deck above (G Deck) held the sealed room for Registered Mail and the Post Office, where mail generated on the ship was received and all the mail was sorted. The five Postal Clerks generally ran the same voyages together, so they were good friends. William J. Gwinn, John S. March and Oscar S. Woody were employed by the

U.S. Post Office while John R.J. Smith and James B. Williamson were employed by the Royal Post Office.

The iceberg created a hole the entire length of the Mail Room on the Orlop Deck, which immediately began to flood all the mail. The five clerks managed to haul about 200 sacks of mail up the ladder to the sorting room on G Deck. The water was coming in so fast, however, that within 20 minutes the Mail Room was completely flooded and the water was beginning to flood the sorting room on G Deck. Smith reported the flooding to Fourth Officer Boxhall, who sent him up to Captain Smith with the news. From there, the clerks started to move the registered mail up to D Deck, but it was all in vain. None of the postal clerks survived.

Substitute Group Notes: It was standard for the time, but with few exceptions, crewmembers were hired on for only one voyage. In fact, all but about 40 of the crewmembers for the voyage were "signed on" on April 6, and told to report back to the ship at 6:00 AM on Wednesday, April 10, or six hours before departure. There was always the possibility that someone would not show up the day of departure, so after the crew had been signed on, additional personnel called substitutes were signed up. The substitutes were assigned to whatever department they would work in, and just before departure if a signed on member did not appear, the first substitute would be signed on in his place, and so on until a complete crew was assembled. A total of 15 individuals signed on as substitutes, replacing someone who didn't show. This was not an unusual number for a crew the size of *Titanic's* crew.

GLOSSARY OF CREW TERMS

What, exactly does a trimmer do? How about a greaser or glory-hole steward? Following is a listing of job functions and terms relevant to the crew of *Titanic*.

Able Bodied Seaman: Assigned to the Deck Department, the 29 Able Bodied Seamen had gone through additional training and usually had seniority. They were trained to operate the lifeboat davits and the lifeboats themselves. Each ABS was assigned to a lifeboat and would be in charge of the lifeboat if an officer wasn't present. Several of the Able Bodied Seamen were lost when they were sent down to open the E Deck gangway, and several more got off on the early lifeboats, so later lifeboats had a shortage of ABS to man them.

Bath Steward: see Steward, responsible for maintaining supplies in the community-type bathrooms utilized by everyone except a select few First Class passengers.

Bedroom Steward: They were assigned to each class, and First Class Bedroom Stewards not only cleaned the rooms and made beds, but they were also available to serve food in the rooms or help in getting dressed. Some of the First Class Bedroom Stewards made substantial tips, and passengers who made frequent trips often requested the same steward. First Class Bedroom Stewards usually were responsible for only 3-5 rooms, Second Class for up to 10 rooms and Third Class for as many as 25 rooms.

Boatswain's Mate: highly trained crewmen who managed the lines, deck cranes, winches, lifeboat davits, etc. on the deck.

Boots Steward: See Steward. These were cobblers and bootblacks, and were responsible for maintaining and polishing the shoes of the passengers.

Deck Department: Sixty-six men (men only) were assigned to the Deck Department. This would include, among others, the eight ships officers, two surgeons, Master at Arms, six lookouts and the 29 Able Bodied Seamen.

Engineering Department: There were 326 men assigned to this department. Most worked as firemen, greasers or trimmers, but it also included storekeepers, plumbers, electricians and the 33 engineers.

Engineers: the engineers were responsible for keeping the engines, generators and other mechanical equipment running. Among the highest paid crew, they had the technical expertise to operate, maintain and repair the engineering plant. Dedicated until the end, the entire engineering staff worked to maintain enough steam to keep the generators running and moving power from one part of the ship to others to keep the lights on until less than two minutes before *Titanic* stood up on its bow and sank. None of the 35 engineers survived. In their honor, in 1914 King George V decreed that all British marine engineers wear the insignia of their rank and profession next to a royal purple background to remember their brave colleagues on *Titanic*.

Fireman: There were 13 Leading Firemen and 160 Firemen assigned to *Titanic*. The ship had 53 boilers, each containing 3 furnaces for a total of 159 furnaces. Each fireman was assigned one boiler and three furnaces. There were six boiler rooms, and each Leading Fireman was assigned to two of them. Shifts for all firemen were four hours on and eight hours off. The heat in the boiler rooms usually exceeded 120 degrees, and there was a continuous cloud of coal dust, so a four-hour shift was extremely demanding. Next to each boiler was a coal chute that deposited coal from the overhead coal bunkers. A fireman with a shovel would continuously feed coal into the three furnaces. Most of the firemen worked shirtless, and often in just shorts. Several of the firemen that survived got into lifeboats dressed only in shorts in the 28-degree weather.

Glory-Hole Steward: These four crewmen were responsible for cleaning and maintaining the common restrooms in the third class and crew areas. (Stewards did the same for the First and Second Class passenger areas.)

Greaser: There were 33 men assigned as a greaser. They were responsible for maintaining and supplying oil and lubricants for all of the mechanical equipment.

Linen Steward: see Steward, responsible for washing and maintaining all of the linen (sheets, towels, table linen, etc.)

Lookout: There were six of them. The lookouts worked two to a shift in the crow's nest. They worked two-hour shifts because of the extreme colds they were exposed to in the open-air crow's nest. Normally supplied with binoculars to help them see, the lookouts on *Titanic* didn't have any because they had been locked up in a cabinet and no one knew. With the air temperature at 28 degrees and a 20-mile headwind, it's speculation as to how much good the binoculars would have been if they had been present.

Master at Arms: There was one Master at Arms and one assistant. They and the Chief Officer had the only keys to the firearms cabinet. It was Master at Arms Joseph Bailey who opened the cabinet and distributed pistols to all of the officers except Captain Smith when it was determined they might be needed to help control any panic.

Purser: This person supervised all of the Victualling Department and was the direct link to the passengers and from the passengers to the deck (ships) officers.

Quartermaster: highly trained crewmen who work on and around the bridge. Quartermasters steer the ship (helmsman), manage signal flags and communications, update charts, and stand watch on the bridge to assist the Duty Officer.

Saloon Steward: see Steward

Scullion: Part of the Victualling Department, they were responsible for washing the dishes.

Steward: (lounge pantry, Saloon, Verandah, etc.) There were 421 personnel assigned to the Victualling Department, and over half of them were stewards in 57 different job functions. Stewards were what we would call waiters, waitresses, maids, etc.

Trimmer: There were 75 trimmers. They had the absolute worst job in the crew, and were paid the least. Trimmers worked inside the coal bunkers, which were located on top of and between the boilers. All the residual heat from the boilers rose up into the coal bunkers. The trimmers used shovels and wheel barrels to move the coal around the bunker to keep the load level. If too much coal built up on one side, the ship would list to that side. Inside the bunker was usually poorly lighted, full of coal dust and the heat from the boilers. It was not a pleasant place to work.

Turkish Bath Steward: See Steward. The Turkish Bath was similar to what we would call a steam bath today. It is a hot, dry steam which causes the user to sweat heavily, then follows a swim in the warm water of a pool, followed by a massage and then a time to relax in a nice, cozy chair in a cooling room.

Vendor Department: As it indicates, personnel assigned to the Vendor Department worked for the à la Carte restaurant. Other vendors include the barbers and postal clerks.

Victualling Department: All of the crew, totaling 421 men and women, whose employment involved working directly with the passengers were assigned to this department. This includes stewards, cooks, pursers, etc. All received a small base salary and most relied mostly on tips from the passengers. First Class Stewards could easily earn substantial amounts of tips.

Bibliography

BOOKS

Ballard, Robert D. *The Discovery of the Titanic.* New York: Warner, 1987.

Beesley, Lawrence. *The Loss of the SS Titanic.* Boston: Houghton Mifflin, 1912.

Bullock, Shane F. *A Titanic Hero: Thomas Andrews, Shipbuilder.* Baltimore: Norman, Remington 1913.

Caplan, Bruce M., editor, *The Sinking of the Titanic,* the original book by Logan Marshall, Seattle: Seattle Miracle Press

Davie, Michael. *Titanic: the Death and Life of a Legend.* London: Bodley Head, 1986.

Eaton, John P. and Charles Haas. *Titanic: Destination Disaster.* New York: W. W. Norton, 1987.

Eaton, John P. and Charles Haas. *Titanic: Triumph and Tragedy.* New York: W. W. Norton, 1988.

Gracie, Archibald. *The Truth About the Titanic.* New York: Kennerly, 1913.

Hoffman, William and Jack Grimm. *Beyond Reach: The Search for the Titanic.* New York: Beaufort, 1982.

Kuntz, Tom. ed. *The Titanic Disaster Hearings: The Official Transcripts of the 1912 Senate Investigation.* New York: Pocket Books, 1998

Lightoller, Charles Herbert. *The Titanic and Other Ships.* London: Nicholson and Watson, 1935.

Lord, Walter. *A Night to Remember.* New York: Holt, Rinehart and Winston, 1955.

Lord, Walter. *The Miracle of Dunkirk.* New York: William Morrow, 1976.

Lord, Walter. *The Night Lives On.* New York: William Morrow, 1986.

Merideth, Lee W. *1912 Facts About Titanic.* Sunnyvale: Historical Indexes, 1999.

Pellegrino, Charles. *Her Name, Titanic.* New York: Avon Books, 1988.

Simpson, Colin. *The Lusitania.* Boston: Little, Brown and Company, 1972.

Wade, Wynn Craig. *The Titanic: the End of a Dream.* New York: Penquin, 1979.

Winocour, Jack, ed. *The Story of the Titanic as told by its Survivors.* New York: Dover Publications, Inc., 1960.

PERIODICALS

Ballard, Robert D. "How We Found *Titanic.*" *National Geographic,* (December 1985).

Carrothers, John C. "Lord of the *Californian.*" *United States Naval Institute Proceedings* 94 (March 1968).

Carrothers, John C. "The *Titanic* Disaster," *United States Naval Institute Proceedings* 88 (April 1962).

Lord, Walter: "Maiden Voyage." *American Heritage,* December 1955.

Titanic Historical Society "The Commutator"

DOCUMENTS

Great Britain, Parliamentary Debates (Commons), 5th series, 37–42, April 15–October 25, 1912.

U.S. Congress, Senate, *Hearings of a Subcommittee of the Senate Commerce Committee pursuant to S. Res. 283, to Investigate the Causes leading to the Wreck of the White Star Liner "Titanic."* 62nd Congress, 2nd session, 1912. S. Doc 726 (#6167).

U.S. Congress, Senate, *Loss of the Steamship 'Titanic': Report of a Formal Investigation...as conducted by the British Government, Presented by Mr. Smith,* 62nd Congress, 2nd session, 20 August 1912, S. Doc. 933 (#6179).

U.S. Congress, Senate, *Report of the Senate Committee on Commerce pursuant to S. Res. 283, Directing the Committee to Investigate the Causes of the Sinking of the 'Titanic' with speeches by William Alden Smith and Isador Rayner,* 62nd Congress, 2nd session, 28 May 1912, S. Rept. 806 (#6127).

INTERNET SITES

Encyclopedia Smithsonian:
    www.si.edu/resource/faq/nmah/titanic.htm

Encyclopedia Titanica
    www.encyclopedia-titanica.com

Molly Brown House:
    www.mollybrown.com

RMS *Titanic* (*Titanic* Artifacts Display)
    www.titanic-online.com

Rocklin Press Publishing Company (publisher of this book)
    www.factsabouttitanic.com

Titanic Books
    www.titanicbooksite.com

Titanic Diagram:
    members.aol.com/lorbus

Titanic Historical Society:
    titanic1.org

If you enjoyed *Titanic Names: A Complete List of the Passengers and Crew,* you will also enjoy two other books by Lee W. Merideth

1912 Facts About Titanic

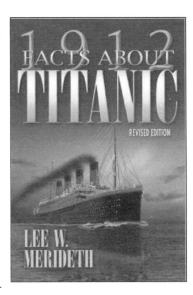

The world's most famous ocean liner carried to the bottom of the ocean a treasure trove of secrets, myths, and legends. Who built RMS *Titanic*? Was it really an American owned ship? Who were the hundreds of passengers who traveled on the maiden voyage? Why weren't there enough lifeboats? What if Captain Smith hadn't delayed a major course change the day *Titanic* struck the iceberg? What about the fire that smoldered for two weeks in a coal bunker and weakened a major structural bulkhead? What if *Titanic* had missed the iceberg? How were the bodies of the dead collected and where are they buried?

Rather than a standard narrative format, *1912 Facts About Titanic* uses easy-to-read fact "groups" that allow the reader to open the book on any page and read a rousing story. Many of the lesser-known passengers and crew are introduced and their fate is immediately divulged. Loading and launching each of the lifeboats is listed chronologically, as is the entire story of the great, but doomed, ship.

1912 Facts About Titanic is jammed with little known, hard to find and often-shocking information, including a complete deck-by-deck walking tour of *Titanic* and 50 photographs. It will please both the serious student as well as the casual reader. This is a "must have" book if you are interested in the *Titanic* story. First published in February 1999, to date over 75,000 copies have been sold. The book is 240 pages, 6" x 9" with 50 photographs, printed on recycled acid-free paper.

Order your signed copy of *1912 Facts About Titanic* by sending a check or money order for $18.00 for the paper cover edition (ISBN 978-0-9626237-9-2) or $22.00 for the hard cover with dust jacket edition (ISBN 978-0-9626237-8-4), tax and postage included, to Historical Indexes, P O Box 64142, Sunnyvale, CA 94088. Indicate how you would like the book signed.

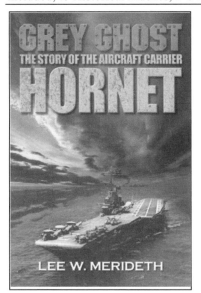

Grey Ghost: The Story of the Aircraft Carrier Hornet

The remarkable story about one of the United States Navy's most decorated combat ships. USS *Hornet*, CV-12, CVA-12, CVS-12, holds the record for the number of enemy ships and aircraft destroyed during World War II. During 15 months of combat, *Hornet's* pilots shot down 668 enemy planes, destroyed 742 more on the ground, and sank or damaged 486 ships accounting for 1,269,710 tons. After being decommissioned for a brief period, *Hornet* was brought back into service and modernized three times. She served in Vietnam and was the Prime Recovery Vessel for the Apollo 11 and Apollo 12 moon missions.

The stalwart warship was decommissioned again in 1970 and languished in reserve and disposal status for almost three decades before a dedicated group of volunteers saved the gallant old ship from the cutter's torch in 1997 and moved her to the former Alameda Naval Air Station, California for conversion into a floating museum. *Hornet* has been preserved so future generations can walk her decks and ponder the sacrifices made by thousands of her former crewmen to preserve the freedom we enjoy today.

In addition to providing a full illustrated history of this magnificent ship, *Grey Ghost: The Story of the Aircraft Carrier Hornet* serves as a complete self-guided tour of the Aircraft Carrier Hornet Museum, and includes fifteen special "How It Works" sections full of comprehensive information about aircraft carriers and how their sub-components work. The book is 264 pages, 6" x 9" with almost 100 photographs, printed on recycled acid-free paper, and over 9,000 copies sold.

Order your signed copy of *Grey Ghost: The Story of the Aircraft Carrier Hornet* by sending a check or money order for $18.00 (paper edition only, ISBN 978 0-9626237-5-X), postage included, to Historical Indexes, P O Box 64142, Sunnyvale, CA 94088.

About the Author

Lee W. Merideth is the acclaimed author-compiler of several historical magazine indexes, including *Civil War Times and Civil War Times, Illustrated 30-year Comprehensive Index* (1989) and the mammoth two-*volume Guide to Civil War Periodicals* (1991 and 1995). These combined 110,000 entries have helped thousands of students of the Civil War better access and utilize their extensive libraries and collections of Civil War-related periodicals.

In addition to the Civil War, Lee has been deeply interested in the *Titanic* disaster for over 45 years. In the process of his research he accumulated over 4,000 index cards with facts and figures, all of which formed the foundation for his best *selling 1912 Facts About Titanic* (1999) currently in its 16th printing with over 75,000 copies sold.

Lee has also had an abiding interest in World War II naval history, and is currently a docent on the Aircraft Carrier *Hornet* in Alameda, California. This interest led him to author and publish *Grey Ghost: The Story of the Aircraft Carrier Hornet* (2001), which is a history of the United States Navy's most decorated warship and a self-guided tour of the Aircraft Carrier Hornet Museum.

Lee's latest book is *Titanic Names: A Complete List of Passengers and Crew* which is a listing of all of the passengers and crewmembers who were on the maiden voyage of the RMS *Titanic.* In addition to names, the book includes, where known, the age, home, destination, embarkation point. Additionally, if saved, the lifeboat the person was on and if their body was recovered, where it was buried. Additionally, the list includes a brief description of many those people.

A graduate of California Polytechnic State University in San Luis Obispo, California and a retired United States Army officer, Lee has been in the printing and publishing business for more than 25 years. He currently lives in San Jose, California where he is "semi" retired and spends several months a year traveling to the Titanic Artifact Exhibits (over 45 to date), signing books, giving lectures, teaching *Titanic,* doing radio and television interviews and most recently, he is on the cruise ship travel circuit speaking about both the *Titanic* and the *Hornet.*

* * *

To receive a personally inscribed copy of any of Lee's books or to schedule Lee to speak to your organization, email him at historyindex@earthlink.net or write him at P.O. Box 64142, Sunnyvale, CA 94088